Bhakti Vijñāna Gosvāmī

HEALING PRAYERS
Reflections on Queen Kuntī's Prayers

This book is dedicated to

His Divine Grace
A.C. Bhaktivedanta Swami Prabhupāda
who revealed the path of devotional service
to people of the West

and to my spiritual master

His Holiness Rādhānāth Swami
whose life exemplifies and teaches
how to follow this path

Bhakti Vijñāna Gosvāmī

HEALING PRAYERS
Reflections on Queen Kuntī's Prayers

What is the secret of true love? How can we properly pass through the tests God sends us? How do we temper our hearts? What shouldwe ask for in our prayers? We learn the answersby reading Queen Kuntī's prayers, reflectingon her life and trying to empathize with her.

TULSI BOOKS (A division of Sri Tulsi Trust) 7. K. M. Munshi Marg, Girgaum Chowpatty,Mumbai, India – 400007
www.tulsibooks.com
Email: info@tulsibooks.com

VIRA BOOKS (a division of the Vaishnava International Relief Association, Inc.)
www.virabooks.org
Email: 108virabooks@gmail.com

ISBN: 978-81-970552-8-7
First Edition – October 2024, 1000 copies
Second Edition – March 2025, 2000 copies

Published by: Tulsi Books Printed in USA by: VIRA BOOKS

Content Page

Reviews

Throughout the ages, struggling spiritual aspirants and the most God-intoxicated *ācāryas* (saints) have recited, contemplated and sought shelter in the prayers of Queen Kuntī. Kuntī was a devoted, loving mother who had encountered severe and inconceivable heartbreaks throughout her life. Lord Krishna was her only shelter. She had realized that to be without loving remembrance of Krishna was the ultimate tragedy, and that in seeking shelter of humble, pure love for Krishna, she was blessed with the infinite joy of her soul and supreme victory over hardship, sorrow and death. The prayers offered by Queen Kuntī to Lord Krishna, as found in the *Śrīmad-Bhāgavatam*, reveal to us the true import of surrender in unconditional loving service to the Lord.

In this erudite, authentic, and heartfelt book, *Healing Prayers, Reflections on Queen Kuntī's Prayers*, His Holiness Bhakti Vijñāna Gosvāmī leads us deep into the meaning of true love of God and the prayerful state of mind and heart to approach God's love. He takes us on a journey into the extraordinary life of Queen Kuntī and into the essence of her historic prayers. This precious book is an invaluable boon in today's turbulent times. Bhakti Vijñāna Gosvāmī's own incredible life and all that he has seen, along with his scholarship, realizations and compassion make this book a profound contribution. I am deeply grateful to him.

HH Rādhānāth Swami

This unique book offers us a treasure chest of devotional reflections upon the prayers of Queen Kuntī. We receive a special opportunity to glimpse into her sacred sentiments and see Krishna from her eyes. Bhakti Vijñāna Gosvāmī unpacks her words to show the depth and beauty of the inner dealings between God and his beloved devotees.

The book takes us on a journey of healing. We learn how to address our loneliness, despair, and troubles. We understand that real wholeness and completeness come only when we reunite with the Complete Whole, Krishna. With great clarity, Mahārāja explains how a sadhana of gratitude transforms our crises into moments where our faith can become true love and we meet Krishna in the heart.

Bringing together insights from *ācāryas*, an array of scriptural stories, and of course his personal insights, Mahārāja teaches us how to offer true prayers, develop spiritual emotions, and employ our only real choice: to embrace or reject Krishna's will.

HH Girirāj Swami

The Prayers by Queen Kuntī from *Śrīmad-Bhāgavatam*, Canto One, chapter eight, are a favorite of mine. Now having read His Holiness Bhakti Vijñāna Gosvāmī's new book, *Healing Prayers*, my appreciation for Śrīmatī Kuntī's prayers has expanded exponentially.

In this book Mahārāja gives not only a practical guide for those who wish to deepen their love for Krishna, but also an invaluable overview of the science of devotional service. I will keep this book nearby to read and refer to often.

HG Vaiśeṣika Dasa

The book *Healing Prayers* explores the subtleties of prayer by following the glorious example of Queen Kuntī, a paradigmatic devotee whose character was forged in the extreme circumstances of her eventful life. She had close contact with Krishna throughout, both as her nephew and her ultimate shelter and therefore, is very suited to teach us prayers to the Lord.

HH Bhakti Vijñāna Gosvāmī is known for his deep spiritual insights, learning and willingness – at times even boldness – to explore subjects and fine nuances that need to be addressed, if we are looking for a guideline that helps us to apply the teachings of saints and scriptures in our lives.

Śrīla Prabhupāda wrote about finding Krishna while living in this world: 'This life of material existence is just like hard wood, and if we can carve Krishna out of it, that is the success of our life.' (Letter to Krishna Devī, January 26, 1968) Prayers are definitely a carving tool that induces Krishna to reveal Himself more and more. Mahārāja draws from a vast treasury of Vedic texts, commentaries by the previous *ācāryas*, contemporary philosophers and poets, and perhaps most importantly his own realizations gained during his years of selfless service. I highly recommend this insightful book.

HH Śacīnandana Swami

Foreword

I have found *Healing Prayers* to be a deep insight into the need and practice of prayer. As St. Francis of Assisi once said, 'The result of prayer is life.' By practicing the principles in *Healing Prayers* devotees can find new life in their devotional practice. Bhakti Vijñāna Gosvāmī primarily examines the teachings of Kuntī Devī as found in the eighth chapter of the first canto of the Śrīmad Bhāgavatam.

Mahārāja reveals Kuntī Devī's prayers to be an existential cry that recitation and study of manifests as an echo in the heart of the devotees. These prayers express a heart song relevant for seekers on the devotional path and particularly important for aspiring Vaiṣṇavas. Many devotees are not aware of the depth of attachment felt by His Divine Grace A. C. Bhaktivedanta Swami Prabhupāda for these verses. One of his earliest disciples Brahmānanda Prabhu describes:

> *Even before founding ISKCON in 1966, during Śrīla Prabhupāda's beginning times in New York City, he had recorded himself singing Kuntī's prayers. These prayers are the only section of verses Śrīla Prabhupāda ever recorded from the Śrīmad Bhāgavatam. He was living alone in what was an office on West 72nd Street in New York during the winter of 1965–66, after having come to New York from Butler, Pennsylvania. These were difficult days. Not only was Śrīla Prabhupāda alone, but his quarters offered no shower or kitchen. To bathe and to cook his meals at Dr. Mishra's apartment-cum-yoga studio, Prabhupāda had to walk seven blocks in the frigid cold, tolerating the howling winds blowing off the Hudson River onto Riverside Drive. Although Śrīla Prabhupāda had an overcoat and a sweater,*

his clothes were the thin cloth he had worn from Vṛndāvana and suited for hot, tropical climates, and not New York winters.

It was in those difficult times that Śrīla Prabhupāda found solace in the prayers of Kuntī Devī. Later, on the 31st of June in 1967, Śrīla Prabhupāda had a stroke. At that time, he requested three things from his young disciples. He asked them to bring a painting of Lord Narasiṁhadev; he instructed them to chant the prayers to Lord Narasiṁha and do Hare Krishna kirtana for him; and thirdly he asked his servant to recite the prayers of Queen Kuntī to him.

A few years later in August of 1974, while in Vṛndāvana, Śrīla Prabhupāda had another health crisis. At that time, he developed a high fever and collapsed. Many doctors came, but none of them were able to heal Śrīla Prabhupāda. Once again, Śrīla Prabhupāda requested devotees to pray to Lord Narasiṁha, and chant Hare Krishna, and once again he requested his servant Brahmānanda Prabhu to recite to him the prayers of Queen Kuntī. Śrīla Prabhupāda later wrote a letter to Brahmānanda commenting on that experience:

> *I thank you for your concern for my well-being. Actually I was very ill. I was falling down. But, by your prayers Krishna has kindly made me recover. Because you have prayed to Krishna, therefore I have recovered. Just like Śrīmatī Kuntī Devi, when there was difficulty, she prayed to Krishna. That is Krishna consciousness. Not that when there is difficulty I shall forget Krishna. Whatever the material condition may be, we should just cling to Krishna's lotus feet.*
> Written from Mayapur. 7 October 1974

In *Healing Prayers*, Bhakti Vijñāna Gosvāmī illuminates these important verses spoken by Kuntī Devī through the lens of commentaries by the previous *ācāryas* as well as the poems of contemporary Christian saints. Mahārāja begins in a classical way by examining the three types of prayers described by Śrīla Rūpa Gosvāmī in his *Bhakti-rasāmṛta-sindhu* and explains the first category known as *samprārthanā* as: '... the sincere, fervent prayer for complete surrender and for overcoming the abyss that separates us from God. It is where true *bhakti* begins because it is a prayer from a heart that has realized its indifference and disconnection from God. This painful truth is our starting point.'

It is *samprārthanā* prayers which Mahārāja later explains as, 'articulating the call of a divided heart for undivided love.' Which he explains as, 'the main topic of Queen Kuntī's prayers and her conclusion.'

This book is a classic. I highly recommend it to anyone who wants to go deeper into a life of prayer.

Madhāvananda Das

Preface

This book is about love. About love of God. Or, rather, how to attain it. Everyone wants to talk about love, but rarely can anyone understand real, pure, divine true love. It is far from a cheap thing. Love is God's primordial energy through which He creates the spiritual and material worlds. A single droplet of it can inundate the entire universe with bliss. The great saints and mystics of the past considered themselves most successful if, after years and years dedicated to fasting and prayer, they succeeded in the slightest contact with that miracle and experienced a semblance of all-consuming and all-purifying love, even for a moment. Nowadays, however, so-called 'divine' love has become a widely advertised commodity, an object of trade. The greatest problem of our time is that people believe they understand the nature of true love. Many wish to attain it, but few are willing to pay the correct price. Instead, people fall for all kinds of counterfeits.

True love has nothing to do with New Age fantasies of 'universal divine love' or with the saccharine preaching of so-called followers of Vedic culture who pass off ordinary worldly piety as love of God. Indoctrinated by such sermons and after slightly changing external aspects of their lives, people imagine themselves to have obtained or be on the verge of obtaining 'divine love.' But just as a ruddy papier-mâché apple cannot nourish us, so counterfeit 'love' is unable to quench the soul's eternal thirst and relieve it of parching loneliness. Nothing but a genuine experience of pure spiritual love can make us truly happy.

From the outset, *Śrīmad-Bhāgavatam* declares that nothing but pure love, unmarred by any self-interest, which unites the tiny soul with its source, God, and nothing else, can bring true satisfaction to the soul:

sa vai puṁsāṁ paro dharmo
yato bhaktir adhokṣaje
ahaituky apratihatā
yayātmā suprasīdati

'The supreme occupation [dharma] for all humanity is that which leads to loving devotional service unto the transcendent Lord. Such devotional service must be unmotivated and uninterrupted to completely satisfy the self.'
Śrīmad-Bhāgavatam 1.2.6

Everything else, including the desire for spiritual liberation, is deception, *kaitava-dharma*. The entire *Śrīmad-Bhāgavatam* is about how to attain devotional love free from the slightest taint of self-interest, the price we must pay for it, and how to distinguish it from counterfeits. Therefore, Queen Kuntī's prayers are intentionally in the first chapters of this great scripture. In them, she shows the path we must take to prepare our hearts for the descent of pure love.

Queen Kuntī and her sons, the Pāṇḍava brothers, endured unimaginable trials of infamy, humiliation, poverty, and death of loved ones. They knew that Krishna is God Himself and ultimately He had sent all the adversities and trials. This in no way shook their confidence in Him, which on the contrary, grew stronger and purer. Never did they curse their fate, but joyfully welcomed it as a blessed gift of God. The happiness of true love that illuminated and blazed in their hearts more than compensated for all the suffering that befell them.

Just as a mother-in-law teaches her daughter-in-law by instructing her own daughter, Krishna teaches us – the rebellious souls of this world – by sending adversities to His eternal companions. By weighing our so-called adversities against what they had to go through, we can begin to strengthen our weakened hearts.

What is the secret of true love? How can we properly pass the tests God sends us? How do we temper our hearts? What should we ask for in our prayers? We learn the answers by reading Queen Kuntī's prayers, reflecting on her life, and trying to empathize with her.

The original scriptures of mankind, the Vedas, tell of three paths of spiritual development – the path of *jñāna* (renouncing the world and realizing the unified spiritual nature of all things) which awards liberation, the path of karma (ritual purificatory activities) which leads to purification of the heart, and the path of *bhakti* (loving service to God) which leads to pure love of God. Krishna has Himself created these paths and without following one of them we are destined for degradation.

yogās trayo mayā proktā
nṛṇāṁ śreyo-vidhitsayā
jñānaṁ karma ca bhaktiś ca
nopāyo 'nyo 'sti kutracit [1]

'My dear Uddhava, because I wish for human beings to achieve perfection, I have presented three paths of advancement – the path of knowledge, the path of work and the path of devotion. Besides these three there is absolutely no other means of elevation.'
Śrīmad-Bhāgavatam 11.20.6

To help people develop spiritually, these paths and their combinations have always existed in human society, in various forms of religious and philosophical systems. However, in Kali-yuga, spirituality has become a commodity of mass consumption, and like all other values, rapidly devalued.

1 Classical *aṣṭāṅga-yoga* (mystical yoga) is sometimes considered a separate path, but it is a type of *jñāna-yoga*.

In earlier ages, those who chose *karma-yoga* had to strictly fulfill their duties, observe numerous rules of purity, follow severe vows, and perform Vedic rituals with impeccable accuracy. This purified their consciousness and awarded residence in heavenly planets after death. Nowadays, we have dubious tantric practices, cleansing diets, 'prosperity mantras,' astrological fortune-telling and cheap 'good luck' rituals left.

The path of *jñāna-yoga* sought empirical knowledge of the Absolute Truth and meant renunciation of the world, mastering the mind and senses, exercising repentance and austerity, profound study of the scriptures, and more. Those following this path achieved liberation by realizing their spiritual nature and severing all ties to the material world. In popular culture, this path has deteriorated into simplified versions of mindfulness practices and 'transcendental' meditation, gym yoga, experimentations with psychedelic substances, and psychotherapeutic techniques of 'letting go.'

Due to total degradation, the true paths of *karma-yoga* and *jñāna-yoga* are practically inaccessible to the people of Kali-yuga. Our undisciplined and unclean lifestyles make it impossible to perform *karmic* rituals accurately, and our minds, weighed down by stress and contaminated by impure food and water, are ill-equipped for deep meditation.

Under such circumstances, tangible spiritual transformation can only be achieved by following the path of *bhakti*. This path seems outwardly simple. It requires neither strict adherence to ritual purity, nor complete immersion in the inner self, nor renunciation of the world. Success on this path depends not so much on one's own efforts as on the grace of God, to whom one entrusts oneself.

However, this path implies a profound inner transformation, a cardinal transformation of the ego. The ego of man, preoccupied with his own happiness, must be transformed into the ego of a servant who wishes to do the will of God, and nothing else. Bhakti requires our absolute and exclusive focus on God and the abandonment of all plans for material happiness that are independent of Him. True *bhakti* begins where material hankerings end. Humility, patience, and willingness to serve everyone are the price for genuine devotion to God.

We cannot be misled by the external simplicity of devotional service. The path allows no room for negligence or inattention; it is narrow paths not highways that lead to the kingdom of God. The *Upaniṣads* warn:

> *uttiṣṭhata jāgrata*
> *prāpya varān nibodhata*
> *kṣurasya dhārā niśitā duratyayā*
> *durgaṁ pathas tat kavayo vadanti*

> 'O soul residing in the material world, you have sunk into a deep sleep. Wake up and take advantage of the gift of human form! Great sages say the path of attaining spirit is difficult to tread. Indeed, it is sharp like a razor's edge.'
> *Kaṭha Upaniṣad* 1.3.14

Of course, mass culture has not spared the path of devotion, either. True *bhakti* has been displaced by entertaining recitations of *Śrīmad-Bhāgavatam*, disco-like chants, stadium prayers, mechanized worship in temples, and lavish promises of instant 'divine love' dispensed by various '*avatāras*' of our age.

Seldom do such preachers of *bhakti* speak of inner transformation and chastity of the heart, without which the practice of devotional service is impossible. Few explain how to temper and cleanse the heart or how to tear our attention away from a world brimming with temptations and selflessly focus it inwards upon the source of all things. This lack of guidance makes Queen Kuntī's prayers even more valuable to us because she teaches what we need to do so that God entrusts us with His most precious gift – the pure energy of love.

Sometimes, the followers of karma and *jñāna* disdainfully call the practice of *bhakti* 'the path for women and *śūdras*.' We see nothing shameful in this conclusion. Firstly, because the individual soul, constituted of God's energy, is of a feminine nature, and secondly, because the soul's purpose is to serve God, just as a *śūdra's* purpose is to serve the master. Executing one's obligations, even imperfectly, is much better than doing someone else's obligations perfectly. By walking the path of *bhakti*, we are learning to manifest our original feminine nature. This is far better than trying to fulfill demoniac dreams of becoming God, obtaining mystical powers, or enjoying prosperity in this world of death.

Unfortunately, pride forbids most of us from recognizing our true nature and realizing it in fullness. True love does not tolerate the slightest alloy of selfishness. Therefore, it cannot enter a heart polluted with pride. That is the primary difficulty of the journey in *bhakti*.

Addressing Krishna, Queen Kuntī poses a rhetorical question, 'So, what are we women supposed to do?' She offers her own answer to show us, the debilitated and pampered people of *Kali-yuga*, how to cast aside pride and gradually transform our false ego into a true one. Furthermore, by her prayers and personal example, she, along with many personalities of the *Śrīmad-Bhāgavatam*, demonstrates what Sūta Gosvāmī describes at the commencement of the scripture – the way pure *bhakti* bestows the soul with unclouded happiness. When Queen Kuntī prays to God, she seeks what all living beings desire – happiness. The difference between her prayers and ours is that she knows what brings about true happiness, while we do not.

The process of healing

Without transforming our false ego as an enjoyer into the true ego of a devoted servant, we can never become happy, that is, be cured of our fundamental disease of identifying with our material body and mind as the instruments for our enjoyment. A soul afflicted by this fatal disease will experience unfathomable feelings of separation from God, separateness from others, loneliness, desolation, and despair at the finiteness of existence.

Although immortal by nature, the tiny and enfeebled soul, a spark of spirit, is forced to continually 'take birth and die' in the material world because of its incompleteness and incomprehension of its true self. Having turned away from God, the soul condemns itself to a petty, miserly, conceited, vindictive and powerless existence. It can restore its wholeness only through connection with God, the Infinite, by aligning its finite and limited will to His will and aligning its desires to His desires. Then, reestablished as a little part of the Complete Whole, the soul recovers its completeness and is freed from death, weakness, and loneliness.

> *bālāgra-śata-bhāgasya*
> *śatadhā kalpitasya ca*
> *bhāgo jīvaḥ sa vijñeyaḥ*
> *sa cānantyāya kalpate*

> 'When the tip of a hair is divided into one hundred parts, and then each of those parts is divided into another hundred parts, the size of one such part equals the size of the eternal soul. However, this tiny, finite soul is capable of attaining an infinite state of immortality by serving the infinite God.'
> *Śvetāśvatara Upaniṣad* 5.9

To heal is to reunite with the Complete Whole. This is the only way to reestablish our wholesome state of being. The price to pay is to give up our independent will and accept God's will. In her prayers, Queen Kuntī teaches us the way to achieve this . Hence, the title of this book, *Healing Prayers*.

The remaining question to address, 'Why do we need another book on Queen Kuntī's prayers when Śrīla Prabhupāda has already written purports on these in the *Śrīmad-Bhāgavatam* and expounded their meaning in a series of lectures published as a separate book?'

Śrīla Prabhupāda wished his followers, especially the *sannyāsīs*, to write books. This is the best way to engage the restless mind – by reflecting on the words of the *Śrīmad-Bhāgavatam* and explanations by *ācāryas*. In this book, we have collected precious crumbs from their feast table. We have supplemented these with quotations from Russian poets, the weakness for which we have tried to turn into a strength by engaging the words in the service of *grantha-raj*, the king of all books, the *Śrīmad-Bhāgavatam*.

As in all such cases, the main benefit, i.e., purification of the heart, goes to the writer. However, if any reader feels induced afterwards to study Śrīla Prabhupāda's books deeper, or if the reasoning provided in this book prompts a re-evaluation of the beauty and grandeur of the path of devotional service, then our goal might be considered achieved. We claim to have accomplished nothing more.

Queen Kuntī's Prayers

1.8.18

kunty uvāca
namasye puruṣaṁ tvādyam
īśvaraṁ prakṛteḥ param
alakṣyaṁ sarva-bhūtānām
antar bahir avasthitam

Śrīmatī Kuntī said: O Kṛṣṇa, I offer my obeisances unto You because You are the original personality and are unaffected by the qualities of the material world. You are existing both within and without everything, yet You are invisible to all.

1.8.19

māyā-javanikācchannam
ajñādhokṣajam avyayam
na lakṣyase mūḍha-dṛśā
naṭo nāṭyadharo yathā

Being beyond the range of limited sense perception, You are the eternally irreproachable factor covered by the curtain of deluding energy. You are invisible to the foolish observer, exactly as an actor dressed as a player is not recognized.

1.8.20

tathā paramahaṁsānāṁ
munīnām amalātmanām
bhakti-yoga-vidhānārthaṁ
kathaṁ paśyema hi striyaḥ

You Yourself descend to propagate the transcendental science of devotional service unto the hearts of the advanced transcendentalists and mental speculators, who are purified by being able to discriminate between matter and spirit. How, then, can we women know You perfectly?

1.8.21

kṛṣṇāya vāsudevāya
devakī-nandanāya ca
nanda-gopa-kumārāya
govindāya namo namaḥ

Let me therefore offer my respectful obeisances unto the Lord, who has become the son of Vasudeva, the pleasure of Devakī, the boy of Nanda and the other cowherd men of Vṛndāvana, and the enlivener of the cows and the senses.

1.8.22

namaḥ paṅkaja-nābhāya
namaḥ paṅkaja-māline
namaḥ paṅkaja-netrāya
namas te paṅkajāṅghraye

My respectful obeisances are unto You, O Lord, whose abdomen is marked with a depression like a lotus flower, who are always decorated with garlands of lotus flowers, whose glance is as cool as the lotus, and whose feet are engraved with lotuses.

1.8.23

yathā hṛṣīkeśa khalena devakī
kaṁsena ruddhāticiraṁ śucārpitā
vimocitāhaṁ ca sahātmajā vibho
tvayaiva nāthena muhur vipad-gaṇāt

O Hṛṣīkeśa, master of the senses and Lord of lords, You have released Your mother, Devakī, who was long imprisoned and distressed by the envious King Kaṁsa, and me and my children from a series of constant dangers.

1.8.24

viṣān mahāgneḥ puruṣāda-darśanād
asat-sabhāyā vana-vāsa-kṛcchrataḥ
mṛdhe mṛdhe 'neka-mahārathāstrato
drauṇy-astrataś cāsma hare 'bhirakṣitāḥ

My dear Kṛṣṇa, Your Lordship has protected us from a poisoned cake, from a great fire, from cannibals, from the vicious assembly, from sufferings during our exile in the forest and from the battle where great generals fought. And now You have saved us from the weapon of Aśvatthāmā.

1.8.25

vipadaḥ santu tāḥ śaśvat
tatra tatra jagad-guro
bhavato darśanaṁ yat syād
apunar bhava-darśanam

I wish that all those calamities would happen again and again so that we could see You again and again, for seeing You means that we will no longer see repeated births and deaths.

1.8.26

janmaiśvarya-śruta-śrībhir
edhamāna-madaḥ pumān
naivārhaty abhidhātuṁ vai
tvām akiñcana-gocaram

My Lord, Your Lordship can easily be approached, but only by those who are materially exhausted, because one who is on the path of [material] progress, trying to improve himself with respectable parentage, great opulence, high education and bodily beauty, cannot address You with sincere feeling.

1.8.27

namo 'kiñcana-vittāya
nivṛtta-guṇa-vṛttaye
ātmārāmāya śāntāya
kaivalya-pataye namaḥ

My obeisances are unto You, who are the property of the materially impoverished. You have nothing to do with the actions and reactions of the material modes of nature. You are self-satisfied, and therefore You are the most gentle and are master of the monists.

1.8.28

manye tvāṁ kālam īśānam
anādi-nidhanaṁ vibhum
samaṁ carantaṁ sarvatra
bhūtānāṁ yan mithaḥ kaliḥ

My Lord, I consider Your Lordship to be eternal time, the supreme controller, without beginning and end, the all-pervasive one. In distributing Your mercy, You are equal to everyone. The dissensions between living beings are due to social intercourse.

1.8.29

na veda kaścid bhagavaṁś cikīrṣitaṁ
tavehamānasya nṛṇāṁ viḍambanam
na yasya kaścid dayito 'sti karhicid
dveṣyaś ca yasmin viṣamā matir nṛṇām

O Lord, no one can understand Your transcendental pastimes, which appear to be human and so are misleading. You have no specific object of favor, nor do You have any object of envy. People only imagine that You are partial.

1.8.30

janma karma ca viśvātmann
ajasyākartur ātmanaḥ
tiryaṅ-nṝṣiṣu yādaḥsu
tad atyanta-viḍambanam

Of course it is bewildering, O soul of the universe, that You work though You are inactive, and that You take birth though You are the vital force and the unborn. You Yourself descend amongst animals, men, sages and aquatics. This is very bewildering.

1.8.31

gopy ādade tvayi kṛtāgasi dāma tāvad
yā te daśāśru-kalilāñjana-sambhramākṣam
vaktraṁ ninīya bhaya-bhāvanayā sthitasya
sā māṁ vimohayati bhīr api yad bibheti

My dear Kṛṣṇa, Yaśodā took up a rope to bind You when You committed an offense, and Your perturbed eyes overflooded with tears, which washed the mascara from Your eyes. And You were afraid, though fear personified is afraid of You. This sight is bewildering to me.

1.8.32

kecid āhur ajaṁ jātaṁ
puṇya-ślokasya kīrtaye
yadoḥ priyasyānvavāye
malayasyeva candanam

Some say that the Unborn has taken birth for the glorification of the great pious king, and others say that You took birth to please King Yadu, one of Your dearest devotees. You appeared in his family as sandalwood appears in the Malaya Hills.

1.8.33

apare vasudevasya
devakyāṁ yācito 'bhyagāt
ajas tvam asya kṣemāya
vadhāya ca sura-dviṣām

Others say that since both Vasudeva and Devakī prayed for You, You have taken Your birth as their son. Undoubtedly You are unborn, yet You take Your birth for their welfare and to kill those who are envious of the demigods.

1.8.34

bhārāvatāraṇāyānye
bhuvo nāva ivodadhau
sīdantyā bhūri-bhāreṇa
jāto hy ātma-bhuvārthitaḥ

Others say that the world, being overburdened like a boat at sea, is much aggrieved, and that Brahmā, who is Your son, prayed for You, and so You have appeared to diminish the trouble.

1.8.35

bhave 'smin kliśyamānānām
avidyā-kāma-karmabhiḥ
śravaṇa-smaraṇārhāṇi
kariṣyann iti kecana

And yet others say that You appeared in order to renovate the devotional service of hearing, remembering, worshiping and so on in order that the conditioned souls suffering from material pangs might take advantage and gain liberation.

1.8.36

śṛṇvanti gāyanti gṛṇanty abhīkṣṇaśaḥ
smaranti nandanti tavehitaṁ janāḥ
ta eva paśyanty acireṇa tāvakaṁ
bhava-pravāhoparamaṁ padāmbujam

O Kṛṣṇa, those who continuously hear, chant and repeat Your transcendental activities, or take pleasure in others' doing so, certainly see Your lotus feet, which alone can stop the repetition of birth and death.

1.8.37

apy adya nas tvaṁ sva-kṛtehita prabho
jihāsasi svit suhṛdo 'nujīvinaḥ
yeṣāṁ na cānyad bhavataḥ padāmbujāt
parāyaṇaṁ rājasu yojitāṁhasām

O my Lord, You have executed all duties Yourself. Are You leaving us today, though we are completely dependent on Your mercy and have no one else to protect us, now when all kings are at enmity with us?

1.8.38

ke vayaṁ nāma-rūpābhyāṁ
yadubhiḥ saha pāṇḍavāḥ
bhavato 'darśanaṁ yarhi
hṛṣīkāṇām iveśituḥ

As the name and fame of a particular body is finished with the disappearance of the living spirit, similarly if You do not look upon us, all our fame and activities, along with the Pāṇḍavas and Yadus, will end at once.

1.8.39

neyaṁ śobhiṣyate tatra
yathedānīṁ gadādhara
tvat-padair aṅkitā bhāti
sva-lakṣaṇa-vilakṣitaiḥ

O Gadādhara [Kṛṣṇa], our kingdom is now being marked by the impressions of Your feet, and therefore it appears beautiful. But when You leave, it will no longer be so.

1.8.40

ime jana-padāḥ svṛddhāḥ
supakvauṣadhi-vīrudhaḥ
vanādri-nady-udanvanto
hy edhante tava vīkṣitaiḥ

All these cities and villages are flourishing in all respects because the herbs and grains are in abundance, the trees are full of fruits, the rivers are flowing, the hills are full of minerals, and the oceans are full of wealth. And this is all due to Your glancing over them.

1.8.41

atha viśveśa viśvātman
viśva-mūrte svakeṣu me
sneha-pāśam imaṁ chindhi
dṛḍhaṁ pāṇḍuṣu vṛṣṇiṣu

O Lord of the universe, soul of the universe, O personality of the form of the universe, please, therefore, sever my tie of affection for my kinsmen, the Pāṇḍavas and the Vṛṣṇis.

1.8.42

tvayi me 'nanya-viṣayā
matir madhu-pate 'sakṛt
ratim udvahatād addhā
gaṅgevaugham udanvati

O Lord of Madhu, as the Ganges forever flows to the sea without hindrance, let my attraction be constantly drawn unto You without being diverted to anyone else.

1.8.43

śrī-kṛṣṇa kṛṣṇa-sakha vṛṣṇy-ṛṣabhāvani-dhrug-
rājanya-vaṁśa-dahanānapavarga-vīrya
govinda go-dvija-surārti-harāvatāra
yogeśvarākhila-guro bhagavan namas te

O Kṛṣṇa, O friend of Arjuna, O chief amongst the descendants of Vṛṣṇi, You are the destroyer of those political parties which are disturbing elements on this earth. Your prowess never deteriorates. You are the proprietor of the transcendental abode, and You descend to relieve the distresses of the cows, the brāhmaṇas and the devotees. You possess all mystic powers, and You are the preceptor of the entire universe. You are the almighty God, and I offer You my respectful obeisances.

Introduction

The Choice of the Heart

Each time we face complex or tragic situations in life, a question arises which is oftentimes difficult to answer. Why has this happened? Why? Carl Jung said, 'Man positively needs general ideas and convictions that will give a meaning to his life and enable him to find a place for himself in the universe. He can stand the most incredible hardships when he is convinced that they make sense; he is crushed when, on top of all his misfortunes, he has to admit that he is taking part in a "tale told by an idiot."'[1]

If we find ourselves amid an absurdity of no meaning whatsoever, then our patience is limited. Conversely, we can endure the worst ordeals if we can make sense of what is happening and be able to see God's will behind it. Theoretically, we know that the ultimate answer to all whys and wherefores is one: 'it' happens because that is what God wants, and we should gratefully accept His will.

But theory is one thing, practice is another. Life invariably poses difficult questions that test our readiness to accept a higher will over our lives. Every now and then, certain challenges impact large masses of people, and an entire nation can face the same question, 'Why is this happening to us?' Each person has to find their own answers.

Queen Kuntī endured her share of trials. The brutal war ended with her eldest son, Karṇa, killed. Although her five other sons miraculously survived as victors, her grandsons, mere teenagers

1 Carl Jung, 'Approaching the Unconscious', Man and his Symbols, Anchor Press, New York, 1964.

who had fought valiantly before even coming of age, were viciously slaughtered. All her nephews and other relatives were also killed. Unlike us, Queen Kuntī knew perfectly well the cause of everything. He was standing before her – Krishna. She honestly confessed to Him, 'I cannot understand what is going on. It is impossible to understand Your intention.'

Nevertheless, she tried to understand the Incomprehensible One and gratefully accept His will. In truth, this is the only choice we have – to reject God's will or accept it. Not just to resign ourselves to all that is going on and reluctantly accept things as inevitable, but to joyfully accept the circumstances, understanding that the all-benevolent Lord, who wishes us well, is behind it all.

We are not obliged to accept God's will. He personally bestows on us that freedom. We can reject it and curse Krishna or try to understand His will and feel deep gratitude towards Him. We may become spiteful towards Krishna as Queen Gāndhārī did, or love Him, as Queen Kuntī did. It is up to us to choose whether the outcome of our difficult life (and life is never simple or easy) is love or spite. For those who wish to choose love, Sūta Gosvāmī presents Queen Kuntī's prayers, in which she shows us how to understand God, trust Him, and accept His will in our lives.

Prayers in the Śrīmad-Bhāgavatam

Śrīmad-Bhāgavatam is our primary *pramāṇa*, the impeccable testimony of truth, and guide to action. At the same time, it is a collection of prayers by devotees. In almost every chapter, and certainly in every canto, someone is praying to Krishna or praising Him. Sometimes these prayers extend over dozens of verses, which we can find difficult to assimilate because we lack a background in prayer. They can seem cumbersome, conceptual, or overly pompous. We might feel they slow down the pace. We might prefer more dynamic action as in the *Mahābhārata* or *Rāmāyaṇa*. Compositionally, these prayers may seem redundant, and we struggle to grasp their profundity or immerse ourselves in their mood. To help us appreciate these prayers and fathom their meaning, let us ask, 'Why are there so many prayers in *Śrīmad-Bhāgavatam*?

To find the answer, we need to recall the origins of the book. Nārada Muni instructed Vyāsadeva, 'Write a book in which the glory of the Supreme Lord will be the main theme. Describe His greatness, His qualities and His pastimes (*līlās*).' Thus, *Śrīmad-Bhāgavatam* appeared.

Everyone sees the boundless Absolute Truth from different angles; each devotee sees it from their perspective. In their prayers, the great Vaiṣṇavas, the heroes of *Śrīmad-Bhāgavatam*, bring to light various facets of the Absolute Truth. Unlike us, they have direct experience of God's association; so, they share their understanding of Krishna's identity, His qualities and how He manifests in life.

Our spiritual experience is limited. Sometimes, for a moment, we might feel: 'God is here, in my heart, He hears me and guides me through life,' but the doubt shortly follows, 'is this just my imagination?' Sometimes, while chanting we get goosebumps, or our hair stands on end, or tears well up, and our heart overflows with gratitude. But this is seldom the norm. Mostly, we do not feel Krishna's direct presence, nor His qualities, nor His involvement in our lives. By immersing ourselves in the prayers of *Śrīmad-Bhāgavatam*, we can get a clearer sense of Him and become imbued with feelings for Him, seeing Him through the eyes of those offering their prayers.

When Nārada Muni advised Vyāsadeva on how to write the scripture, he calls Krishna *mahā-anubhāva*[1], to mean 'master of the greatest power and influence.' A literal translation would be the 'greatest experience,' which implies that direct contact with God is an amazing experience – the greatest. This is why, when reading *Śrīmad-Bhāgavatam* prayers, we should remember that they convey the lived spiritual experience of great devotees. We should try to share in these. Then the meaning of the scripture is gradually revealed to us.

All the prayers are beautiful in their own way because they glorify 'the highest truth … reality distinguished from illusion for the welfare of all.' (*Śrīmad-Bhāgavatam* 1.1.2) In fact, Krishna alone is worthy of praise. Everyone is familiar with the embarrassment and unease that involuntarily comes over us when we hear excessive praise, either for ourselves or others. Rarely do people praise one another sincerely. Praise of the material world always carries an element of artificiality, manipulation, and a touch of flattery, whether gross or subtle. Therefore, Krishna censors the condemnation or glorification of others' actions and qualities, *para-svabhāva-karmāṇi/na praśaṁsen na garhaye*t – 'One should neither praise nor criticize the conditioned nature and activities of other persons.' (*Śrīmad-Bhāgavatam* 11.28.1)

1 *mahānubhāvābhyudayo 'dhigaṇyatām* – 'Therefore, describe the transcendental pastimes of the Supreme Personality of Godhead, Śrī Kṛṣṇa more vividly.' *Śrīmad-Bhāgavatam* 1.5.21.

Praise of conditioned living beings is inappropriate because we owe everything we have to others – God, the spiritual master, father, mother, the people around us, teachers, and philosophers whose books we have read, etc. We are influenced in so many ways that none of our merits are ours and therefore, any praise addressed to us is misplaced.

Of all living beings, Krishna is *svarāṭ-tattva* – absolutely independent. When explaining Krishna's nature, Vyāsadeva describes Him as *abhijñaḥ svarāṭ*[1], which means 'omniscient and independent.' God is the only person who does not depend on anyone else. Therefore, He alone deserves praise.

In scripture, *ācāryas* explain that even when a demon showers curses upon Krishna, he glorifies Him. When the condemnations touch the Supreme Lord, they miraculously turn into praise. Just as any praise of God is truth, any praise of conditioned living beings is a lie, for all the attractive qualities in us reflect God's qualities.

Thus, through the fervent prayers flowing from the lips of exalted devotees, *Śrīmad-Bhāgavatam* offers exquisite detail of the original, infinitely charming, multifaceted nature of the Absolute Truth – a person abounding in astonishing qualities and attributes. The prayers are imbued with *sambandha-jñāna*, knowledge of God, and our relationship with Him. This is the first reason there are so many prayers in the scripture.

The Courage to Pray

Certainly, these prayers do not just glorify Krishna – they always contain some kind of request, which, in turn, reflects the petitioner's binding relationship with God, and the degree of

1 *Śrīmad-Bhāgavatam* 1.1.1.

their intimacy and trust in Him. Queen Kuntī's prayers occupy a special place in the long list of exalted prayers because in them she asks for something that no one has ever asked of God.

'Send me dangers, one after another,' she says, turning to Krishna. 'Let them pour down upon my head as if from a horn of plenty. Let adversities and trials come to me every day, for they help me remember You and feel Your presence in my life.'

Everyone knows this prayer, but few can utter it with proper feeling. Which sane person would ask God to send difficulties? What if the prayer is answered? Many Vaiṣṇavas superstitiously circumvent this verse, afraid not only to feel this prayer, but even to consider the concept behind it. Actually, it is a good prayer, because Queen Kuntī has invested in it her most profound sense of trust in God. When devotees follow in Queen Kuntī's footsteps and utter it, they ask Krishna to grant them the same trust.

Whether we pray to Krishna or not, adversities and trials will come to us – that is the way of this world. Hearing this prayer, Krishna will hardly send us difficulties beyond our due karma. Rather, He may give us strength to overcome our difficulties. This prayer helps us see God's mercy behind the calamities of our lives and accept it with gratitude. Otherwise, the mercy will pass us by, leaving us with nothing but our misery which only further hardens our heart.

As a rule, people ask God for well-being. I know many people who have prayed to Krishna seeking relief from their hardships but then utterly lost faith in Him. 'When I was in need, He did not answer my prayers. He didn't hear me!'

Queen Kuntī's prayers are meant to help us understand why Krishna sends adversities in our lives. If we can grasp this, we will cease to be light-headed seekers of happiness who pray for nothing else. One who asks God only for happiness is like a child who constantly demands candy from a parent. Eating an excess of sweets extinguishes the fire of digestion. Likewise, a too-easy life without any hardships prevents us from learning lessons and transforming them into wisdom. Besides, can a person be truly happy without accessing the wisdom of the creator of this complex world?

By citing the prayers of great devotees, *Śrīmad-Bhāgavatam* teaches us how to pray; that is, it explains how we should conduct ourselves in relationship with the Lord and what moral obligations we must fulfill once we understand His nature. This is the second reason there are so many prayers; they teach us what to ask of God and give us an understanding of *abhidheya-tattva* – the means and ways to traverse the devotional path.

A Step into the Abyss

Finally, the third reason for so many prayers in the *Śrīmad-Bhāgavatam* is to teach us the proper way of praying to God. *Bhakti-yoga* is the path of spiritual emotions that culminate in overwhelming love, while prayer is the way of expressing these emotions. Prayer, *vandanaṁ*, is one of the nine methods of *bhakti*, and not the simplest one. Before we become able to offer prayers with feeling, we need to master *śravaṇam*, *kīrtanaṁ* and even *smaraṇam*, which precede it. Therefore, Śrī Caitanya Mahāprabhu taught that we can enter into the true meaning of *Śrīmad-Bhāgavatam* only by studying it under the guidance of a qualified Vaiṣṇava, who is capable of experiencing the spiritual emotions contained in its verses: *śrīmad-bhāgavatārthānām āsvādo rasikaiḥ saha.*[1]

1 'One should taste the meaning of *Śrīmad-Bhāgavatam* in the association of pure devotees, and one should associate with the devotees who are more advanced than oneself and who are endowed with a similar type of affection for the Lord.' *Caitanya-caritāmṛta, Madhya-līlā* 22.131.

If we read the prayers of great devotees, not with our heads, but with our hearts, then to a certain extent we will be able to feel the love for Krishna contained in them. The heart is like a mirror. If it is pure enough, it can reflect the feelings invested by great devotees into their prayers and experience a spiritual greed (*lobha*) and desire to love Krishna as purely as they do. This is how the prayers of *Śrīmad-Bhāgavatam* impart to us the knowledge of *prayojana-tattva*, the ultimate goal of all our spiritual aspirations.

While we lack love, we will find it difficult to pray sincerely. Our prayers are seldom genuine or fervent because our hearts are closed to God. In my youth, I was struck by the verses of Alexander Galich: 'I don't know how to pray, forgive me, my Lord; I don't know how to pray, forgive me and help me.'[1]

This is a prayer to learn how to pray. Back then I was not yet a Vaiṣṇava, nor even a believer in God. However, I read these lines and felt a strange sadness, longing, and shame that I, too, was unable to pray, although I desperately needed forgiveness and help. I remember the thought flashing through my mind, 'How nice it would be to learn to pray sincerely.' Now, years later, I am still acutely aware of my inability to pray; however, I know whom to learn from.

Of course, spontaneous prayers such as, 'Save me!' 'Help me!' 'Have mercy on me!' 'Punish my enemies!' to an abstract or specific God sometimes spring from our hearts. These are as spontaneous as the emotions of fear, guilt, sadness, or resentment inherent in any conditioned soul, and they can be most fervent and sincere.

Nevertheless, these are not yet prayers in the fullest sense because in all these pleas the center is still occupied by 'me'

1 A kaddish by Alexander Galich, a Soviet poet, singer, songwriter, and dissident of the 20th century.

and 'my needs.' True prayer expresses our conscious attempt to 'generously' make way for God at the center of our consciousness as we take our appropriate place on the periphery. It can only be born in a heart that feels God's constant presence and connection with Him (*sambandha*). Until that connection is there, we are not actually praying but merely learning to pray and trying to harmonize our hearts with the prayerful words of great devotees.

Genuine prayer is an act of profound inner humbleness and trust in God, where we transcend ourselves, our pride, and our concepts of what is right and wrong for our lives. In true prayer, we dare to feel our helplessness and dependence on God to the utmost extent. *Kīrtanīyaḥ sadā hariḥ*[1] – only a humble heart is capable of constant prayer. Only a humble heart is ready to recognize the Lord as the only person worthy of praise (*kīrtanīyaḥ*). If we seek independence, which we all do, then we cannot direct our prayers to anyone because by praying to someone we give up our independence. It is with the renunciation of independence that true prayer begins. Until that happens, we can pray that someday we will learn to pray, that is, we will be able to give up our independence. Thus, in prayer we gradually grasp the meaning of our existence – *abhidheya.*[2]

By seeing the way God's will manifests in our lives, we can gradually learn to trust Him enough to stop bothering Him with pleas for happiness. Śrīla Prabhupāda made a seemingly contradictory statement that speaks to this point:

> *'One should not, therefore, look for help from imperfect living beings or demigods, but one should*

1 'One can chant the name of God constantly,' *Śrī Śikṣāṣṭaka* 3.

2 The Sanskrit word *abhidheya* means 'purport,' 'meaning,' 'subject to be explained.' In the teachings of Śrī Caitanya Mahāprabhu, the main subject is *sādhana* (a set of means to achieve love of God), which becomes the meaning of our existence.

> *look for all help from Lord Kṛṣṇa, who is competent to save His devotees. Such a chaste devotee also never asks the Lord for help, but the Lord, out of His own accord, is always anxious to render it.'*
> *Śrīmad-Bhāgavatam* 1.8.17, purport

First, he says that devotees should not seek help from imperfect living entities or demigods but exclusively pray to Krishna as the only one who can save them. Then he adds that devotees should never ask the Lord for help. Are these two points not contrary? No. Śrīla Prabhupāda explains that the Lord is Himself always anxious to give help. Devotees show their highest trust in Him by understanding, 'God knows better what I need.' Therefore, genuine prayer is to some extent, a step into the abyss; a step validated by the experience of a lifetime. Once we learn to invest gratitude and love into our prayers, they will change from being a means into the goal of our existence, becoming our *prayojana.*

In fact, our entire life should gradually become a prayer. Krishna answers the prayers of those devotees who turn to Him not just in trouble, but remember Him every moment, confiding all thoughts and actions to Him. That is true prayer. Queen Kuntī paid for her prayers with her entire life. Who better should we learn from? Who better than her can teach which feelings should direct us when we pray to God or chant His holy name, especially at the outset of our journey to Him?

Three Types of Prayers

Another reason for our difficulties in praying is that we often do not understand our personal level of spiritual advancement and therefore do not know which feelings should imbue our prayers. Our spiritual journey can be divided into three stages: initially from *śraddhā* to *anartha-nivṛtti*, then the intermediate phase up to *ruci*, and finally attainment of *bhāva*, perfection on the spiritual path. Corresponding to these levels of development are three types of prayers. Śrīla Rūpa Gosvāmī describes them in *Bhakti-rasāmṛta-sindhu* 1.2.152.

First Type of Prayer: *samprārthanātmikā*

The Sanskrit word *samprārthanā* consists of the prefix *sam* (*samyak*), meaning 'completely, entirely,' and the word *prārthana*, 'prayer,' 'supplication,' or 'request.' *Samprārthanā* is the sincere, fervent prayer for complete surrender and for overcoming the abyss that separates us from God. It is where true *bhakti* begins because it is a prayer from a heart that has realized its indifference and disconnection from God. This painful truth is our starting point.

In essence, we don't care about God. We need Him only to serve our interests. We constantly beg Him for something. Without realizing it, we put what we want to obtain from God above God Himself, as did Duryodhana who preferred to have Krishna's army rather than Krishna by his side. The thinking behind this: it is not God that matters but what He can give. We do not need Him on His own. A poet once expressed this most honestly, 'What kind of God is He when he does not help?' Even on the path of *bhakti*, many continue to expect something from God, regularly billing Him for their so-called service.

Our ambivalence towards God is not always clear to us. Only through association with Vaiṣṇavas do we come to realize that our heart is dead, and that we have nothing to say to Krishna. Then we can begin to pray that He bestows upon us attachment to Himself. Actual spiritual life begins with the awareness of our heart's duplicity, our disunion from God. Within us, two opposing forces tear us apart. Our soul wants to get closer to God. It seeks Him and hankers for Him, but its voice falls weak to the imperious demands of the flesh for material pleasures. It is not by chance that Śrīla Rūpa Gosvāmī illustrated a *sam-prārthanātmikā* prayer in *Bhakti-rasāmṛta-sindhu* by citing a verse from the *Padma Purāṇa*:

yuvatīnāṁ yathā yūni
yūnāṁ ca yuvatau yathā
mano 'bhiramate tadvan
mano me ramatāṁ tvayi

'O my Lord, may my mind always find pleasure in You, just as the mind of a maiden finds pleasure in the thoughts of a youth, and the mind of a youth finds pleasure in the thoughts of a maiden.'
Bhakti-rasāmṛta-sindhu 1.2.153

Each of us knows how material attachments can hold us hostage. Theoretically, we understand that we should be attached to Krishna, but the reality of our heart is different – and the heart cannot be commanded. It wants what it wants.

At the beginning, our attempts to get closer to God are dictated not by the heart, but by the intellect. When we become aware of our duality (the split between the mind and heart) we feel acute pain – and this pain should pour out in the form of prayers, for the reinstatement of our lost integrity and restoration of our wholeness. We should wish and petition to feel attraction for God as spontaneously and naturally as we feel attraction for material pleasures.

Affection for Krishna and the desire to entirely devote ourselves to His service does not come from our own efforts. Only Krishna or His devotee can impart this to us. We are unable to squeeze it out of ourselves for we have no power over our desires. Therefore, we might pray to Krishna that:

> 'Please heal me, restore my entirety. I'm tired of feeling split. I understand that I am spiritual by nature, but I am divided into matter and spirit. A part of me wants to relish material enjoyment while the other part yearns for You. O Krishna, You are all-attractive. The only person You don't attract is me. Gift me the chance to be captivated by Your beauty!'

Queen Kuntī's prayers belong to this category. In essence, they say, 'Please make it possible that my attachment to You is never interrupted by anything else! Then I can constantly remember You.'

Of the three types, the most important for us is *samprārthanātmikā* prayers. They help us to feel attachment towards Krishna and offer all of ourselves – our body, mind, and speech – to Him. Hence, the prefix *sam* for *samyak* which denotes 'completely.' When Krishna believes us, He will answer our prayers and heal us, enabling us to move to the next level of prayer.

Second Type of Prayer: *dainya-bodhikā*

In Sanskrit, the noun *dainya* comes from the adjective *dina* which means 'beggarly,' 'stupid,' or 'fallen.' The word *bodhikā* means 'acknowledgment.' Thus, a person who has realized the extent of their fallen state can offer *dainya-bodhikā* prayers. These sentiments can only spring from the heart of one who has fostered a speck of attachment for Krishna.

At the start of our spiritual journey, we are unable to soberly assess the degree of our fallen state. Thank God! Otherwise, we would be dejected if we were able to see it. For a time, Krishna does not reveal reality to us. Looking into the distorted, constantly flattering mirror of our minds, we see a Vaiṣṇava with *tilaka* on the forehead and admire ourselves.

Broadly speaking, the second stage of our devotional path begins with *niṣṭhā*, when a person gains stability and is truly eager to serve God. Nothing material makes any sense to such a person for they have reestablished their spiritual integrity. The heart no longer oscillates between God and the world of matter. At the same time, such a devotee understands:

> 'My dear Lord! I have wasted so much time in vain! I have done so many stupid things even while engaged in "devotional service!" I have said so many ridiculous things and insulted, offended so many people!'

The practitioner wakes up to the realization of who they are and faces the judgment of their conscience. Śrīla Bhaktivinoda Ṭhākur discusses this state of heart in *Bhajana-rahasya*, in the chapter where he explains the third verse of the *Śikṣāṣṭaka*. He quotes Yāmunācārya's prayer to emphasize his point:

> *na ninditaṁ karma tad asti loke*
> *sahasraśo yan na mayā vyadhāyi*
> *so'haṁ vipākāvasare mukunda*
> *krandāmi saṁpraty-agatiḥ tavāgre*

> 'There is not a single offensive or sinful act that I have not committed in this world, and not just once, but thousands of times. Now the day has come when shedding tears of repentance, I stand before You, my Lord, seeing all this within myself. The day of

judgment has come, and I have no other shelter but You, O Mukunda, the Lord who bestows salvation!'
Stotra-ratna, 23

At first, it seems strange that *samprārthanātmikā* prayers precede *dainya-bodhikā*. Often, we think prayer begins with humility and repentance. In reality, we are unable to admit our sins simply because we do not see them, having learned to justify and excuse ourselves. True humility is a matter of growing up. Genuine remorse is a result of mercy and not our own endeavors. That is the opinion of Śrīla Śrīdhara Svāmī in his gloss to *Śrīmad-Bhāgavatam*.

Initially in our spiritual journey, our humility is a pose, a coquetry. 'I am the most fallen!' usually means, 'Admire me, look how humble I am.' This self-centred, self-effacement is another side of pride. Sometimes, this posture turns into an oppressive feeling of hopelessness and guilt, which is also a facet of pride. Eventually, by the mercy of Krishna and His devotees, humility ceases to be a pose, and true, unfeigned humility stirs in our hearts. Feelings of repentance, softened by hope for God's mercy, pour out in the shape of prayers that acknowledge the full depth of one's fall.

Third Type of Prayer: *lālasāmayī*

This prayer arises in one who has attained deep love for God and for serving Him, at the level of *āsakti* or *bhāva*. The devotee is imbued with *lālasā*, an insatiable desire to serve Krishna in a particular way. Prayer suffused with such a desire is called *lālasāmayī*.

Sometimes, devotees rush to *Rādhā-kuṇḍa*, the lake whose waters have mixed with the tears of our *sampradāya's prayojana ācārya*, *Raghunātha dāsa Gosvāmī*, hoping to quickly reach such perfection. There, all who want it are initiated into *rāgānuga-sādhana* and 'discover' their *siddha-svarūpa*, their perfect personal spiritual form in service to Radha and Krishna in the spiritual world. They are handed a slip of paper that lists eleven *bhāvas* (aspects of one's spiritual *svarūpa*): one's name, age, village, and eternal service in transcendental Vraja.

Oh, if only it were that simple! Not just service itself, but even the right to pray for eternal service must be deserved. Śrīla Prabhupāda liked to repeat, 'First deserve, then desire' – the right to desire must be earned. Once, Śrī Caitanya Mahāprabhu sent Raghunātha dāsa Gosvāmī home with the injunction:

antare niṣṭhā kara, bāhye loka-vyavahāra
acirāt kṛṣṇa tomāya karibe uddhāra

'First, gain firm inner faith (*niṣṭhā*), while outwardly continuing to live like an ordinary man. Then, pleased with you, Krishna will soon liberate you from the shackles of material existence.'
Caitanya-caritāmṛta, Madhya-līlā 16.239

Being our *ācārya*, Raghunātha dāsa Gosvāmī showed by example what price is paid to receive eternal service: day and night he would cry and roll in the dust of Vṛndāvana, begging everyone he met to bestow upon him love for Radha and Krishna.

yatha dustatvam me darayati sathasyapi kripaya
yatha mahyam premamritam api dadati ujjvalam asau
yatha sri-gandharva-bhajana-vidhaye prerayati mam
tatha gosthe kakva giridharam iha tvam bhaja manah

'O mind, filled with humility and choked with emotion, worship Lord Krishna, who raised Govardhana Hill to mercifully destroy my deep-rooted sinfulness and strip my heart from falsehood.

> He pours upon me the invigorating nectar of radiant love and inspires me to serve my Lady, Śrī Radha.'
> *Śrī Manaḥ-śikṣā* 8

Before asking Krishna for eternal service unto Him, we must at least tearfully recognize the full depth of our fall and confess it to Krishna and the world. This is a much-elevated state from our present level, and there is no point in trying to jump above our own heads. All will come in its turn. First, we need to undergo heart surgery, restoring its integrity and cutting out the tumour of the false ego, then we take a complete course of the bitter medicine of humility, and only afterwards can we take the tonic of sublime prayers by the great *ācāryas* pleading to Krishna for personal service.

At our level, we should start with *samprārthanā*, the prayer to become able to surrender everything we have – body, speech, and mind – to Krishna. But even this is difficult to do sincerely by one whose heart is divided. Blessed St. Augustine confessed this with utmost frankness:

> 'As a youth I was most wretched, and especially so at the threshold. I would ask You for chastity, saying: "Please, bestow chastity and abstinence onto me, but not immediately." I feared You might instantly hear me and heal me from the evil passion when I preferred to quench it rather than extinguish it.'
> Confessions, Book VIII, 7

However, when a person comes to the profound realization of the meaninglessness of material pleasures and the emptiness of so-called material happiness, he begins to ask God to fill his heart with a genuine longing to come to Him and have no other goal in life. It is no coincidence that in Russian the words 'integrity' and 'entirety' which denote 'completeness' come from the same root as 'goal'. The idea behind this is that we are incomplete by nature, and all our goals are an attempt to become more complete, and more wholesome.

We need to learn to chant the *mahā-mantra* in the mood of complete surrender, striving to utterly devote ourselves to Krishna's service. Simultaneously, we must be aware of the multiple concerns and interests that prevent us from truly focusing on our spiritual goal. Therefore, following in Queen Kuntī's footsteps, we must ask Krishna to take away all unnecessary attachments so our inner integrity, which has been much impaired by contact with matter, can be restored. Should we be lucky, Krishna will believe our prayers and disentangle the knot of material attachments in our heart.

The Prison of the Falso Ego

Let us ask the question: Why does duality take over us? Despite having faith, desire, and a clear goal, why is it so difficult to give our whole heart to God from the beginning? Why do material desires continue to reign over our hearts even though we have awakened to the truth that no measure of material pleasures, honours or opulence can truly satisfy us? Krishna explains in the *Bhagavad-gītā*:

yeṣāṁ tv anta-gataṁ pāpaṁ
janānāṁ puṇya-karmaṇām
te dvandva-moha-nirmuktā
bhajante māṁ dṛḍha-vratāḥ

'Persons who have acted piously in previous lives and in this life and whose sinful actions are completely eradicated are freed from the dualities of delusion, and they engage themselves in My service with determination.'

Bhagavad-gītā 7.28

The sins and offenses committed in this life and earlier ones have left deep marks in our mind that prevent us from fully concentrating on service to God. It takes time to purify oneself of these through the process of devotional service. A Sanskrit word for sin is *agha*,[1] which etymologically denotes 'indelible imprint.' In other words, sin leaves a deep imprint in the mind called a *saṁskāra*, which impels us to repeat the experience.

In this way, sins reinforce the soul's ignorant identification with matter and concentrate our focus on the dualities of this world (*dvandva-moha*). This duality consists of *rāga* and *dveṣa*, attachment and aversion to all that we behold. The stronger these two programs are, the less freedom we have. Enslaved in a cycle of sin, we become unable to serve God because 'the spirit is willing, but the flesh is weak.' A verse from the *Bhakti-rasāmṛta-sindhu* expresses this truth perfectly. The first lines are:

kāmādīnāṁ kati na katidhā pālitā durnideśās
teṣāṁ jātā mayi na karuṇā na trapā nopaśāntiḥ

> 'O my Lord, there is no limit to the unwanted orders of lusty desires. Although I have rendered them so much service, they have not shown any mercy to me. I have not been ashamed to serve them, nor have I even desired to give them up.'
>
> *Bhakti-rasāmṛta-sindhu* 3.2.25.
> Quoted in *Caitanya-caritāmṛta*, *Madhya-līlā* 22.16

The influence of countless past sinful actions weighs down our consciousness and causes the heart to split. The stronger the material attachments, the deeper and more agonizing is the duality and the more severe is the internal conflict. In public we are one person and in private another. We think one thing,

1 From the verbal root *ghna* – 'to destroy.' The word *agha* means indestructible.

say another, and do something else – constantly playing roles and wearing various false faces. Internal duality blocks our understanding of who we really are and separates us from our true self; so much so that at some point we cannot distinguish between our true self and the roles we play. Worst still, this internal disunity separates us from God. Due to the sins and offenses committed, we lose connection with Him.

Those who commit serious crimes are imprisoned or put in solitary confinement. Likewise, those guilty of sins find themselves trapped in the prison of their egos, between walls that separate them from God and other people. Therefore, true human existence begins the moment we relinquish material attachments, restore the spiritual integrity of our 'self', and break free from the prison of the false ego. When our intelligence awakens and we realize our deplorable state, we start begging Krishna to free us from the bondage of sin and allow us to serve Him. The prayer concludes in this way:

utsṛjyaitān atha yadu-pate sāmpratam labdha-buddhis
tvām āyātaḥ śaraṇam abhayam mām niyuṅkṣvātma-dāsye

'O my Lord, O leader of the Yadu dynasty, my
intelligence has recently awakened (labdha-buddhiḥ)
and I have decided to leave my cruel masters.
Through transcendental intelligence, I now refuse
to obey the orders of my material desires. I come
to You to surrender myself in the hope of finding
fearlessness at Your lotus feet. Grant me mercy.
Kindly engage me in Your personal service
and save me.'
Bhakti-rasāmṛta-sindhu 3.2.25

These verses capture the essence of *samprārthanā* prayers by articulating the call of a divided heart for undivided love. This is the main topic of Queen Kuntī's prayers and her conclusion:

tvayi me 'nanya-viṣayā
matir madhu-pate 'sakṛt
ratim udvahatād addhā
gaṅgevaugham udanvati

'O Lord of Madhu, as the Ganges forever flows to the sea without hindrance, let my attraction be constantly drawn unto You without being diverted to anyone else.'
Śrīmad-Bhāgavatam 1.8.42

Freedom from Loneliness and Death

It is no coincidence that the above verse from *Bhakti-rasāmṛta-sindhu* speaks of awakened intelligence. If our intelligence is sleeping, then it's impossible to realize we're imprisoned in the dungeon of the false ego, trapped in duality. Incognizant, we don't pray for liberation and restoration of our integrity. Instead, we pray for material well-being for ourselves and loved ones. Instead of begging for freedom from prison, we beg God for a more comfortable cell. As we all know, a prison remains a prison – with its prisoners doomed to loneliness and death.

These are the two prime existential problems that all of us face: loneliness and fear of our impending death. Fear of death arises from the clash between our soul's intuitive sense of our immortality and deep identification with a material body that is doomed to die. Every particle of our consciousness cries out against the idea of dying, but cruel time prevails, inexorably bringing us closer to death.

The other existential problem of loneliness is also generated by the clash of our spiritual and material natures. The eternal soul, generous by nature, wants nothing but to love, serve and give infinitely, while the false ego builds walls between itself and others, forcing us to appropriate everything possible. The false ego vigilantly guards our independence, depriving us of intimate relationships with others and condemning us to pangs of loneliness. '...And no one knew how great was the torment behind the closed door of my solitude.'[1]

Both problems are especially acute for those brought up in Western civilization, which is materialistic in its essence. Directed outwardly and extroverted, Western culture has 'successfully' dominated material energy, winning Pyrrhic victories one after another. It distracts and prevents us from looking deep within ourselves to gain a sense of immortality. At the same time, individualism, enthroned as the greatest value, has made us unhappy, unwanted, and lonely. Drugs, alcohol, sex, and computer games temporarily help us forget death, while social networks generate the illusion of fighting loneliness. However, none of these solve the problems.

In the Third Canto[2], Kapiladeva explains that the false ego builds walls around itself to keep out God and feel like an independent supreme ruler. This turns us into individualists who separate our interests from those of God. The same walls also separate us from other people, and we face this block every time we try to enter deep relationships. Our efforts crash against the wall of pride and arrogance, which deprives us of the real love and closeness we crave. Imprisoned in our cells, we don't know we are dying of desolation and loneliness. Inherently, we long to give ourselves and forget ourselves in love, but because we have separated ourselves from God, we have lost the ability to understand others, love others, associate with others, and serve others. In this state of total existential alienation, one constantly

1 Bella Akhmadulina, 'It so happened that twenty-seven.' Akhmadulina was a major Soviet and Russian poet of the 20th century.

2 *Śrīmad-Bhāgavatam* 3.29.9.

fears. Kapiladeva discussed the reason for this in his instructions to Devahūti:

ātmanaś ca parasyāpi
yaḥ karoty antarodaram
tasya bhinna-dṛśo mṛtyur
vidadhe bhayam ulbaṇam

'As the blazing fire of death, I cause great fear to whoever makes the least discrimination between himself and other living entities because of a differential outlook.'
Śrīmad-Bhāgavatam 3.29.26

Loneliness and fear of death are interdependent. After separating us from God and other living beings, the false ego reinforces a false sense of independence and pride. This dooms us to death since our temporary material identity is false and destined to die. As soon as we restore our connection with God, we at once feel inextricably related to all other living beings; and at the same time, we stop fearing death.

Boris Pasternak's poem, 'Dawn'[1] illustrates this state of mind. After reading the New Testament throughout the night, the protagonist is filled with a sense of new life, the true life of the soul. Only connection to God can awaken this. Early morning, he rushes into the crowded street and sees the world anew. He feels empathy and kinship for people rushing to work in the snowy blizzard:

You were my life some time ago.
Then came the war, the devastation.
You vanished, leaving me alone,
Without a trace or explanation.

1 Boris Pasternak, Dawn, 1947, translated by Andrey Kneller.

When many years had passed me by,
Your voice awakened me by chance.
I sat and read Your Word all night
And came to life out of a trance.

Since then, I feel more drawn to people,
To blend into the morning crowd.
I'll cause commotion and upheaval
And send the sinners bowing down.

Outside I rush for this alone.
Like for the first time, standing speechless,
I see these streets and snowy roads,
These desolate, abandoned bridges.

I'm welcomed everywhere I visit.
There's light and comfort, and time flies.
And in a matter of just minutes,
The landscape can't be recognized.

The blizzard's weaving by the gate
From falling snow that won't diminish.
In haste, not wanting to be late,
The people leave their meals unfinished.

For all of them, I feel compassion,
As if their troubles are my own.
I melt, myself, like snowflakes ashen,
And knit my brows like the dawn.
I walk among these nameless men.
Before my eyes, the world is spinning!
I lose myself in all of them,
And only in this is my winning.

The poem depicts two contrasting feelings – fearless energy after contact with the Truth, conveyed in the lines: 'I'll cause commotion and upheaval/And send the sinners bowing down,' and humility expressed in the final lines: 'I lose myself in all of them/And only in this is my winning.'

Both emotions, of delight and reverence for God, are the same. Feelings of love for others, fearlessness, humility, and compassion all coexist and underpin each other. They surface from within when we reconnect with Krishna. This is what Queen Kuntī begs for in her prayers.

Śaranāgati – the Gateway to the Kingdom of Freedom

The first step on the spiritual path is the sincere prayer of one who realizes their helplessness and despairs at solving their existential problems on their own. This step is surrender to God, or *śaraṇāgati*. For us, people of the West, who have imbibed the spirit of independence with our mother's milk, this is most difficult to do. This is why various forms of Buddhism and *Māyāvāda* philosophy, which represent divinity as impersonal, are so popular and appealing.

Impersonalism is nothing more than an attempt to solve the existential problems generated by the false ego with alternatives that avoid submission of the ego to a personal God. To an extent, these practices may relieve us from the fear of death, but they do not solve the problem of loneliness. On the contrary, they award it the status of eternity.

Loneliness and fear of death can be solved on the path of *bhakti*, which begins with *śaraṇāgati*. When a person trusting in God realizes that the root of all their problems is the false ego and identification with matter, and that they have no power to get free from this, they turn to God for help. *Samprārthanā* is our prayer to Krishna in which we plead for Him to crush the fortress of false ego.

'Krishna, come with a massive battering ram! I have constructed this fortress and hidden in it, shooting away everyone. Unbeknown to myself, I have become a prisoner of that bastion. On my own, I am powerless to break down its walls. Please come to me and destroy it! If you do not destroy this fortress, I will remain a pitiful creature doomed to loneliness and fear in the material world. I have tried to find happiness in my independence but have met nothing but boredom and suffering! Take away my independence and make me Your servant!'

Sometimes we equate *śaraṇāgati* with *bhakti*. However, Śrīla Jīva Gosvāmī explains that *śaraṇāgati* is not yet *bhakti* but just a prerequisite necessary to start practicing *bhakti*. Real *bhakti* comes *after* our unreserved surrender to the will of God, which is the gateway out of the prison of the material ego into a realm of love and freedom. There is no other way to that realm. Our problems arise because that same false ego is such a powerful, unrelenting obstacle that does not allow us to pass through the doorway. Not without reason is it said that a camel can more easily pass through the eye of a needle than a rich man can enter the kingdom of God.

This situation seems a logical fallacy. An attentive reader should object, 'You have just said that we can never be rid of our false ego on our own and therefore must helplessly plead to Krishna for help. Now it turns out that we cannot honestly ask for help because of that same false ego. Is there a way out of this vicious circle?'

In fact, there is no fallacy. Queen Kuntī says this in her prayers. It is difficult for a proud person to turn to God. If our false ego is too big, we cannot pass through the doorway of *śaraṇāgati*. In some South Indian temples, the entrance doors are made exceptionally low so that pilgrims must bend to the ground to enter. An upright, proud man cannot go in. Likewise, Krishna generously sends adversities into our lives to help us feel helpless, shake off our excess arrogance, and earnestly pray to Him. It is this kind of prayer that ushers us through the low door frame of *śaraṇāgati*, leading to a realm of genuine spiritual emotions, where we meet Krishna.

Meeting Krishna in the Pages of the Śrīmad-Bhāgavatam

Śaraṇāgati is one of the main themes of the First Canto. We see invincible Arjuna surrender to Krishna after finding himself in a desperate situation where he is deprived of Krishna's physical proximity and defeated by simple cowherd men. Uttarā prays for protection when she is pursued by a deadly weapon. Queen Kuntī attests that Krishna is her only shelter. On his deathbed, Bhīṣmadeva entrusts himself to Krishna. The Pāṇḍavas and chaste Draupadī set out on their final journey, leaving everything behind and surrendering themselves to Krishna. And Parīkṣit Mahārāja renounces his kingdom to completely surrender and immerse his mind in stories of Krishna.

At the end of the first chapter, Śaunaka Ṛṣi asks the question, 'Since Śrī Kṛṣṇa, the Absolute Truth, the master of all mystic powers, has departed for His own abode, please tell us to whom the religious principles have now gone for shelter.' In answer, Sūta Gosvāmī makes clear that in the age of Kali, knowledge and religion have taken shelter in the *Śrīmad-Bhāgavatam*. After Krishna's departure from Earth, darkness befell the world. To illuminate a path for a population blinded by ignorance, the sun of the *Śrīmad-Bhāgavatam* arose.

Hearing this, Śaunaka Ṛṣi wanted to know how the *Śrīmad-Bhāgavatam* came about. Any book is difficult to understand without knowing its author, what he lived for, and his motivations to write the book. The sages of Naimiṣāraṇya were not just interested in hearing about why the author, Vyāsadeva, wrote the scripture and why his son Śukadeva, an absolute renunciate, sought to hear it and became the first narrator to retell it. They were also eager to hear all about Parīkṣit Mahārāja, the primary listener of the narration.

The First Canto contains answers to the sages' questions. The first three chapters are about Vyāsadeva and Śukadeva Gosvāmī, while almost thirteen chapters discuss Parīkṣit Mahārāja – who he is, his family background, and his relationship with Krishna. Because the scripture's narrative is non-linear, along the way, Sūta Gosvāmī includes Bhīṣmadeva's instructions and passing, Dhṛtarāṣṭra's salvation and the Pāṇḍavas' departure from this world. These topics all relate to Mahārāja Parīkṣit.

We might ask why Sūta Gosvāmī pays so much attention to Parīkṣit Mahārāja? One surface answer is that Sūta Gosvāmī does this for our benefit. It is more relevant for us to understand the qualifications of an excellent listener of *Śrīmad-Bhāgavatam* rather than its narrator. After all, narrators of the scripture need to be listeners first. It is our task to hear the scripture in such a way that we meet Krishna in its pages, face to face. Śrīla Prabhupāda prescribes this:

> '*One has to learn* Bhāgavatam *from the representative of Śukadeva Gosvāmī, and no one else, if one at all wants to see Lord Śrī Kṛṣṇa in the pages. That is the process, and there is no alternative. Sūta Gosvāmī is a bona fide representative of Śukadeva Gosvāmī because he wants to present the message which he received from the great learned* brāhmaṇa. *Śukadeva Gosvāmī presented* Bhāgavatam *as he heard it*

> *from his great father, and so also Sūta Gosvāmī is presenting* Bhāgavatam *as he had heard it from Śukadeva Gosvāmī. Simple hearing is not all; one must realize the text with proper attention. The word* niviṣṭa *means that Sūta Gosvāmī drank the juice of* Bhāgavatam *through his ears. That is the real process of receiving* Bhāgavatam. *One should hear with rapt attention from the real person, and then he can at once realize the presence of Lord Kṛṣṇa in every page. The secret of knowing* Bhāgavatam *is mentioned here. No one can give rapt attention who is not pure in mind. No one can be pure in mind who is not pure in action. No one can be pure in action who is not pure in eating, sleeping, fearing and mating. But somehow or other if someone hears with rapt attention from the right person, at the very beginning one can assuredly see Lord Śrī Kṛṣṇa in person in the pages of* Bhāgavatam.'
>
> *Śrīmad-Bhāgavatam* 1.3.44, purport

The main point of the First Canto is to glorify *Śrīmad-Bhāgavatam* and explain the methodology of comprehending it. This great work has been composed to awaken sublime emotions of pure spiritual love for God, that is, to give us the experience of coming into direct contact with God. For this to happen, it is not enough to merely read or hear the scripture – we need to develop an *attachment* to reading and hearing it.

In his *Bhakti-rasāmṛta-sindhu*, Śrīla Rūpa Gosvāmī analyzes why *bhāva-bhakti*, true love of Godhead, is so rare: *sādhanaughair anāsaṅgair alabhyā su-cirād api.*[1] 'If a person engages in the practice of devotional service without being attached to it, then even if he does that for a long time, he will not be able to attain love of God.'

1 *Bhakti-rasāmṛta-sindhu* 1.1.35; *Caitanya-caritāmṛta, Madhya-līlā* 24.172

Purity Gives Access

Unless we develop a true taste for reading *Śrīmad-Bhāgavatam*, it will not reveal its truth within our hearts, and we will be denied access to the spiritual emotions contained therein. Taste for the narratives of *Śrīmad-Bhāgavatam* is far from a cheap thing. The brand-new, hardly opened volumes sitting on bookshelves in devotees' homes are the best evidence of that.

Purity of heart, so rare nowadays, is the precondition to acquire spiritual taste. If we happen to lack purity, and therefore, lack any taste for hearing the scripture, then we need to make this activity a part of our *sādhana*. This *sādhana* will itself purify our hearts: *naṣṭa-prāyeṣv abhadreṣu/nityaṁ bhāgavata-sevayā* – 'By regular attendance of classes on the Bhāgavatam and by rendering service to the pure devotee, all that is troublesome to the heart is almost completely destroyed.' (Śrīmad-Bhāgavatam 1.2.18) In this way, our purified hearts can access the spiritual emotions of this scripture.

Another, less obvious explanation of why *Śrīmad-Bhāgavatam* focuses on its first hearer is that by carefully describing Mahārāja Parīkṣit's story – the way he was born, his qualities and the deeds he performed – Sūta Gosvāmī indirectly glorifies the scripture.

A virtuoso violinist will change the way they perform in a village club to peasants compared to a conservatory hall filled with music connoisseurs. An audience has a magical effect on the performer. Anyone who presents to various audiences can confirm this. The speaker's heart either opens in yearning to share intimate thoughts or closes and limits them to a few formal phrases. This is why, in one sense the hearer has an even greater influence on the depth of narration than the speaker himself. Without such a perfect hearer as Mahārāja Parīkṣit, who was humble, enthusiastic, and attentive, Śukadeva Gosvāmī would not have been able to narrate the *Śrīmad-Bhāgavatam*.

There is nothing more valuable in this world than the craving to hear narrations about Krishna. Responding to such craving, Krishna starts speaking through the narrator. Śrīla Prabhupāda's Godbrother, B.R. Śrīdhara Swami, told an interesting story about Śrīla Bhaktisiddhānta Sarasvatī Ṭhākura.

'From Vrindavan we came to Prayag. At that time, I was with him [Bhaktisiddhānta Sarasvatī]. We were invited to the house of an influential person. [As soon as Guru Mahārāja began to speak], amazingly beautiful, hitherto unheard things began to pour from his lips. Not having the opportunity to write them down, my mind became extraordinarily agitated, so much so that I couldn't concentrate on his lecture attentively. All I wanted was to get hold of some paper and a pencil. After the lecture, I felt terribly embarrassed for not being able to take it down in shorthand. When we left, Guru Mahārāja said about himself, and these were his own words, that he was 'Gobar Ganesha,' that is, Ganesha made of *gobar* (cow dung).'[1]

In other words, Bhaktisiddhānta Sarasvatī Ṭhākura meant to emphasize his passive role as a conduit of revelation coming from above and that he was not aware of what words came to his lips.

Realizing the greatness of Parīkṣit Mahārāja as the first hearer of *Śrīmad-Bhāgavatam*, who in his last days of life fervently yearned to hear about Krishna, allows us to better appreciate the scripture and realize how it can completely free us mortals from the fear of death. Who knows, we might become attentive while hearing it, and at some point, see Krishna descend from its pages.

1 In India there is a custom on festival days to sculpt images of Ganesha from cow dung. Ganesha scribed the *Mahābhārata* as Vyāsadeva dictated it to him.

Now is the time to revisit the scene when Krishna saved Parīkṣit Mahārāja in the womb of his mother Uttarā. Without this story, we will be unable to properly understand Queen Kuntī's prayers.

CHAPTER 1

The Bitter Fruit of Stubbornness

The Night Slaughter

> ***yadā mṛdhe kaurava-sṛñjayānāṁ***
> ***vīreṣv atho vīra-gatiṁ gateṣu***
> ***vṛkodarāviddha-gadābhimarśa-***
> ***bhagnoru-daṇḍe dhṛtarāṣṭra-putre***
> ***bhartuḥ priyaṁ drauṇir iti sma paśyan***
> ***kṛṣṇā-sutānāṁ svapatāṁ śirāṁsi***
> ***upāharad vipriyam eva tasya***
> ***jugupsitaṁ karma vigarhayanti***

> 'When the respective warriors of both camps, namely the Kauravas and the Pāṇḍavas, were killed on the Battlefield of Kurukṣetra and the dead warriors obtained their deserved destinations, and when the son of Dhṛtarāṣṭra fell down lamenting, his spine broken, being beaten by the club of Bhīmasena, the son of Droṇacārya [Aśvatthāmā] beheaded the five sleeping sons of Draupadī and delivered the heads as a prize to his master, foolishly thinking that he would be pleased. Duryodhana, however, disapproved of the heinous act, and he was not pleased in the least.'
> *Śrīmad-Bhāgavatam* 1.7.13-14

Chapter seven of the First Canto describes how Aśvatthāmā, along with Kṛtavarmā and Kṛpācārya, arrived in chariots at the spot where Duryodhana lay dying.

In the predawn twilight, they beheld Duryodhana as they had the evening before. Overnight he had lost much blood and was now as pale as death. Surmounting his agony, he had mustered the last of his strength to raise his golden mace and drive away hyenas snapping for a bite of his flesh. Around him, the grounds were strewn with bodies of soldiers not yet cremated.

A sickening stench hung in the air. Jackals howled ominously, cursing the coming of day after a night of feasting.

To please his master, Aśvatthāmā placed on the ground the terrible trophy of five severed heads. 'My lord, I've killed them all. This is my last offering to you – the heads of the five brothers!'

He was being dishonest for he knew these were the heads of Draupadī's five young sons and not the Pāṇḍavas, but he hoped his dying friend would not notice the fraud. With great difficulty, Duryodhana raised himself on his elbows. Fire flashed once again in his dimming eyes.

Barely audible, he rasped, 'O son of Droṇa! I'm proud of you. You have accomplished what Bhīṣma, Karṇa and even your great father could not do. I die happy.'

Duryodhana pulled the bloody heads of his sworn enemies closer. Oh, how he craved to see the head of hated Bhīma and the face of Arjuna, the prime cause of his defeat, distorted by a dying grimace! But alas, what was this? Duryodhana saw five beardless teenage faces disfigured by death. Refusing to believe his fading eyes, he pressed the blood-smeared heads against his golden-armored chest. One after another, the heads burst with a cracking sound just like coconuts thrown into a sacrificial fire. Duryodhana understood. With a long groan, he dropped to the ground.

'O *Brāhmaṇa*!' he croaked. 'These are not the Pāṇḍavas, but the sons of Draupadī. Woe to us! You have extinguished the last hope of the Kuru dynasty. There is no one left to continue our glorious lineage. All has come to an end. An inglorious end.'

Duryodhana's face contorted with disgust as tears rolled down his cheeks. Death spasms shook through his body. He flailed in agony and breathed his last.

* * *

The previous day – the last, eighteenth day of the battle of Kurukṣetra – at sunset, as night descended, Aśvatthāmā and two surviving friends had emerged from hiding and found Duryodhana bleeding to death. With thighs crushed, he looked like a giant tree overthrown by a hurricane. The mighty warrior, who once ruled the world, possessed untold riches, and commanded eleven *akṣauhiṇī* troops, now lay on the ground soaked in his own blood. His hundreds of servants, always ready to carry out every order, were nowhere to be seen. There was no one to bring him a sip of water. Only hungry hyenas, foxes, and jackals encircled him. With his strength seeping away, only Duryodhana's eyes, red with fury, gleamed.

Beholding such a sight, the three visitors could not hold back tears. Wailing, they fell to the ground before their master. Arduously, Duryodhana saluted them silently with a gesture of his hand. He told them how Bhīma, contrary to all fighting rules, treacherously struck him below the belt and smashed his thighs.

'Don't cry for me. I am dying as a hero. I never showed my back to anyone. No one could beat me in a fair fight. But fate, as always, proved stronger. Now leave me alone. Soon death will come to me, and my soul will ascend to the heavens.'

Hearing the story, Aśvatthāmā gritted his teeth. Ever since the Pāṇḍavas dishonestly killed his father, wrath had not abated in his heart. They were all to blame. He could not forgive Yudhiṣṭhira for lying out loud, 'Aśvatthāmā is dead!' which horrified and prompted Droṇācārya to lay down his arms. Nor could he forgive Bhīma for purposely killing the elephant named Aśvatthāmā, or Arjuna for allowing such an injustice to take place, or Dhṛṣṭadyumna for slaughtering his father like a butcher chops up mutton. Duryodhana's tale added fuel to the fire already raging in his heart. Henceforth, nothing but the blood of the Pāṇḍavas could quench the flames.

Chest heaving, Aśvatthāmā said, 'O King, I swear by all I hold sacred that I will avenge you and my father! I will send the Pāṇḍavas to the abode of the God of Death, whatever the cost! All I need is your permission, my master.'

Duryodhana beamed. Immediately, he ordered the *brāhmaṇa,* Kṛpācārya, to conduct a simple ritual to appoint Aśvatthāmā as the fifth and final commander of his army. Taking leave, the three heavy-hearted warriors headed to the Pāṇḍavas' camp. Neither Kṛpācārya nor Kṛtavarmā believed that Aśvatthāmā could keep his promise, but neither could they accept defeat. They were glad that Aśvatthāmā would lead them into a last battle; a glorious death was dearer to them than an ignominious life. In a clearing near to where the Pāṇḍavas' soldiers were noisily celebrating victory, they dismounted their chariots, unharnessed their horses and conferred about what to do next. After they decided that in the morning they would declare war on the remnants of the Pāṇḍavas' army, they lay under a sprawling banyan tree and soon forgot themselves in a heavy sleep.

But Aśvatthāmā was restless. Anger choked him. Again and again, he replayed the moments when Dhṛṣṭadyumna made a wild cry, jumped into the chariot of his father who was immersed in *samādhi*, and chopped off his head. He remembered how Arjuna hid behind Śikhaṇḍī and shot a deadly arrow at Bhīṣma who had already laid down his arms; how Bhīma despicably smashed Duryodhana's thighs. The images boiled his blood. He could not live unless he avenged these crimes!

In the light of the stars, Aśvatthāmā saw a huge owl silently swoop onto the banyan tree where hundreds of crows were sleeping. The owl began killing the sleeping birds one after another with its sharp talons. The ground beneath was soon bloody. Aśvatthāmā was struck with an idea.

'Providence itself is prompting me to take action! This is

my chance to kill the Pāṇḍavas and fulfill the vow to my dying king. I must attack right now, while they sleep carefree.'

Immediately, Aśvatthāmā's devious mind began its persuasions to undertake an ignominious plan, and in a matter of minutes he was convinced that it was the only right course of action. Rejoicing, he woke up Kṛtavarmā and Kṛpācārya and shared his plan. In disbelief, the two great warriors lowered their heads in shame.

Kṛpācārya, his maternal uncle, tried to reason with Aśvatthāmā, 'Believe me, son, I wish you well. You are a great warrior, and your glory is impeccable. Should you do as you intend, you will smear your name with indelible disgrace. You will regret it, but it will be too late. Go to sleep now, and in the morning, if you like, we will confer with Dhṛtarāṣṭra and engage in a fair fight. Trust me, your determination is so great that no one will be able to resist you.'

'Wise as you are, O teacher, I have grown out of living by others' wisdom,' Aśvatthāmā replied. 'I don't need anyone's advice. I am convinced of my rightness, and no one can dissuade me. You go on sleeping. But I can't sleep – my master's moans still echo in my ears. Nothing but the death cries of Dhṛṣṭadyumna and the Pāṇḍavas can silence them.'

Thus, that night, while asleep, the underaged sons of Draupadī were murdered, along with Dhṛṣṭadyumna, Śikhaṇḍī and other heroes of the Pāṇḍavas' army who had survived the battle.

* * *

Indeed, Aśvatthāmā's determination outweighed all arguments of reason and conscience. We suspect however, it wasn't determination but rather stubbornness.

When describing the birth of Aśvatthāmā, the *Mahābhārata* says, 'The lotus-eyed son of Droṇa, named Aśvatthāmā, was born. He was a partial incarnation of Lord Śiva, and of the God of Death and of the personifications of lust and anger.'[1] What could we expect from him? Four destructive forces converged in his heart. It is no wonder that the passion for murder took over him – as if Rudra himself had taken possession of him.

Determination Versus Stubbornness

We will explore the *Mahābhārata* personalities in greater depth by referring to great *ācāryas* who have mined the *Mahābhārata* for its gems. In his analysis,[2] Śrīpad Madhvācārya explains that the book contains three layers of meaning: historical, allegorical, and metaphysical. The historical (*astika*) describes actual events that took place five thousand years ago in the great war in Kurukṣetra. On the allegorical level (*mānavdi*), the battle between the Pāṇḍavas and the Kauravas enacts the eternal conflict between the forces of good and evil, and between faith in God versus the God-averse tendencies in our hearts. The third level of narration (*upari-cara*) is the spiritual one. From this perspective, the *Mahābhārata* describes the nature of the Supreme Personality of Godhead, Krishna, and His relationships with His devotees. According to Madhvācārya, the main objective of the *Mahābhārata* is to prove the superiority of God, the director of universal drama.

It is important to remember that when speaking of allegorical meaning, characters do not merely symbolize certain cosmic forces; they *are* those cosmic forces embodied as people of this

1 *Mahābhārata*, *Adi-parva*, ch. 61.

2 *Mahābhārata-tātparya-nirṇaya*, ch. 2.

epic who enter mortal combat on the battlefield of Kurukṣetra. Krishna, the brilliant director, stages the drama to show through the characters' examples what happens if we allow Duryodhana or Aśvatthāmā to prevail over our hearts. The same combat goes on in our hearts today. Therefore, we must understand Duryodhana, Aśvatthāmā, Bhīma and Arjuna so that we can recognize their voices within.

Duryodhana is the personification of the age of *Kali*, which is an era of enmity, quarrel, intrigue, and hypocrisy. He started the Kurukṣetra war as a forerunner of the endless wars of *Kali*. Envious and ambitious, Duryodhana sowed enmity among kin to trigger a fratricidal war. Self-important and arrogant, he schemed, cheated, and boasted. We, the people of the age of *Kali*, living in its atmosphere impregnated with pride and hypocrisy, can hardly resist imbibing his qualities. This is why the *Mahābhārata* warns us so emphatically that whoever follows Duryodhana's example will face an inglorious end.

Aśvatthāmā, the personification of death, lust, and anger, served Duryodhana truly and faithfully. The name in Sanskrit means 'one who fights with the tenacity of a horse.'[1] *Aśva* means 'horse' and *sthāmā* means 'strength' or 'stubbornness.' In other words, Aśvatthāmā's dominant quality is stubbornness, or if you will, determination worthy of better application. He became the last commander of the Kaurava army and was Duryodhana's last hope. He could not accept defeat and went on fighting – stupidly, meanly, in total exhaustion – when the war was already over. Even Duryodhana turned away from him in disgust.

The vengeful Aśvatthāmā, ready to serve *Kali* until his last breath, lives in the heart of each of us. At times we might hear his warlike whoop. We people of *Kali* must confess that we like

1 *Aśvasyeva sthāma balaṁ asya aśvaiva tiṣṭhati yuddhe sthiratvāt stha.* From the *Śabda-kalpadruma* Dictionary.

quarrels. We readily start them, sometimes for no reason. At the slightest provocation, we foam at the mouth and defend our case.

Recently, Kurukṣetra has been replaced by the endless expanses of the internet. Unfortunately, when fighting our brothers across the cyber plane, we imagine we are fighting for Krishna. But if we have the courage to look deeper into our hearts, we will recognize a small Aśvatthāmā, hurt, stupid and stubborn, whose answer to all arguments of reason and conscience is the same: 'You are wise, my teacher, but I have grown out of living by others' wisdom. I don't need anyone's advice. I am convinced of my rightness, and no one can dissuade me.'

If in our battles over 'the truth' we are driven by pride, resentment, or stubbornness, or if we envy the Vaiṣṇavas, then we fight on Duryodhana's side, defending his cause though it is already lost. If we refuse to hear our seniors' advice and are firmly convinced of our own views, we have become servants of *Kali*, despite the *tilaka* on our foreheads and *kaṇṭhī-mālā* around our necks.

How easy it is to confuse ignorant stubbornness with determination, and the blindness of self-righteousness with sincerity! In *Bhagavad-gītā* 2.41, Krishna praises the fixed resolution born of intelligence, *vyavasāyātmikā buddhir/ekeha kuru-nandana* – 'Those who are on this path are resolute in purpose, and their aim is one.' But resolutions are worthy, based on their aims. If we strive to achieve false goals then our resolve turns into blind, ignorant stubbornness that brings about spiritual death. This is Aśvatthāmā's lot. He resolves upon immoral goals, generated not by reason but by pride, anger and lust. His goal is to defy, destroy, wipe out, humiliate the devotees and take revenge. If we allow Aśvatthāmā to prevail in our hearts, we are bound to face the same terrible end he met.

The Payback for Stubbornness

The seventh chapter of Canto One narrates the aftermath of the terrible night of massacre. At dawn, news of the bloodshed reached the Pāṇḍavas who had stayed overnight elsewhere some distance away. The five brothers returned to camp. Draupadī followed. It is impossible to even imagine her pain at the sight of the decapitated bodies of her five sons. Her exquisite face turned black with grief, resembling an eclipsed sun. Sobbing, she collapsed and writhed in agony. Yudhiṣṭhira stood with face downcast. Bhīma bit his lips, and the twins looked away, unable to bear the sight.

At once, to console Draupadī in some way, Arjuna vowed to lay the head of Droṇa's vile son at her feet. Wasting no time, he jumped into his chariot and flew in pursuit of Aśvatthāmā. Seeing Arjuna charging towards him, Aśvatthāmā was horror-struck and in stubborn retaliation released a *brahmāstra*, a terrible weapon capable of mass destruction. The secret of its release was known only to him and Arjuna, but Aśvatthāmā had violated the will of his father by using it. To explain why requires us to take a short diversion into the past.

Droṇa had received the *brahmāstra* from his teacher Agniveśa,[1] a disciple of Agastya Ṛṣi. Droṇa trained the Pāṇḍavas, Kauravas and Aśvatthāmā together but he decided to reveal the secret of the *brahmāstra* only to Arjuna, his most diligent student.

Sharing the secret mantra, Droṇa said, 'This weapon can destroy the entire Earth. Only you are worthy of receiving it. However, always remember that my teacher forbids its use against ordinary people.'

1 *Mahābhārata*, *Adi-parva*, ch. 121.

Envious of Arjuna, Aśvatthāmā began nagging at his father for the weapon. Where there is lust and anger, there will always be envy. Droṇa was aware of his son's unbridled nature but could not resist his requests.[1] He reluctantly agreed to share the use of the weapon but warned Aśvatthāmā that he mustn't resort to it, even in deadly danger. 'By using it against ordinary people, you will destroy yourself,' he warned.

Droṇa's fears were justified. Angry and terrified, Aśvatthāmā ended up releasing the *brahmāstra*, although he knew it could burn down the entire world. Śrīla Prabhupāda comments:

> 'The heat created by the flash of a brahmāstra resembles the fire exhibited in the sun globe at the time of cosmic annihilation. The radiation of atomic energy is very insignificant in comparison to the heat produced by a brahmāstra. The atomic bomb explosion can at utmost blow up one globe, but the heat produced by the brahmāstra can destroy the whole cosmic situation. The comparison is therefore made to the heat at the time of annihilation.'
>
> *Śrīmad-Bhāgavatam* 1.7.30, purport

Knowledge imposes a huge responsibility on a person, and Arjuna was aware of that. Only once did he use this weapon in the battle of Kurukṣetra when fighting with Karṇa, and only because Krishna threatened to summon his *Sudarśana cakra* against Karṇa if Arjuna did not act.

After Aśvatthāmā released the weapon, Krishna ordered Arjuna to neutralize it. After doing so, Arjuna arrested Aśvatthāmā, tied him up and drove him to the camp. Dirty, beaten down, terrified and rancorous, Aśvatthāmā stood before Draupadī with his head cast down.

1 *Mahābhārata*, *Sauptika-parva*, ch. 16.

What a pitiful sight he must have been if after looking at him Draupadī forgot her own grief. Seized by sympathy, she asked Arjuna to release him. Yudhiṣṭhira, Nakula and Sahadeva also felt pity for their defeated enemy and supported her request. Bhīma, however, insisted that Aśvatthāmā be killed. Krishna indicated that Arjuna must respect all requests. Krishna often wants us to do the impossible. Even more amazing is that true devotees always manage to fulfill His desire!

Arjuna found a solution. He grabbed Aśvatthāmā by the hair, unsheathed his razor-sharp sword and cut off from the *brāhmaṇa*'s forehead the mystic stone with which he was born. Cutting the hair off a warrior's head is equivalent to killing him. Aśvatthāmā's humiliation was worse as Arjuna stripped him of his precious, much-prized gem, which had endowed him with many amazing abilities: he never got hungry or thirsty; no gods, demons, *nāgās* or *rākṣasas* could harm him; and no disease could afflict his mighty body. Deprived of all these powers, Aśvatthāmā stumbled to the ground, while Arjuna placed the precious stone at Draupadī's feet.[1]

At that moment, Krishna addressed Aśvatthāmā: 'O son of Droṇa! You have smeared your name with shame. You will have to dearly pay for the crimes you have committed. Everyone will turn their back on you. From now on, you will wander alone in impenetrable forests and wild deserts like a ghost. No one will ever open their doors to you to let you rest for the night. You will be bereft of what is most precious in the world – love. Struck down by diseases, your body will be covered with ulcers and rot alive. The bleeding wound on your head will never heal. For every moment of your life, you will curse the hour you were born and pray for death. But life will not leave you until the end of *Kali-yuga* when your sufferings will finally atone for your crimes.'

1 When Arjuna set off in pursuit of Aśvatthāmā, Draupadī asked for this stone to be brought to her as proof of the perpetrator's death.

It is worth remembering Krishna's curse the next time the little indignant Aśvatthāmā incites us in our hearts to fight with devotees. Who knows, out of fear, the troublemaker might finally hold his tongue?

* * *

Cursed with such a long life, Aśvatthāmā is said to still wander the Earth. High in the mountains, in desolate jungles or along deserted riverbanks, people still occasionally meet an old man of enormous height with a bleeding wound on his forehead. A certain *brāhmaṇa* has even written a version of the *Mahābhārata* in the *Tulu* language, which he says was dictated to him by Aśvatthāmā. That *brāhmaṇa* had prayed to Krishna that a witness tells him what had happened on the battlefield of Kurukṣetra. Krishna answered his prayers and Aśvatthāmā began visiting him at night to retell his version of that great historical battle. Evidently, Aśvatthāmā has not found peace of mind and wants to prove his righteousness to the world.

CHAPTER 2

Krishna, the Saving Grace

Aśvatthāmā Retaliates Again

We are now fast approaching the part of the story where Queen Kuntī makes her prayers though we need to delve a little further into events that unfolded after Krishna cursed Aśvatthāmā. Krishna and the Pāṇḍavas, headed by Yudhiṣṭhira, along with Kuntī, Dhṛtarāṣṭra, Gāndhārī, Draupadī, Subhadrā and others offered sacred Ganges water to the warriors who had died in battle, for their peace and liberation. The party then bathed in the river to purify themselves. Fulfilling Krishna's will, Yudhiṣṭhira ascended the throne, which had come at such a great cost. Celebrations were concluded after he performed three great horse sacrifices.

Having honoured all His responsibilities in Hastināpura, Krishna took permission from Vyāsadeva and other sages to return to Dvārakā. He mounted His chariot ready to leave when Uttarā suddenly rushed over in terror. Her hair and clothes disheveled, eyes wide, and face flushed, she cried out to Krishna desperately.

Unbelievably, Aśvatthāmā had wreaked havoc again! After being driven out of the Pāṇḍavas' camp, he had retired into the jungle to begin his long exile. But the passion for revenge haunted him. Arjuna might have cut out the precious stone from his head and deprived him of his mystic powers, but not of his stubbornness. Even Krishna's curse did not sober him. We may lose everything, but our false ego remains. Stung to the depths of his soul, Aśvatthāmā resolved to make one last attempt to take revenge on the Pāṇḍavas – he had nothing to lose. A wounded snake becomes even more dangerous because it loses its caution. Aśvatthāmā decided this time to destroy not just the Pāṇḍavas but also Mahārāja Parīkṣit, the last and sole successor of the dynasty. Parīkṣit, who was the child of Abhimanyu, Arjuna's slain son, had not been born yet and was still in the womb of his mother, Uttarā.

Commenting on this episode, Śrīpad Vallabhācārya writes that Aśvatthāmā released a main *brahmāstra* aimed at Mahārāja Parīkṣit, while a cluster of other *brahmāstras* split from it towards the Pāṇḍavas. Aśvatthāmā wanted to destroy the whole clan right down to the last surviving seed. Nothing else could appease his wounded pride and quench his heart-burning hatred.

The Pāṇḍavas were unaware of the deadly arrows headed towards them. Uttarā was first to feel the heat of the fiery arrow flying towards her. Shaking with horror, she rushed towards Krishna. She knew only He could save her and the child she carried.

uttarovāca
pāhi pāhi mahā-yogin
deva-deva jagat-pate
nānyaṁ tvad abhayaṁ paśye
yatra mṛtyuḥ parasparam

'Uttarā said: "O Lord of lords, O Lord of the universe! You are the greatest of all mystics. Please protect me, for there is no one else who can save me from the clutches of death in this world of duality."'

Śrīmad-Bhāgavatam 1.8.9

Uttarā's plea rings with fear. Each line carries layers of emotions in dialogue with Krishna. We will attempt to unpack the words to appreciate the devotion laden within them:

'Save me! Save me!' she repeats.

'How can I save you? The deadly arrow has been released. It must hit its target,' Krishna might reply.

'Yes, You can save me, because You are a great mystic, a *mahā-yogin*!'

'But in this world, there are many great yogis. Lord Śiva, for example, or Lord Brahmā – it is his arrow that is flying towards you now. Why not seek their help?'

'No, You are *deva-deva*. All the demigods, including Lord Śiva and Lord Brahmā, worship You and approach You for protection. Why would they hear me?' insists Uttarā.

'If you doubt the demigods, then why not seek Mahārāja Yudhiṣṭhira for protection? He is now the king, and it is his direct duty to protect his subjects.'

Uttarā says, 'He rules over some wretched kingdom on earth, while You rule over the entire universe, O *jagat-pati*! To whom, if not You, should I turn for protection?'

'But there is also Arjuna, your father-in-law. Not long ago, he protected the entire world from Aśvatthāmā's *brahmāstra*. He is a great warrior and a great yogi. Even the demigods look to him for protection. In a battle, he even defeated Lord Śiva,' reasons Krishna.

'How can someone who is not free from fear protect me? In this world, everyone fears death. Driven by fear and envy, they do nothing but kill each other: *yatra mṛtyuḥ parasparam*. Shouldn't I know this best? Arjuna could not protect his son, my husband Abhimanyu from death. I see no one in this world but You who can rescue me from death's claws.'

In his purport, Śrīla Prabhupāda stresses the point that *only* the Lord, and nobody else, can save us from inevitable death:

> *'In the world of duality everyone is envious of all others, and death is inevitable due to the dual existence of matter and spirit. The Lord is the only shelter of fearlessness for the surrendered soul. One cannot save himself from the cruel hands of death in the material world without having surrendered himself at the lotus feet of the Lord.'*
> *Śrīmad-Bhāgavatam* 1.8.9, purport

Uttarā goes on to tell Krishna that she is not afraid for herself:

> ***abhidravati mām īśa***
> ***śaras taptāyaso vibho***
> ***kāmaṁ dahatu māṁ nātha***
> ***mā me garbho nipātyatām***

> 'O my Lord, You are all-powerful. A fiery iron arrow is swiftly approaching me. My Lord, let it burn me personally, if You so desire, but please do not let it burn and abort my embryo. Please do me this favor, my Lord.'
> *Śrīmad-Bhāgavatam* 1.8.10

A plea for personal salvation, even when addressed to Krishna, may seem a departure from the ideal of pure devotion: *any-ābhilāṣitā-śūnyaṁ,*[1] which is defined as worship, free of desire for one's own personal comfort, happiness, and liberation. This is why Uttarā says:

'I am not asking You to save me. I may die, but the child in my womb must survive. Otherwise, You will be blamed for allowing Your friends' family to be destroyed right before Your eyes when You could have saved them.'

1 *Bhakti-rasāmṛta-sindhu* 1.1.11.

Uttarā turns to Krishna and offers humble arguments in anticipation of His objections:

'You are the Almighty! You can do all things. My life is not precious to me, only the life of my child – the son and grandson of great devotees. Save him!' she says.

'But how can I save a child who is in your womb? The radiation of the *brahmāstra* has already burned the baby's tender body to ashes. You can feel that it is already dead,' Krishna says.

'You are omnipresent. You are in my womb. You can bring him back to life with one glance.'

'The laws of this world are inexorable. Death is irreversible,' Krishna rationalizes.

'For all else, but not for You. You are nātha, the Master of death itself.'

How can Krishna not fulfill such a request?

sūta uvāca
upadhārya vacas tasyā
bhagavān bhakta-vatsalaḥ
apāṇḍavam idaṁ kartuṁ
drauṇer astram abudhyata

'Sūta Gosvāmī said, "Having patiently heard her words, Lord Śrī Kṛṣṇa, who is always very affectionate to His devotees, could at once understand that Aśvatthāmā, the son of Droṇācārya, had thrown the brahmāstra to finish the last life in the Pāṇḍava family."'

Śrīmad-Bhāgavatam 1.8.11

Krishna calmly listened to Uttarā. No storms in this world can disturb His serenity, but Bhagavān is one who is ready to sacrifice everything for the sake of helping the devotee (*Bhagavān bhakta-vatsalaḥ*). Remembering this, we, too, can remain imperturbable in any situation.

Krishna instantly understood everything – that the foolish son of Droṇa had released a deadly arrow. In the verse, Aśvatthāmā is described as *abudhyata*, which means one who has completely lost his mind and ceases to understand the goals he should strive towards. Aśvatthāmā wasn't satisfied with slaughtering the Pāṇḍavas but wanted to destroy their offspring to efface all trace of the family.

Krishna Comes to the Rescue

In the next verse, Sūta Gosvāmī describes how the Pāṇḍava brothers also realise what is going on.

> ***tarhy evātha muni-śreṣṭha***
> ***pāṇḍavāḥ pañca sāyakān***
> ***ātmano 'bhimukhān dīptān***
> ***ālakṣyāstrāṇy upādaduḥ***

> 'O foremost among the great thinkers [Śaunaka], seeing the glaring *brahmāstra* proceeding towards them, the Pāṇḍavas took up their five respective weapons.'
>
> *Śrīmad-Bhāgavatam* 1.8.12

Devotees try to defend themselves and are careful not to bother the Lord with needless requests. At the same time, they are confident in His protection. On this occasion, Krishna personally protected the Pāṇḍavas.

vyasanaṁ vīkṣya tat teṣām
ananya-viṣayātmanām
sudarśanena svāstreṇa
svānāṁ rakṣāṁ vyadhād vibhuḥ

'The almighty Personality of Godhead, Śrī Krishna, having observed that a great danger was befalling His unalloyed devotees, who were fully surrendered souls, at once took up His *Sudarśana* disc to protect them.'

Śrīmad-Bhāgavatam 1.8.13

We may question why Krishna didn't advise Arjuna to ward off the *brahmāstra* with a counter mantra, the way He had when the first one was released. No other Pāṇḍava could neutralize the weapon but Arjuna. Śrīla Prabhupāda points out that this time Arjuna may not have had enough time to defend everyone against six *brahmāstras* shot simultaneously to six different targets. Therefore, Krishna, the hero for His devotees, came to the rescue.

The omnipresent Lord (*vibhu*) is more than capable of protecting everyone all at once without getting off His chariot. He summoned His *Sudarśana cakra*, which easily fought off Aśvatthāmā's weapon. Simultaneously, He entered Uttarā's womb.

A *brahmāstra* never fails to hit its target. Nothing but another *brahmāstra* can stop its course. But Krishna warded it off effortlessly with His *Sudarśana cakra*. The *brahmāstra*, the weapon of Brahmā, is by far the most powerful material weapon, but the *Sudarśana cakra* is the weapon of the Lord Himself. It renders all other weapons powerless.

* * *

In the *Mahābhārata*,[1] Krishna tells Mahārāja Yudhiṣṭhira an interesting story about *Sudarśana cakra*.

Long before the Kurukṣetra battle, while the Pāṇḍavas were living in forests, Aśvatthāmā had settled for a while in Dvārakā. The inhabitants of the city received him with great honor and respect as the only son of the famous Droṇācārya, providing him with a luxurious apartment and taking care of all his needs.

Everyone knew that the war between the Pāṇḍavas and the Kauravas was inevitable. Aśvatthāmā forged an insidious plan. Seizing a moment when Krishna was sitting by the ocean shore immersed in thought, Aśvatthāmā put on his best ingratiating smile and said, 'My respected father gave me a *brahmāstra*, the weapon of Brahmā. It is worshiped by the gods and the gandharvas. I could give it to You in exchange for Your disk, the *Sudarśana*.'

Krishna answered with a smile, 'Why only the disc? I also have the *Śārṅga* bow, a dart which strikes without ever missing, and the *Kaumodakī* mace. I am ready to give you whatever you want, provided it benefits you. I do not need anything in return from you.'

God needs nothing from us but our love. He is willing to give us anything, but He knows that not everything will benefit us. Without hesitation, the overjoyed Aśvatthāmā chose *Sudarśana*. He took a jump for the disk and clutched at it. But no matter how hard he tried, he could not move it. He tried with his left hand, right one and then both but the disc remained immovable. Krishna sympathetically watched. Aśvatthāmā

1 *Mahābhārata*, *Sauptika-parva* ch. 16.

blushed and strained, to no avail. Vexed and ashamed, he gave up.

Krishna smiled on and said, 'May I ask you a question? Arjuna, who defeated Lord Śiva in single combat, is my beloved friend whom I am willing to give everything, including my wives and children. He has never asked Me for this disc. Neither has my beloved son Pradyumna ever made such a request. Even my elder brother Balarāma has never thought to ask. No Vṛṣṇi or Andhaka has ever claimed possession of it. May I ask what you were going to do with it?'

Aśvatthāmā confessed, 'O Krishna, no other weapon can compare with Your disc. It strikes terror in the entire world. Because of it, everyone is in awe of You. By pleasing You, I wanted to have it and kill You with it to please my friend and master Duryodhana! But only You can harness it, so I have no other business here. Allow me to take leave, O Govinda.'

* * *

The word *su-darśana* means 'benevolent glance,' i.e., the *Sudarśana cakra* is God's personified glance. With a fleeting look, invested with incredible potency, God creates this entire world, setting in motion the modes of material nature: *sa aikṣata tat-tejo 'sṛjata*: 'He glanced at His energy, who then manifested the creation,'[1] Brahmā is only the secondary creator. The true creator (and therefore, destroyer) of the material realm is *Sudarśana*, God's glance.[2] Of course, Aśvatthāmā's *brahmāstra* could not withstand it.

Returning to the scene of Aśvatthāmā's crime, it's important to highlight why Krishna made such a valiant rescue. Sūta

1 *Aitareya Upaniṣad*, 3.11.

2 *'tvaṁ tejaḥ pauruṣaṁ param,' Śrīmad-Bhāgavatam* 9.5.5.

Gosvāmī uses keywords in *Śrīmad-Bhāgavatam* 1.8.13: *ananya-viṣayātmanām. Viṣaya* refers to 'objects of the senses' and *ātmānaṁ* means 'attached.' Combined, the phrase describes the Pāṇḍavas as 'those who had no other attachment than attachment to Krishna.' In the purport, Śrīla Prabhupāda explains that Krishna protected the Pāṇḍavas with *Sudarśana* because they never looked to anyone else but Him for protection.

Although the Pāṇḍavas were themselves great warriors and did whatever was necessary to protect themselves, in their heart, they relied on the Lord alone: *māre kṛṣṇa rākhe ke, rākhe kṛṣṇa māre ke* – 'Whom Krishna protects, no one can kill, and whom Krishna wants to kill, no one can protect.'

This is the first precondition to gain the Lord's protection. Śukadeva Gosvāmī comments in the Fifth Canto, 'Those who already know that the soul is separate from the body, who are liberated from the invincible knot in the heart, who are always engaged in welfare activities for all living entities and who never contemplate harming anyone are always protected by the Supreme Personality of Godhead, who carries His disc [*Sudarśana*] and acts as supreme time to kill the demons and protect His devotees.' (*Śrīmad-Bhāgavatam* 5.9.20)

The Lord will protect us if we do not turn to anyone else. If we place our trust in Him, He will be there for us in all situations. Even if undesirable things happen, we should understand that this is another manifestation of His protection. Krishna states, *kaunteya pratijānīhi/na me bhaktaḥ praṇaśyati* – 'He [the devotee] quickly becomes righteous and attains lasting peace. O son of Kuntī, declare it boldly that My devotee never perishes.' (*Bhagavad-gītā* 9.31)

In the purport to 1.8.13, Śrīla Prabhupāda comments:

> *'When the Lord saw that there was no time for the Pāṇḍavas to counteract the brahmāstra of*

> *Aśvatthāmā, He took up His weapon even at the risk of breaking His own vow. Although the Battle of Kurukṣetra was almost finished, still, according to His vow, He should not have taken up His own weapon. But the emergency was more important than the vow. He is better known as the bhakta-vatsala, or the lover of His devotee, and thus He preferred to continue as bhakta-vatsala than to be a worldly moralist who never breaks his solemn vow.'*

The next verse says:

antaḥsthaḥ sarva-bhūtānām
ātmā yogeśvaro hariḥ
sva-māyayāvṛṇod garbhaṁ
vairātyāḥ kuru-tantave

> 'The Lord of supreme mysticism, Śrī Kṛṣṇa, resides within everyone's heart as the Paramātmā. As such, just to protect the progeny of the Kuru dynasty, He covered the embryo of Uttarā by His personal energy.'
>
> *Śrīmad-Bhāgavatam* 1.8.14

Krishna protected the Pāṇḍavas with His *Sudarśana* and personally rushed to the rescue of Mahārāja Parīkṣit, the future emperor, by encircling him with His energy *(sva-māyayā)*. Invisible to everyone, Krishna appeared before Parīkṣit in Uttarā's womb to save him from the intolerable heat of the *brahmāstra*.

Krishna's Inconceivable Power

yadyapy astraṁ brahma-śiras
tv amoghaṁ cāpratikriyam
vaiṣṇavaṁ teja āsādya
samaśāmyad bhṛgūdvaha

> 'O Śaunaka, glory of Bhṛgu's family, although the supreme *brahmāstra* weapon released by Aśvatthāmā was irresistible and without check or counteraction, it was neutralized and foiled when confronted by the strength of Viṣṇu [Lord Kṛṣṇa].'
>
> *Śrīmad-Bhāgavatam* 1.8.15

Krishna possesses inconceivable potency that is not subject to the laws of material nature. The *brahmāstra*, also called *brahma-śiraḥ*, which means 'Lord Brahmā's head,' is invested with the energy of the creator, and therefore has two properties: *amoghaṁ* – it always hits the target, and *apratikriyam* – it is impossible to avert. (Modern missiles with ultra-precise aim are our closest imitation.) The warrior who knows the secret of the *brahmāstra* recites the mantra and pronounces the name of the person to be destroyed. If the mantra is pronounced correctly, the named person is destined to be killed. However, having clashed with Lord Viṣṇu's energy, Aśvatthāmā's *brahmāstra* lost its power.

In this verse, Sūta Gosvāmī deliberately addresses Śaunaka Ṛṣi as 'the adornment of the Bhṛgu dynasty.' What is Bhṛgu Muni famous for? To the entire world, he proved Viṣṇu's superiority over Brahmā and Śiva. The story is retold in the Tenth Canto.[1] By calling Śaunaka Ṛṣi 'the best of the Bhṛgu dynasty,' Sūta Gosvāmī reminds him (and readers) that Viṣṇu's superiority has long ago been established by the family ancestor, and that it should hardly be a surprise to know that Krishna has accomplished the impossible and defeated Brahmā's invincible weapon. Sūta Gosvāmī emphasizes the point again in the next verse:

1 *Śrīmad-Bhāgavatam*, 10.89. Bhṛgu Muni visited the three Gods to test their tolerance. He deliberately offered no gesture of respect, which enraged Lord Brahmā. He insulted Lord Śiva with harsh words and narrowly escaped with his life. Finally, he marched into Vaikuṇṭha and kicked Lord Viṣṇu in the chest. The Lord showed no reaction, welcomed the sage, and apologized for not greeting him properly.

mā maṁsthā hy etad āścaryaṁ
sarvāścaryamaye 'cyute
ya idaṁ māyayā devyā
sṛjaty avati hanty ajaḥ

'O *brāhmaṇas*, do not think this to be especially wonderful in the activities of the mysterious and infallible Personality of Godhead. By His own transcendental energy, He creates, maintains and annihilates all material things, although He Himself is unborn.'

Śrīmad-Bhāgavatam 1.8.16

The definition of Īśvara, the Personality of Godhead, is *kartum akartum anyathā kartum/yah samarthah sa eva isvaraḥ*[1] – 'God can do whatever He wants. He can change everything He did previously and do it all in a different way.' He creates this world, destroys it, but remains unchanged. That is why He is Acyuta, the infallible, the unchanging, and the unborn. Sūta Gosvāmī is amazed that people mistrust and doubt when they hear of miracles performed by God but take the great miracle of creation for granted. Krishna is *sarva āścarya-maye*, the reservoir of all wonderful and inconceivable qualities.

In other words, He is incomprehensible if we try to understand Him with logic and reason. The only way to understand Him is to bow down before Him and accept His inconceivable omnipotence. With this verse, Sūta Gosvāmī wants to reiterate that the Lord enacted another miracle by protecting Mahārāja Parīkṣit in Uttarā's womb. It is to this Lord and not to her nephew that Queen Kuntī will address her prayers.

1 *Paramātma-sandarbha* 93.

CHAPTER 3

Chastity that Grants Fearlessness

The Point of Silence

We have described everything up to this point in detail so we can properly understand Queen Kuntī's prayers. It is crucial for us to know the wider context and Queen Kuntī's emotional state. Right before her eyes, Krishna has saved her sons twice: by advising Arjuna to neutralise the first *brahmāstra* and then by personally intervening. Love, gratitude and reverential admiration unite in Queen Kuntī's heart and pour from her lips as prayer.

Sliding through life, we usually notice only the superficial meanings of things and events; petty worries and joys obscure truth from us like ripples on a lake, preventing us from seeing what is beneath. However, a severe shock or great sorrow can reveal to us the underlying intricacies of events previously hidden from sight. Something shifts in our consciousness, and we suddenly begin to see that behind everything in this world is God. Suffering has a sobering effect on a pure person. The veil of *māyā*, the Lord's illusory energy, drops from their eyes, and momentarily the truth is disclosed. At such a moment, prayer is born in the heart.

One Vaiṣṇavī shared her experience with me. Tragedy entered her life with the death of a dear one. Feeling unbearable pain, she cried day and night. Drowning in sorrow, by some mercy, she met a wise old devotee lady who was a deep believer. This wise lady's attitude, deep soft voice, and glance of great compassion blessed the grieving Vaiṣṇavī with an incredible transformation.

Something amazing happened. Something changed inside her heart and her perception transformed. She realized that God is all-mercy and love, and she could see and feel the situation and herself in a completely different light. She felt she could see the three modes of material nature in operation – *rajas*, which creates everything in this world, *tamas*, which brings about death and destruction, and *sattva*, which sustains the creation. She could look at a flower, and as if in a movie, its entire life would unfold in her inner vision: the way it sprouted from a small seed, became a seedling, flowered, blossomed with pride and then would wither. She would look at a person and somehow visualize the imprint of predestination on their forehead. She could sense how the past had shaped their present, and how the future would bring death. She could feel the passing of inexorable time. The cheerful, cozy, and glossy world to which she was accustomed crumbled, and instead she saw a terrible force, a force that nothing can resist. This revelation filled her heart with exultation and fear. She realized she was seeing how God acts in this vast world. She felt an urge to return to her familiar, habitual world, where everything was trivial and simple.

In one sense, this Vaiṣṇavī's experience is like Arjuna's experience on the battlefield when Krishna displayed His universal form. Arjuna beheld the entire universe in a single spot: *tatraika-sthaṁ jagat kṛtsnaṁ,*[1] and when he asked Krishna, 'Who are You?' he heard a thunder-like reply: *kālo 'smi loka-kṣaya-kṛt pravṛddho* – 'Time I am, the great destroyer of the worlds.' (*Bhagavad-gītā* 11.32)

Arjuna rejoiced at what he saw and at the same time felt scared. The difference between him and us is that the veil of *Yoga-māyā*, Krishna's internal energy, fell from his eyes, while the veil of *Mahā-māyā*, the external illusory energy of the Lord, must fall for us to be able to see the truth. Whichever way, the spectacle that unfolds is the same – the observer beholds death, including his own.

1 *Bhagavad-gītā* 11.13. Translation: 'At that time, Arjuna could see in the universal form of the Lord, the unlimited expansions of the universe situated in one place although divided into many, many thousands.' These words evoke the modern scientific theory of the Big Bang where the whole universe burst from a single point in which energy and matter are compressed to infinity (the so-called state of singularity).

When the terrible sight of the Lord's majesty was revealed to Arjuna, he began to pray. What else is to be done at such a moment? Prayer spontaneously pours from the lips of an overwhelmed person when the familiar world collapses and an abyss opens before them. At that moment, one's consciousness is catapulted out of external reality. The chattering, ever-agitated mind, swarming with thousands of thoughts and desires, falls silent. Out of that silence of the heart emerges prayer.

Usually, the chatter of our material mind prevents us from praying to God. Prayers born from the melting pot of such a material mind are like bubbles of putrid gas rising from the bottom of a swamp. True prayer can only be born out of a silence beyond the mind.

At the epicenter of any hurricane, there is a point of silence, the so-called 'eye of the hurricane.' Likewise, any tragedies that come into our lives carry a point of silence where we can feel God's presence, find ourselves face to face with Him, and begin to pray.

In Orthodox Christianity, there is the tradition of Hesychasm, or 'intellectual labor,' a contemplative practice of continuous recitation and concentration on the Jesus prayer. It is similar to the practice of chanting the Hare Krishna *mahā-mantra* brought by Lord Caitanya. The word 'hesychasm' comes from the Greek '*hesychia*,' which means 'silence,' or 'stillness.' True chanting of mantras or praying to God can only take place beyond the chatter of the mind, in an internally silent state, when, listening to our hearts, we begin to feel God's presence.[1]

Currently, our consciousness focuses on the events and objects of this world, which agitate the mind and create a sense

1 The verse *manaḥ saṁharaṇaṁśaucaṁ maunaṁ* (Hari-bhakti-vilāsa 17.129) also speaks of silence (*mauna*) as a pre-condition for receiving the benefit of chanting the holy name.

of happiness or grief. We take these storms, which occur on the mind's surface, to be life. We are afraid of silence and solitude because we fear emptiness and nothingness. Accustomed to living on the surface of our consciousness, we are afraid to plunge into the depths of the heart. What if we look inside and find out no one is there?

These fears and doubts are unfounded because all scriptures of the world unanimously state that God resides in the imperturbable depths of the heart, beyond happiness and grief.

tam durdasam gūdham anuprāviṣtaṁ
guhahitam gahvarestam
ādhyātma-yogadhigamena devaṁ
matva dhīraṁ dhīro harṣa-śokau jahāti

'The Supreme Personality of Godhead, the most ancient of the ancients, who is being worshiped in the dense jungle of this world, hides in the cave (*guhāhitam*) of our heart. Meditating on Him in a spiritual trance, the wise (*dhīra*), becomes free of material happiness and sorrow.'

Kaṭha Upaniṣad 1.2.12

By Krishna's grace, a devotee gains access to that innermost cave of the heart. This happens at the time of turmoil, when our consciousness rushes towards God, or when we find our way there through the process of *sādhana* – the daily conscious efforts to remain alone with God, turning off the talkative and ever-agitated mind.

Nephew or God?

Queen Kuntī's prayers, like those of Arjuna in the Eleventh Chapter of *Bhagavad-gītā*, begin with astonishment at the sight of the Almighty, in whose hands are the destinies of all living beings. However, even in this state she does not forget that this almighty God is her nephew and her sons' best friend. It seems incompatible at first sight but both maternal love for Krishna and adoration for Him as the Supreme coexist in her heart. For Queen Kuntī, Krishna is first Arjuna's friend and only then *Īśvara* and *Bhagavān*, the Almighty Lord and Supreme Person, as she says at the end of her prayers:

> ***śrī-kṛṣṇa kṛṣṇa-sakha vṛṣṇy-ṛṣabhāvani-dhrug-***
> ***rājanya-vaṁśa-dahanānapavarga-vīrya***
> ***govinda go-dvija-surārti-harāvatāra***
> ***yogeśvarākhila-guro bhagavan namas te***

> 'O Kṛṣṇa, O friend of Arjuna, O chief amongst the descendants of Vṛṣṇi, You are the destroyer of those political parties which are disturbing elements on this earth. Your prowess never deteriorates. You are the proprietor of the transcendental abode, and You descend to relieve the distresses of the cows, the *brāhmaṇas* and the devotees. You possess all mystic powers, and You are the preceptor of the entire universe. You are the almighty God, and I offer You my respectful obeisances.'
>
> *Śrīmad-Bhāgavatam* 1.8.43

In his purports in the First Canto,[1] Śrīla Prabhupāda writes that Queen Kuntī is the incarnation of the success potency of the Personality of Godhead. By material standards, her hard and bitter life is in no way successful. But from a spiritual perspective,

1 *Śrīmad-Bhāgavatam* 1.13.3-4, purport.

we can hardly imagine a greater fortune than hers: that the Supreme Lord Himself agrees to become her nephew and her sons' friend.

Queen Kuntī's life was hard from childhood. Some say that Kuntī or Pṛthā,[1] as she was named at birth, lived as many as three lives in one lifetime. She was the daughter of Mahārāja Śūrasena, Krishna's grandfather. In a disposition of generosity, the King promised his first daughter to his childless friend, the leader of the Bhoja clan. Therefore, as an infant she was torn from her mother's breast to be given to the household of Mahārāja Kuntībhoja. For an infant to be separated from their mother is tantamount to death. Thus, ended Kuntī's first life.

Kuntī's second life, her carefree childhood, ended the day she summoned the Sun God, Sūrya, out of curiosity. This life ended in shame, the feeling of burning guilt and irreparable separation from her illegitimate son.

Subsequently, her third life began, the hardest one – as wife of the King of Hastināpura, Mahārāja Pāṇḍu, and mother of his five sons. Shortly after the wedding, her husband set off on a military campaign. She waited for him for a year. After returning victorious, unexpectedly, Pāṇḍu decided to become an ascetic. He gave up the throne and retired to the forest. Both his wives, Queens Kuntī and Mādrī, followed him. There, in the Himalayan forests, Queen Kuntī's sons were born.

A few years later, she witnessed her husband's tragic death and watched her dear friend, Mādrī, voluntarily ascend the funeral pyre. Alone, with five little sons to care for, she returned to the royal family in Hastināpura, hoping for some peace and protection. Instead, she faced jealousy, intrigue, treachery, and humiliation. Those who were supposed to be protectors during

1 To pronounce Pṛthā, stress the last syllable.

her widowhood repeatedly tried to kill her and her sons. Eventually, she and her children were forced to leave for the forests and live on alms.

Several years later, when they returned to Hastināpura, before her eyes, a crowd of whooping warriors tried to publicly undress her daughter-in-law. Thereafter, her sons were ignominiously exiled to the forests. For thirteen long years, Queen Kuntī lived deprived of filial support, and depended on the kind but half-impoverished Vidura. When the terrible war broke out, her eldest son and all her grandchildren were killed.

However difficult all these situations were, Queen Kuntī's mysterious nephew, the lotus-eyed Krishna, son of her elder brother, Vasudeva, would come to the rescue. She knew that He was God, though He would do everything to make her forget this. Upon meeting her, He would bow to the ground before her. In response, she would tightly embrace Him, moistening His shoulder with her tears. Sometimes, He would ask her advice, console her in grief, wipe away her tears, or ask for her blessings. It was as if He yearned to receive her love while generously bestowing on her His love. That explains why affection and reverence for Krishna always conflicted in Queen Kuntī's heart – though affection always prevailed.

* * *

There are two categories of the Lord's devotees: the inhabitants of Vṛndāvana and all the rest. Nothing can obscure the love of the Vṛndāvana inhabitants for Krishna, for it is based on their experience of Krishna's sweetness (*mādhurya-mayi-jñāna*). Knowledge of His greatness and omnipotence (*aiśvarya-mayi-jñāna*) is also present in their hearts but almost never manifests in their relationship with Him.

In Vṛndāvana, Krishna may display His might as much as He likes, but the cowherd men, women, boys, and girls only exclaim in delight, 'Wow, just look at our Gopāla!' He may kill a terrible demoness, smash a large cart into pieces, uproot century-old trees, or even hold a mountain on his little pinky, but the *Vrajavāsīs* will go on believing that it is the prayers and sacrifices of their village *brāhmaṇas* or His father's piety that helps their darling perform the miracle. Even when Krishna shows His universal form, it only heightens their love for Him.

When Krishna's friends complain to Yaśodā that He has eaten earth, He becomes afraid. To avoid punishment, Krishna decides to distract His mother's attention and finds no better way than showing her the whole universe within His mouth.

He seems to excuse Himself by saying, 'What if I ate some earth? The entire planet Earth as well as all the planets of the Universe are in My mouth!' When Yaśodā looked into His mouth, she saw the material elements in their original form – the mind, the senses, the modes of material nature, the boundless expanses of space, the innumerable stars, planets, and galaxies. Like Arjuna, she beholds how merciless time brings the fruits of karma to all living beings. Finally, she sees Vṛndāvana and herself looking into Krishna's mouth. Dizzy, she thinks, 'Either I'm imagining things, or something is threatening my boy again!' Her maternal love never diminishes even slightly; on the contrary, it intensifies. When she is about to pray to Lord Viṣṇu for her son's welfare, Krishna closes His mouth with a grin, and she instantly dismisses the 'delusion.'

Krishna can do whatever He pleases but the Vṛndāvana inhabitants maintain that He is *just* Gopāla, their friend, son, relative or lover. Noone can dissuade them from this – not even Krishna. They love Him the way He is, and they couldn't care less whether He's God or not.

trayyā copaniṣadbhiś ca
sāṅkhya-yogaiś ca sātvataiḥ
upagīyamāna-māhātmyaṁ
hariṁ sāmanyatātmajam[1]

'The glories of the Supreme Personality of Godhead are studied throughout the three *Vedas*, the *Upaniṣads*, the literature of *Sāṅkhya-yoga*, and other Vaiṣṇava literature, yet ***mother Yaśodā considered that Supreme Person her ordinary child.'***
Śrīmad-Bhāgavatam 10.8.45

Krishna's other devotees from Mathurā, Hastināpura and Dvārakā also love Krishna, but their feelings are mixed with awareness of His greatness. This overshadows their love with a reverence and even fear of Him. This is also true for Queen Kuntī though Śrīla Jīva Gosvāmī explains that love for Krishna always prevailed in her heart. To prove this, he quotes her conversation with Akrūra when he visits Hastināpura. She is eager to know if family members in Dvārakā remember her.

bhrātreyo bhagavān kṛṣṇaḥ
śaraṇyo bhakta-vatsalaḥ
paitṛ-ṣvasreyān smarati
rāmaś cāmburuhekṣaṇaḥ

'Does my nephew Kṛṣṇa, the Supreme Personality and the compassionate shelter of His devotees, still remember His aunt's sons? Does lotus eyed Rāma remember them also?'
Śrīmad-Bhāgavatam 10.49.9

Śrīla Jīva Gosvāmī notes, 'a*iśvarya-jñāna-mayi bhakti* is incompatible with Queen Kuntī's position as Krishna's aunt. *Vātsalya*

1 Śrīla Viśvanātha Cakravartī calls this verse *paribhāṣā-sutra*, the key to understanding all of Krishna's pastimes in which He manifested His opulences (*aiśvarya*)

was more befitting her. Although she calls Him '*Bhagavān*' which implies *dāsya-bhāva, vātsalya* overshadows this bhāva, as shown by the words of *bhrātreyaḥ* (nephew), *paitṛ-ṣvasreyān* (aunt) and *cāmburuhekṣaṇaḥ* (lotus-eyed). Because *vātsalya rasa* is predominant by far, there is no clashing combinations of *rasas* in this verse.'(*Prīti-sandarbha, Anuccheda* 192)

For Queen Kuntī, Krishna always remains primarily the son of her brother Vasudeva and her sons' bosom friend. But every time she encounters a manifestation of Krishna's greatness and power, she recalls that He is God. Just as the full moon fades in the light of the rising sun, for a moment, her *mādhurya-jñāna*, the memory of Krishna's sweetness and beauty, of His love and kindness, is obscured by *aiśvarya-jñāna*, knowledge of His omnipotence. During her prayers, this is the case too.

When Faith Turns into Trust

The terrible, brutal war had just ended. After thirteen years of waiting, Queen Kuntī was once again able to embrace her sons. Cradling them in her arms, she recalled when she had followed them into the forests years ago. Drenched in sorrowful tears, she had fallen into the dust and laid there for a long, long time, finding no strength to rise or receive her sons' care. Now all her sons, except the eldest, were back from war. Safe and unharmed, they could finally relax and celebrate victory.

However, the sky and earth were suddenly illuminated by the ominous radiance of Aśvatthāmā's terrible arrow. It threatened to destroy all living creatures. Once again, Krishna intervened and saved everyone. Without moving from His chariot, He effortlessly protected all five Pāṇḍava brothers at once. Simultaneously, He rescued Parīkṣit who was about to be parched in Uttarā's womb by a *brahmāstra*.

In that moment of tremendous tension and relief, Queen Kuntī's understanding of God's greatness came to the fore. A full view of reality revealed itself before her shocked eyes. She clearly saw that Krishna was behind everything. She saw Him inside and outside everything that existed. She saw how He punishes some and protects others, how His material energy acts obediently to His will. The truth, as Krishna explains it in the *Bhagavad-gītā* came alive for her: *mayādhyakṣeṇa prakṛtiḥ/ sūyate sa-carācaram.*[1] She saw how Krishna, in the form of Paramātmā, resides in the hearts of all living beings, prompting everyone to act according to their karma. Overwhelmed with sacred awe, she ran to Krishna to offer her prayers.

> ***brahma-tejo-vinirmuktair***
> ***ātmajaiḥ saha kṛṣṇayā***
> ***prayāṇābhimukhaṁ kṛṣṇam***
> ***idam āha pṛthā satī***

> 'Thus, saved from the radiation of the *brahmāstra*, Kuntī, the chaste devotee of the Lord, and her five sons and Draupadī addressed Lord Kṛṣṇa as He started for home.'
>
> *Śrīmad-Bhāgavatam* 1.8.17

Meanwhile, Krishna behaved as if nothing extraordinary had happened. Moments earlier, Uttarā had charged over in distress, but now His friends were safe, Krishna decided to continue His journey. His charioteer Dāruka had already taken the reins and raised his whip. In a frenzy, Queen Kuntī, the Pāṇḍavas and Draupadī surrounded Krishna's chariot and begged Him to postpone His departure.

1 'This material nature, which is one of My energies, is working under My direction, O son of Kuntī, producing all moving and nonmoving beings. Under its rule this manifestation is created and annihilated again and again.' *Bhagavad-gītā* 9.10.

Usually, when faced with God's omnipotence (*brahma-tejo-vinirmuktair*), a person becomes painfully aware of their helplessness and insignificance. The reaction to this feeling varies from person to person. The ungodly react with arrogance, as seen in the Kauravas's assembly years back when Krishna came as peace envoy. When Vidura began glorifying Krishna's omnipotence, the indignant Duryodhana ran out in defiance, slamming the door behind him. Whenever anyone would even begin to say that Krishna is God in Duryodhana's presence, he would start shaking. Krishna's proximity infuriated him. A proud person finds it extremely difficult to come to terms with his own helplessness. He violently reacts and hides away, feeling insecure.

However, that same sense of helplessness that arises from contact with God's greatness pleases the devotees. They are happy to feel helpless in His presence. On this, Śrīla Prabhupāda says, 'Sometimes the Lord puts His pure devotees in such dangers because in that condition of helplessness the devotee becomes more attached to the Lord,' (*Śrīmad-Bhāgavatam* 1.8.23, purport)

In Hastināpura's royal court, when Krishna showed His universal form, everyone squeezed their eyes shut in horror and collapsed to the floor. Only the sages present – Nārada, Kaṇva, Paraśurāma and others – jumped from their seats and began to offer prayers. Dhṛtarāṣṭra, Kaṁsa, and other kings knew that Krishna was God, but feared Him – 'the impious rulers regarded Krishna as their judge and chastiser.'[1] The Pāṇḍavas and Queen Kuntī also knew that Krishna is God but loved Him dearly.

In other words, simply knowing about God and His omnipotence is not enough to make us love Him. Knowledge of God may turn either into love for Him or fear of Him, depending on

1 *satāṁ kṣiti-bhujāṁ śāstā*, Śrīmad-Bhāgavatam 10.43.17.

what this knowledge meets in the person's heart. In the heart of a humble person, knowledge turns into trust and love, while in the heart of a proud man it turns into fear. Śrīla Prabhupāda once gave a wonderful definition of humility to his disciple Harivilas Das:

> *'Humility means that you are convinced beyond any doubt that there is nothing in this world, absolutely nothing in this world, not your money, not your family, not your fame, not your gun, not your education, nothing will save you except the mercy of Krishna. When you are convinced like this, then you are humble.'*[1]

This quality is a major indicator of the purity of our *bhakti*. It is no coincidence that Sūta Gosvāmī makes special mention of it three times within such a short passage: first, Uttarā runs straight to Krishna, passing by her father-in-law Arjuna and mighty Bhīma; then, in the thirteenth verse, the Pāṇḍava brothers are called *ananya-viṣayātmanām* which means 'utterly dependent,' and, finally, in 1.8.17, he calls Kuntī *satī*, 'chaste.' Śrīla Prabhupāda further elaborates:

> *'A chaste devotee of the Lord does not look to others, namely any other living being or demigod, even for deliverance from danger. That was all along the characteristic of the whole family of the Pāṇḍavas. They knew nothing except Kṛṣṇa, and therefore the Lord was also always ready to help them in all respects and in all circumstances. That is the transcendental nature of the Lord. He reciprocates the dependence of the devotee. One should not, therefore, look for help from imperfect living beings*

1 Following Śrīla Prabhupāda, Remembrances, August 1973 – March 1974.

or demigods, but one should look for all help from Lord Kṛṣṇa, who is competent to save His devotees. Such a chaste devotee also never asks the Lord for help, but the Lord, out of His own accord, is always anxious to render it.'

Śrīmad-Bhāgavatam 1.8.17, purport

In this way, faith transforms into trust in Krishna when it comes into contact with humility, and fear leaves the heart. Lord Rāmacandra also promised to award fearlessness to anyone who says at least once, 'I am Yours.'

sakṛd eva prapanno yas
tavāsmīti ca yācate
abhayaṁ sarvadā tasmai
dadāmy etad vrataṁ mama

'The Lord says, "If one surrenders unto Me sincerely, saying, 'My Lord, from this day I am fully surrendered unto You,' I always give him protection. That is My vow."'

Rāmāyaṇa, Yuddha-kāṇḍa 18.33

The verse establishes beyond all doubt that fear cannot exist in a humble heart. Let us inspect our own hearts. Should we still see fear within, then we know our faith in God has not yet turned into trust in Him, and, therefore, we are still far from true humility. Queen Kuntī's prayers are so important for us because in them she teaches us how to gradually, step by step, humbly and gratefully accept whatever the Lord sends us. This will allow our faith to develop into absolute trust in Krishna, which is called chastity, *satī*. When this happens fear will disappear from our hearts without a trace.

CHAPTER 4

Queen Kuntī's Prayers Begin

Inconceivable Krishna: Defining God

From the start of her prayers, Queen Kuntī shows a deep understanding of the dynamics of relationships. She reveals the depth of her love in the sharing of her heart. She tells Krishna how she feels about Him, what she knows about Him, and all that He has done for her. Her heartfelt words, keen observations, and unreserved appreciation deepen the intimacy and trust between them. Only after this, does she submit a gentle, humble, ardent request.

There is so much we can learn on so many levels from these prayers. Here, at the start, we should consider the unwritten rules of all sincere and true relationships: we sincerely talk and listen. We offer appreciation that is genuine and specific. We show the other person that we value who they are, have noticed and cherish their qualities, and appreciate all the big and small ways they have been there for us. In short, we express how much we deeply know and truly appreciate the other person. If they are convinced of our sincerity, then they will be ready to shower their blessings upon us without even being asked.

During a Ratha-yātrā festival, Śrī Caitanya Mahāprabhu recited again and again a verse from *Kāvya-prakāśa*, a treatise on mundane poetics: *yaḥ kaumāra-haraḥ* – 'That very personality who stole away my heart during my youth is now again my master.'[1] No one could understand the reason for His doing so, except Śrīla Rūpa Gosvāmī who could fathom what was happening in His heart. Kṛṣṇadāsa Kavirāja writes that Caitanya Mahāprabhu was so pleased with Śrīla Rūpa Gosvāmī that He bestowed profuse blessings upon him.

Feeling understood is essential for us, like breathing fresh air. True intimacy – the intimacy of hearts – begins with this. Without

1 *Caitanya-caritāmṛta*, *Madhya-līlā* 1.58.

mutual understanding, there can be no true relationship, be it with Krishna, a spouse, or with our children.

How much pain and misery individuals in close relationships inflict upon each other! What acute loneliness they experience living in the same space but not understanding each other! Few people think to ask themselves, 'Maybe it's because I have not tried hard enough to understand the other person?' Trying to understand the companion that fate has brought into our lives should be our daily labor, our *sādhana*. Every day, we must invest in the relationships that we hold dear, trying to understand the other person's thoughts, heart movements, and soul. Without this, there can be no question of a relationship. Physical closeness can never replace understanding.

Queen Kuntī submits to Krishna a prayer comprising 26 verses, from 1.8.18 to 1.8.43. She begins in a mood of intimacy, telling Krishna, 'No one can completely understand You. However, I have understood something about You. Let me first tell You the way I know You.'

> ***kunty uvāca***
> ***namasye puruṣaṁ tvādyam***
> ***īśvaraṁ prakṛteḥ param***
> ***alakṣyaṁ sarva-bhūtānām***
> ***antar bahir avasthitam***
>
> 'Śrīmatī Kuntī said: O Kṛṣṇa, I offer my obeisances unto You because You are the original personality and are unaffected by the qualities of the material world. You are existing both within and without everything, yet You are invisible to all.'
> *Śrīmad-Bhāgavatam* 1.8.18

Krishna normally addressed Queen Kuntī as His senior, always asking for her blessings. He always received her motherly love.

Now, here, all of a sudden, she begins a speech with '*namasye*,' 'I offer my obeisance unto You, my Lord.'

In Vedic society, etiquette was strictly practiced. Seniors could not bow to juniors. Mothers could not bow to sons. This would break down the relationship, and cause embarrassment because of the incompatible combination of *rasas* (*rasābhāsa*). In this case, however, there was no *rasābhāsa*: the *aiśvarya-jñāna* that had emerged on the surface of Queen Kuntī's consciousness temporarily overshadowed her maternal *rasa*. What remained was *tattva*, eternal reality: 'You are God, and I am a tiny soul in need of Your protection.' Yet, Viśvanātha Cakravartī explained that upon hearing *namasye*, Krishna felt uneasy.

Years back in Mathurā, after a long separation, Devakī and Vasudeva did the same – they folded their hands in prayer to their sons, Krishna and Balarāma. Tears welled in Krishna's eyes. To shake his parents out of this reverential mood, He began asking for their forgiveness, 'Please, forgive me. I am your son, but all this time I have failed to fulfill My filial duty.' Now, however, standing before His aunt, Krishna only raised his eyebrows in surprise, as if to ask the silent question, 'Why are you suddenly bowing to Me?'

We will unpack Queen Kuntī's words to appreciate a beautiful exchange of feelings. In response to Krishna's gesture, she replies,

'I bow to You because You are the Puruṣa (*namasye puruṣaṁ*).'

The word *puruṣa* means the 'supreme enjoyer' but also 'a man.' Krishna takes the latter meaning and says,

'I agree. I am a man, a puruṣa. But that is not a reason to bow to Me.'

'No! You are not an ordinary *puruṣa*,' Queen Kuntī adds. 'You are the original *puruṣa, ādi-puruṣa, ādyaṁ*.'

'Alright, I am the original, but we are all original. For the soul, there is neither birth nor death. The soul was never born, it is original. This is another unconvincing reason for bowing to Me.'

'But You are God, *īśvaram*,' Queen Kuntī persists.

'But Brahmā is an *īśvara*, Indra is an *īśvara*. Kings of this world are also called *īśvaras*. Yes, I am a king, an *īśvara*. But do you have to bow to Me because of that?' Krishna says.

'You are not an ordinary *īśvara*. You are the *īśvara* who is beyond material nature – *īśvaraṁ prakṛteḥ param*,' Queen Kuntī tries to explain.

Krishna raises His eyebrows in even greater surprise, 'Do you mean to say that I am Paramātmā, the *puruṣa*, located in the heart of all living beings?'

'No, you are not Paramātmā. You are *alakṣyaṁ*!'

Śrīla Prabhupāda translates *alakṣyaṁ* as 'the invisible' but its literal meaning is 'one who cannot be recognized, one who has no visible attributes (*lakṣaṇās*).' Paramātmā can be recognized and felt in the heart. Sometimes, we feel God is present in the heart as the voice of conscience. In meditation, yogis see the Paramātmā in their heart. Therefore, Queen Kuntī means to say, 'No, You are not Paramātmā because You are *alakṣyaṁ*, You are unrecognizable.'

'Ah, I am *alakṣyaṁ*,' says Krishna. 'You mean to say that I am the impersonal all-pervading Brahman? But how can it be if I am right in front of you and you can see Me?'

'No, no, You are not the impersonal Brahman!' Queen Kuntī insists as she concludes, 'You are within and without. You are right in front of me and at the same time You are inside all that exists. You protected my sons from without and at the same time, invisible to anyone, You entered Uttarā's womb – *antar bahir avasthitam.*'

In this sequence, Queen Kuntī eventually arrives at the most comprehensive definition of the Lord's omnipotence (*aiś-varya*). It correlates with Krishna's own explanation in the *Bhagavad-gītā*:

> *...mat-sthāni sarva-bhūtāni*
> *na cāhaṁ teṣv avasthitaḥ*
> *na ca mat-sthāni bhūtāni*
> *paśya me yogam aiśvaram*

> 'All beings are in Me, but I am not in them. And yet everything that is created does not rest in Me. Behold My mystic opulence!'
> *Bhagavad-gītā* 9.4-5

The *Kūrma Purāṇa* describes the Lord's *aiśvarya* in the following way:

> *aiśvarya-yogād bhagavān*
> *viruddhārtho 'bhidhīyate*
> *tathāpi doṣāḥ parame*
> *naivāhāryāḥ kathancana*
> *guṇā viruddhā api tu*
> *samāhāryāś ca sarvataḥ*

> 'Because the Supreme Lord is abounding with all opulence, He is called *viruddha-artha*, "internally contradictory." However, despite the incompatible and clashing qualities that coexist in Him, one should

> never allow even the thought of His having flaws. The Supreme Lord is above everything, therefore all qualities, even the incompatible ones, are contained in Him.'
>
> Quoted from *Bhagavat-sandarbha*, *Anuccheda* 37

This is a distinctive characteristic of Bhagavān. The Lord imparts other living beings with some of His qualities, but the ability to combine the incompatible and reconcile the irreconcilable (*acintya-śakti*)[1] is unique to Him alone.

Krishna is standing right before Queen Kuntī. She can see Him. At the same time, she knows that He dwells in the heart of every living being and in every atom. According to the laws of logic, what is everywhere cannot be in one place. Ether cannot have a specific form because it is omnipresent. Something localized cannot be omnipresent, and something omnipresent cannot be localized. But Bhagavān, the Personality of Godhead, can be both formless and have a specific form. That is, He can be simultaneously unlimited and limited. He can take birth while remaining unborn. He can be the greatest and the smallest. He can be infinitely merciful and at the same time allow the existence of evil and suffering in this world. He can remain omnipotent and suffer defeat at the hands of His friends.

All these are logically incompatible qualities. Their presence in God prove that He cannot be understood by logic and reason: *acintyāḥ khalu ye bhāvā na tāṁs tarkeṇa yojayet*[2] – 'Ordinary logic is not applicable to incomprehensible phenomena.' He can be understood only by love; for love, like God Himself, reconciles all contradictions.

1 *Mahābhārata*, *Bhīṣma-parva* 5.22.

2 Śrīla Rūpa Gosvāmī lists five qualities that are unique to *Viṣṇu-tattvas*, the personal forms of God, in *Bhakti-rasāmṛta-sindhu* 2.1.39. The first of these is *avicintya-mahā-śakti.*

From time immemorial, the fools of this world have been trying to deny God's existence by 'catching' Him in logical contradictions. God can never be captured in the net of their primitive logic. 'Can Almighty God create a stone that He Himself will be unable to lift?' The ignorant have no idea that God is logically contradictory, by definition. Logic rests on the 'law of the excluded middle,' which states that if a statement is true, then the negated form of that statement is, by definition, false. Furthermore, there is no option for any middle position.

But God includes everything in Himself. Logic operates with causal relationships, while God is beyond all causes and effects. Logic is applicable only to the limited phenomena of the material world, and God is unlimited.

Therefore, Queen Kuntī concludes this verse with *antar bahir avasthitam*:

> 'You are the master of everything. Indeed, You are the Supreme Personality, for I personally saw You playfully raise Your disk, the Sudarśana cakra. Spinning madly, Your disk stood between my sons and the brahmāstra, and all the incredible potency of the brahmāstra instantly dissolved in the air, as if it had never existed. At the same time, I saw You enter Uttarā's womb and protect her fetus from within. The main brahmāstra was aimed at her child, but You protected him in a way that no one else could see, for You are inside and outside of everything. You miraculously combine these qualities within Yourself. So, I have nothing to do but bow before You.'

Actor on Stage

Queen Kuntī's next verse is about the futility of all our attempts to perceive God and decipher His plan.

> ***māyā-javanikācchannam***
> ***ajñādhokṣajam avyayam***
> ***na lakṣyase mūḍha-dṛśā***
> ***naṭo nāṭyadharo yathā***

> 'Being beyond the range of limited sense perception, You are the eternally irreproachable factor covered by the curtain of deluding energy. You are invisible to the foolish observer, exactly as an actor dressed as a player is not recognized.'
> *Śrīmad-Bhāgavatam* 1.8.19

Acknowledging God's inconceivable nature is the first step to understanding Him. Queen Kuntī takes this step by explaining why Krishna is incomprehensible.

'You are hidden by the veil of *māyā*, the illusory energy – *māyā-javanikācchannam*,' she says.

'Oh! Am I covered by *māyā*?' The Lord's eyebrows arch higher. 'Are you a proponent of the *Māyāvāda* philosophy? Do you really think *māyā* can cover the infinite Brahman?'

'No, no! You are covered only from the ignorant, *ajña*. The veil of *māyā* does not 'cover' You, for You are inexhaustible, infinite, *avyayam*. It covers the eyes of the ignorant, thus making You imperceptible to the material senses, *adhokṣajam*. No cloud can block out the sun, but it can block our eyes from seeing the sun. I cannot come in touch with You because You are beyond sensory perception, and I receive all my knowledge through the senses – the eyes, ears, tongue. Therefore, I am doomed to remain in ignorance.'

'You contradict yourself by calling Me incomprehensible. You have understood Me, haven't you?' Krishna seems to object. 'You see Me right in front of you. You praise Me and know that I am beyond material energy. Why do you call yourself ignorant?'

'Even seeing You with my own eyes, I do not see You, because one sees the world through the prism of their mind, and not through the eyes alone,' Queen Kuntī replies.

Śrīla Prabhupāda has translated *mūḍha-dṛśā* as a 'foolish observer.' A fool cannot recognize God even if He appeared in all His glory and majesty. Ignorance and sin cause such foolishness that deprives us of the ability to understand God. Śrīla Prabhupāda explains:

> *'...a class of men with demoniac mentality who are always reluctant to accept the Lord as the Supreme Absolute Truth. This is partially due to their poor fund of knowledge and partially due to their stubborn obstinacy, which results from various misdeeds in the past and present. Such persons could not recognize Lord Śrī Kṛṣṇa even when He was present before them.'*
>
> *Śrīmad-Bhāgavatam* 1.8.19, purport

Queen Kuntī employs a simile to illustrate the point, 'To foolish observers, You are like the disguised actor on stage (*nāṭyadharo yathā*).' The Sanskrit word *nāṭa* can mean 'actor,' 'dancer,' or 'singer,' that is, anyone who performs on stage. To understand this example, we need to know the specifics of traditional Indian drama.

Unlike modern drama, in India, actors wore heavy layers of costume and jewelry as well as thick dramatically painted makeup. Men played female parts and in such attire were difficult to recognize. Thus, Queen Kuntī says, 'You are *nāṭa*, an actor. You play a variety of roles, which is why we, the audience, cannot recognize You even when we see you.'

Viśvanātha Cakravartī Ṭhākura gives another important interpretation of the line (*na lakṣyase mūḍha-dṛśā, naṭo nāṭyad-haro yathā*) – that a good actor knows what he must do on stage to stir an aesthetic pleasure in the audience. Through rhythm, gesture and creative emotive means, he influences the spectator to feel delight, to laugh, or weep. However, if the audience is uncultured and oblivious to the finer expressions of music, song, and dance, then all they see are meaningless movements that leave them indifferent. Only a connoisseur of developed aesthetic taste, and who has a deep heart, will be able to appreciate the actor's performance.

In Sanskrit classical drama, there is the concept of *sadṛśa*, 'the compassionate spectator' who is 'a person with a responsive heart.' This educated spectator watches the performance and experiences refined emotional bliss, *rasa*. Such a connoisseur must, first of all, have a sufficiently pure mind (be under the predominant influence of s*attva-guṇa*); secondly, be able to control the mind and senses; thirdly, be focused on the action taking place on stage (and be able to identify with the characters) and, finally and most importantly, be well educated in the *rasa-śāstra*. Then their heart will sing and cry with the actor. In contrast, the heart of an ignorant spectator (*mūḍha-dṛśā*) remains cold and apathetic.

If we draw this all together, Queen Kuntī wants to tell Krishna,

'You are a magnificent actor. You play Your part brilliantly and You truly relish it. You are eager to share bliss with everyone, but few of us are able to appreciate Your performance. It finds no response in our hearts. We are all so ignorant and incapable of understanding what You want to tell us. Yes, I did see how You protected my sons, but why did You take Your disc to do that? Before the battle, You promised You would not touch any weapon, but You have just broken Your word needlessly. You could have protected them just as you have protected them many times before and as you have just protected Parīkṣit – from within. Moreover, You are in the heart of all living beings, so who else but You incited Aśvatthāmā to release the *brahmāstra* in the first place? Who can understand why You did that?'

'Is it so difficult to understand?' Krishna might reply. 'I just wanted to protect My devotees, and for that I am ready to break My word.'

'Okay, then explain why You told the Pāṇḍavas how to kill Bhīṣma? You said Yourself in *Bhagavad-gītā, paritrāṇāya sādhūnāṁ*[1] – 'I come here to protect the pious.' If there was ever a true *sādhu* in this world, it was Bhīṣma. You could hardly find a more pious person, but instead of protecting him, You instructed Arjuna to kill him.'

Satisfied, Krishna mysteriously smiles, 'Alright, what else do you not understand?'

'My dear Krishna, I might find a way to understand even that but why didn't You protect my grandson Abhimanyu? He grew up in Your lap. He was the only son of Your beloved sister Subhadrā, whom You gave in marriage to your beloved friend Arjuna. You were so fond of Abhimanyu. He was killed unjustly, in front of You. Who can understand why that happened?'

Queen Kuntī goes on, 'That is not all. Everyone knows how much You love Draupadī! Among female devotees, she is most dear to You. But what did You do to her five sons? You knew what was going to happen that ill-fated night when Aśvatthāmā slaughtered her sons. That is why You persuaded my sons

1 *Bhagavad-gītā* 4.8.

to stay overnight elsewhere. Who can understand and appreciate the way You act? Certainly not those who look at You through the prism of their defiled mind. Only a person with a most pure heart is capable of that.'

* * *

God is *rasa* – *raso vai saḥ* – 'He, the Supreme, is the source of transcendental bliss (*rasa*).'[1] To understand Him, one must become *rasikā*, a connoisseur of *rasa*. Material intelligence cannot grasp the unlimited Lord. Empirical methods of cognition are feeble before Him. Out of compassion for human beings, He descends to this world and like an actor on stage He manifests His amazing *līlās*. However, fools contemptuously laugh at Him: *avajānanti māṁ mūḍhā mānuṣīṁ tanum āśritam* – 'Fools deride Me when I descend in the human form. They do not know My transcendental nature as the Supreme Lord of all that be.' (*Bhagavad-gītā* 9.11)

When scriptures or great devotees tell stories about Krishna to us sinful and foolish listeners, we consider them fiction or myth. Unless our hearts are cleansed through spiritual practice and scriptural study, we cannot come into contact with God. He will remain blocked off by the veil of *māyā*. There is no other way to comprehend Him except by feeling His presence with a pure and humble heart that starts to serve Him. Later in her prayers, Queen Kuntī explains how fools (*mūḍhas*) can gradually purify their hearts and stop being fools. Meanwhile, she reiterates that only those with pure hearts can understand Krishna.

1 *Taittirīya Upaniṣad* 2.7.1.

To Whom are the Gates of God's Kingdom Open?

Loving God is the only way to understand the Absolute Truth. But how can pure love spring in an impure heart? Śrīla Raghunātha dāsa Gosvāmī laments the problem in verse seven of *Śrī Manaḥ-śikṣā: kathaṁ sādhu premā spṛśati śucir etan nanu manaḥ* – 'O mind, tell me, how can pure divine love even come close to my contaminated heart?' In a similar way, Queen Kuntī prays:

> ***tathā paramahaṁsānāṁ***
> ***munīnām amalātmanām***
> ***bhakti-yoga-vidhānārthaṁ***
> ***kathaṁ paśyema hi striyaḥ***

> 'You Yourself descend to propagate the transcendental science of devotional service unto the hearts of the advanced transcendentalists and mental speculators, who are purified by being able to discriminate between matter and spirit. How then can we women know You perfectly?'
>
> *Śrīmad-Bhāgavatam* 1.8.20

She asks, 'Who is capable of feeling the sweetness of Your *līlās* and sharing the *rasa* contained within them?' and answers, 'Only those who are pure in heart.' She uses three words to describe such people: '*paramahaṁsānāṁ*,' '*munīnām*,' and '*amalātmanām*,' which could refer to three categories of people or simply describe purity of heart with three adjectives. She means to say, 'O Krishna, for the sake of such people You come to this world and manifesting Your pastimes, sow the seeds of *bhakti* (*bhakti-yoga-vidhānārthaṁ*) in their hearts.'

'*Paramahaṁsa*' is a person who has developed the ability to distinguish spirit from matter. Śrīla Prabhupāda explains:

> *'The word* parama *means "ultimate," and* haṁsa *means "swan." So paramahaṁsa means "the perfect swan." If we give a swan milk mixed with water, the swan will take the milk and leave aside the water. Similarly, this material world is made of two natures – the inferior nature and the superior nature. The superior nature means spiritual life, and the inferior nature is material life. Thus a person who gives up the material part of this world and takes only the spiritual part is called paramahaṁsa.'*
> Teachings of Queen Kuntī, ch. 3

A '*muni*' is a sage or philosopher. Here, Śrīla Prabhupāda chooses the specific translation of 'mental speculator.' In another purport, (*Bhāgavatam* 1.7.10), he details seven other shades of meanings for '*muni*': 1) those who are thoughtful, 2) those who are grave and silent, 3) ascetics, 4) the persistent, 5) mendicants, 6) sages, and (7) saints. In other words, *munis* are those who focus on spirit and not interested in the gloss of material nature.

'*Amala-ātmā*' means 'pure soul.' The word '*amalātmanām*' refers to one who has no dirty things in their heart. The heart of a materialistic person is full of dirty things, specifically lust and greed. An '*amalātmanām*' is free from these contaminations.[1]

The essence of all three definitions is the same – that pure intelligence gives one the ability to understand the real nature of the soul, as a part of God. Queen Kuntī says *bhakti-yoga* can be learned by those who have no other desires and who are completely focused on Krishna. For them, Krishna comes to Earth. 'But what are we women supposed to do?' she humbly laments.

It is pertinent to ask why *śāstras* sometimes speak disdainfully about women. Is it because men authored the books in distant, unenlightened times, in a society where everything was

1 Teachings of Queen Kuntī, ch. 3.

settled by brute force, and women were mercilessly exploited? Unfortunately, sometimes we hear such ideas. In fact, repeatedly, *śāstras* proclaim the supreme spiritual equality of all living beings:

vidyā-vinaya-sampanne
brāhmaṇe gavi hastini
śuni caiva śva-pāke ca
paṇḍitāḥ sama-darśinaḥ

> 'The humble sages, by virtue of true knowledge, see with equal vision a learned and gentle *brāhmaṇa*, a cow, an elephant, a dog and a dog-eater [outcaste].'
> *Bhagavad-gītā* 5.18

For this reason alone, authors of these sacred writings cannot be suspected of primitive chauvinism. *Śāstra* condemns not women as such, but a certain mentality that impedes spiritual development. Kapiladeva explains this in the Third Canto:

yāṁ manyate patiṁ mohān
man-māyām ṛṣabhāyatīm
strītvaṁ strī-saṅgataḥ prāpto
vittāpatya-gṛha-pradam

> 'A living entity who, as a result of attachment to a woman in his previous life, has been endowed with the form of a woman, foolishly looks upon *māyā* in the form of a man, her husband, as the bestower of wealth, progeny, house and other material assets.'
> *Śrīmad-Bhāgavatam* 3.31.41

In other words, according to *śāstra*, the living being gets a woman's body due to attachment to material enjoyment. That attachment makes the soul fully identify with matter, *prakṛti*, and forget its original pure spiritual nature. Attachment to matter weakens the soul, for weakness is nothing but attachment to pleasures and indulging one's desires.

The female mentality (no matter who inhabits it – a weak woman or a capricious man) is opposite to the mentality of '*paramahaṁsas*', '*munis*' and '*amalātmas*' who have cleansed their hearts from the dirt of material desires and passions. Therefore, when speaking of women, Queen Kuntī also means all of us, the weak and sissified people of *Kali-yuga*.

'Can we, weak living beings shamefully attached to material enjoyment, hope to understand You?' she asks Krishna. Fortunately, as she explains later, there is still hope for us – hope in God's mercy, which He bestows upon the humble. Those who are pharisaically proud of their purity are deprived of it. Therefore, in his commentary of this verse, Śrīla Prabhupāda flips the purport a hundred and eighty degrees:

> *'Even the greatest philosophical speculators cannot have access to the region of the Lord. It is said in the* Upaniṣads *that the Supreme Truth, the Absolute Personality of Godhead, is beyond the range of the thinking power of the greatest philosopher. He is unknowable by great learning or by the greatest brain. He is knowable only by one who has His mercy. Others may go on thinking about Him for years together, yet He is unknowable. This very fact is corroborated by the Queen, who is playing the part of an innocent woman. Women in general are unable to speculate like philosophers, but they are blessed by the Lord because they believe at once in the superiority and almightiness of the Lord, and thus they offer obeisances without reservation.'*
> *Śrīmad-Bhāgavatam* 1.8.20, purport

To enter the Kingdom of God, purity of heart is needed which only *bhakti* can bestow. That is why, for Śrīla Prabhupāda, true purity of heart is not in the ostentatious absence of desires, but in the humility that Queen Kuntī manifests when asking her question. Humility, in turn, forms unshakable faith in Krishna's mercy and thus enables us to practice *bhakti* and purify our hearts. Remnants of material desires are not a disqualification. Krishna states this when describing the qualities of one ready to take the path of *bhakti*:

> *jāta-śraddho mat-kathāsu*
> *nirviṇṇaḥ sarva-karmasu*
> *veda duḥkhātmakān kāmān*
> *parityāge 'py anīśvaraḥ*
> *tato bhajeta māṁ prītaḥ*
> *śraddhālur dṛḍha-niścayaḥ*
> *juṣamāṇaś ca tān kāmān*
> *duḥkhodarkāṁś ca garhayan*

> 'Having awakened faith in the narrations of My glories, being disgusted with all material activities, knowing that all sense gratification leads to misery, but still being unable to renounce all sense enjoyment, My devotee should remain happy and worship Me with great faith and conviction. Even though he is sometimes engaged in sense enjoyment, My devotee knows that all sense gratification leads to a miserable result, and he sincerely repents such activities.'
> *Śrīmad-Bhāgavatam* 11.20.27-28

Thus, in the first three verses of her prayers, Queen Kuntī has listed the reasons why it is so difficult for ordinary people to understand God.

1. He cannot be understood by the material mind.
2. He is unattainable by the material senses.
3. Ignorance, inherent to us all, obscures God from us.
4. The consequences of our sinful activities make us foolish and blur our vision.

5. Attachment to material enjoyment contaminates the heart.

By her own example, Queen Kuntī showed the one quality that helps to overcome all obstacles and understand God – humility, hope for Krishna's mercy. In her following verses, she describes what a humble person must do to understand the inconceivable Lord.

CHAPTER 5

The First Step in Comprehending the Incomprehensible

Opening the Lotus of the Heart

Sādhana is the set of methods to engage our senses otherwise chained to matter, in such a way to receive love of God. It is a practice that restructures our consciousness, enabling us to feel God's presence and feel devoted to Him: *kṛti-sādhyā bhavet sādhya-bhāvā sā sādhanābhidhā.*[1]

The *śruti-śāstra* defines the general principle of *sādhana*: *yatha yathopasate tad eva bhāvantiti*[2] – 'One becomes what he meditates on [in the process of practice].' Therefore, the main instruction Krishna gives in *Bhagavad-gītā is man-manā*[3] – 'Think of Me.' *Śrīmad-Bhāgavatam* defines this principle even more precisely:

yatra yatra mano dehī
dhārayet sakalaṁ dhiyā
snehād dveṣād bhayād vāpi
yāti tat-tat-svarūpatām
kīṭaḥ peśaskṛtaṁ dhyāyan
kuḍyāṁ tena praveśitaḥ
yāti tat-sātmatāṁ rājan
pūrva-rūpam asantyajan

'If out of love, hate or fear an embodied soul fixes his mind with intelligence and complete concentration upon a particular bodily form, he will certainly attain the form that he is meditating upon. O King, once

1 *Bhakti-rasāmṛta-sindhu* 1.2.2, Translation from *Caitanya-caritāmṛta, Madhya-līlā* 19.177: 'The process of devotional service – beginning with chanting and hearing – is called *sādhana-bhakti*. This includes the regulative principles intended to awaken one to devotional service.'

2 *Śatapatha Brāhmaṇa*. Quoted from *Prīti-sandarbha, Anuccheda* 51.

3 *Bhagavad-gītā* 9.34.

> a wasp forced a weaker insect to enter his hive and kept him trapped there. In great fear the weak insect constantly meditated upon his captor, and without giving up his body, he gradually achieved the same state of existence as the wasp. Thus, one achieves a state of existence according to one's constant concentration.'
>
> *Śrīmad-Bhāgavatam* 11.9.22-23

This law has recently been rediscovered by modern scientists studying the workings of the brain. Neurophysiologists have confirmed that regular meditation on a certain object physically changes the structure of the brain, creating new neural networks. Through neurotransmitters, the brain turns on new genes, thereby affecting the body. Thus, the practice of meditation gradually changes a person's consciousness, state of being (*bhāva*) and even physical body.

Everything we think about in meditation eventually manifests in external reality. If we focus and reflect on a particular form of God, as described in *śāstras*, our consciousness spiritualizes, and God appears before us in that form. Lord Brahmā reflects upon this in his prayers:

> *tvaṁ bhakti-yoga-paribhāvita-hṛt-saroja*
> *āsse śrutekṣita-patho nanu nātha puṁsām*
> *yad-yad-dhiyā ta urugāya vibhāvayanti*
> *tat-tad-vapuḥ praṇayase sad-anugrahāya*

> 'O my Lord, Your devotees can see You through their ears by the process of bona fide hearing, and thus their hearts become cleansed, and You take Your seat there. You are so merciful to Your devotees that You manifest Yourself in the particular eternal form of transcendence in which they always think of You.'
>
> *Śrīmad-Bhāgavatam* 3.9.11

In Eastern Catholic and Orthodox traditions, this process is called Theosis – to become 'God-like' and have union with God. The process is gradual because our ability to remember God depends on the purity of the heart. The first step in purifying the heart is feeling our helplessness and surrendering to the Lord – *śaraṇāgati*. From that level, one can gradually focus his consciousness on the Lord's name, form, qualities, and pastimes.

> *atha śaraṇapaty-ādibhih suddhāntah-karanas cet*
> *etan-nirvidyamānānām icchhatām akuto-bhayam ity-*
> *adyuktatvan nāma-kirtanāparityāgena smaraṇam kuryāt*

> 'If one's heart has become pure by surrender, service to devotees who embody truth, and hearing and singing the names, forms, attributes and pastimes of the Lord, one can perform *smaraṇam*, or remembrance of the Lord. The practice of remembrance, however, should be undertaken without giving up *nāma-kīrtana*, because the indispensability of singing the Lord's names has already been expressed in *Śrīmad-Bhāgavatam* 2.1.11: "O King, constant chanting of the holy name of the Lord after the ways of the great authorities is the doubtless and fearless way of success for all, including those who are free from all material desires, those who are desirous of all material enjoyment, and also those who are self-satisfied by dint of transcendental knowledge."'
>
> *Bhakti-sandarbha*, *Anuccheda* 275

In verses to come, Queen Kuntī describes the stages of meditation that gradually spiritualize our consciousness, detach it from matter, and focus it on God.

1) *nama-smaraṇam* – meditation on the holy name

2) *rūpa-smaraṇam* – meditation on God's form
3) *guṇa-smaraṇam* – meditation on God's qualities
4) *līlā-smaraṇam* – meditation on His pastimes.

In *Bhakti-sandarbha*, Śrīla Jīva Gosvāmī explains what takes place in the *sādhaka*'s mind through the course of practice and why it is so crucial to follow a proper sequence of deepening meditation:

> *tatra yadyapi ekatareṇāpi vyutkramenapi*
> *siddhir bhāvaty eva tathāpi prathamam nāmnaḥ*
> *śravaṇam antaḥkaraṇa-śuddhy-artham apekṣyam*

'Although any, even a sporadic (*vyutkramenapi*) contact with God's name, form, etc., may bring about success (*siddhir bhāvati*) in order for the heart of a practicing devotee (*antaḥ-karaṇa*) to begin purifying, he should start by hearing the holy name.'

Chanting the holy name gradually prepares our heart for meditation on the Lord's form, qualities, and pastimes, making it natural.

> *prathamaṁ nāmnaḥ śravaṇam antaḥ-karaṇa-śuddhy-artham apekṣyam*
> *śuddhe cāntaḥ-karaṇe rūpa-śravaṇena tad-udaya-yogyatā bhavati*
> *samyag udite ca rūpe guṇānāṁ sphuraṇaṁ sampadyeta*
> *sampanne ca guṇānāṁ sphuraṇe parikara-vaiśiṣṭyena tad vaiśiṣṭyaṁ sampadyate*
> *tatas teṣu nāma-rūpa-guṇa-parikareṣu samyak sphuriteṣu līlānāṁ sphuraṇaṁ*
> *suṣṭhu bhavatīty abhipretya sādhana-kramo likhitaḥ*
> *evaṁ kīrtana-smaraṇayor jñeyam*

'First one hears the Lord's holy name, and in that way one's heart becomes purified. When one's heart is

> purified, by hearing about the Lord's transcendental form, the form appears in one's heart. When the Lord's form appears in this way, the Lord's transcendental qualities are then clearly manifested (*guṇānāṁ sphuraṇaṁ*) will start revealing themselves to some extent. When the Lord's qualities are fully revealed in the heart, the qualities and names of the Lord's associates start revealing themselves (*nāma-rūpa-guṇeṣu tat-parikareṣu*). When the Lord's name, form, qualities, and associates enter the heart of the *bhakta*, the Lord's *līlās* become revealed to his inner vision in all their splendor (*suṣṭhu*).
> *Bhakti-sandarbha, Anuccheda* 256 [1]

We are describing this gradual path so that the practicing devotees understand how the Lord manifests Himself in one's heart during *sādhana*. The same can be said regarding the chanting the Lord's name, glorifying His form, qualities and pastimes and their remembrance. Indeed, all practicing devotees should understand this process. The Lord's form, already contained within the holy name, is gradually revived in our hearts as we hear and chant the holy name. The symptom of successfully completing a stage of spiritual practice is the spontaneous, flash-like revelation in the heart (*sphūrti*) of the object of meditation. This should take place before we contemplate moving to the next stage.

In other words, we should always begin our practice by chanting and hearing the holy name. At the same time, we can and should study scriptures and listen to exalted Vaiṣṇavas describe Krishna's form, qualities, and pastimes. Our sincere efforts to engage our senses and mind in Krishna's service will at some point induce the Lord's name to reveal His form (*rūpa*).

1 Śrīla Jīva Gosvāmī writes practically the same in *Krama-sandarbha* (7.5.18), his commentary on the *Śrīmad-Bhāgavatam*. Śrīla Bhaktisiddhānta Sarasvatī quoted this passage often.

By the Lord's grace, when His form becomes imprinted in our hearts, in all its details, it will bring forth a reflection of His qualities (*guṇas*). Then, while chanting the holy name, the devotee will spontaneously remember Krishna's qualities with tears of gratitude. At the next stage, the Lord's associates and pastimes will begin to reflect in the mirror of the heart spontaneously.

However, if we try to force premature meditation on Krishna's pastimes, then we inevitably project our material experiences onto them and only commit offenses. Our conscious effort should be in serving Krishna sincerely by hearing and serving exalted Vaiṣṇavas and studying scriptures. The Lord's *svarūpa-śakti*, his inner energy, accomplishes everything else.

ataḥ śrī-kṛṣṇa-nāmādi na
bhaved grāhyam indriyaiḥ
sevonmukhe hi jihvādau
svayam eva sphuraty adaḥ

'Therefore, material senses cannot appreciate Krishna's holy name, form, qualities and pastimes. When a conditioned soul is awakened to Krishna consciousness and renders service by using his tongue to chant the Lord's holy name and taste the remnants of the Lord's food, the tongue is purified, and one gradually comes to understand who Krishna really is.'

Padma Purāṇa.
Quoted from *Caitanya-caritāmṛta, Madhya-līlā* 17.136

Thus, all our efforts to focus on the Lord's *nāma*, *rūpa*, *guṇa* and *līlā* in the form of *śravaṇam*, *kīrtanaṁ* or *smaraṇaṁ*, should spring from a revelation (*sphūrti*), that comes when the Lord is pleased with our efforts and agrees to manifest more fully in our hearts, which have been purified by spiritual practice. The revelation is a symptom that our attempts to serve have been accepted and we can go deeper in our efforts to understand the Lord. Śrīla Prabhupāda describes this process in one of his letters:

> *'Generally it is the process to simply chant and hear, but if Krishna's līlā comes into remembrance, that is very good. It should come automatically. Not that you are remembering artificially.'*
>
> Letter to Prahlādananda das 17.06.1971

In Lord Brahmā's prayer, (quoted above, *Śrīmad-Bhāgavatam* 3.9.11) the heart is compared to a lotus (*hrit-saroja*). Lotuses bloom only in the daytime, in sunlight. Similarly, without the grace of the sun-like holy name, the lotus of our heart will never bloom. When it is in full flourish, Krishna, His form, qualities, *līlās*, the entire spiritual world will be revealed in it. However, a lotus opens slowly as it saturates light and heat from the sun. This process cannot be accelerated artificially, otherwise the lotus simply withers. Therefore, at the heart of *bhakti* are always two qualities, two adornments of a surrendered soul – humility and patience.

The Philosopher's Stone of the Holy Name

As mentioned, meditation on Krishna always begins with hearing and chanting His holy name, but Śrīla Jīva Gosvāmī emphasizes that we must go on chanting throughout all the stages of spiritual development. There is an important reason for this. Scriptures compare the holy name to the philosopher's stone:

> *nāma cintāmaṇiḥ kṛṣṇaś*
> *caitanya-rasa-vigrahaḥ*

pūrṇaḥ śuddho nitya-mukto
'bhinnatvān nāma-nāminoḥ

'The holy name of Kṛṣṇa is transcendentally blissful. It bestows all spiritual benedictions, for it is Kṛṣṇa Himself, the reservoir of all pleasure. Kṛṣṇa's name is complete, and it is the form of all transcendental mellows. It is not a material name under any condition, and it is no less powerful than Kṛṣṇa Himself. Since Kṛṣṇa's name is not contaminated by material qualities, there is no question of its being involved with *māyā*. Kṛṣṇa's name is always liberated and spiritual; it is never conditioned by the laws of material nature. This is because the name of Kṛṣṇa and Kṛṣṇa Himself are identical.'

Padma Purāṇa.
Quoted from *Caitanya-caritāmṛta*, *Madhya-līlā* 17.133

The philosopher's stone turns iron into gold by its touch. Similarly, God's holy name, being non-different from Him, transforms the conditioned soul. Instead of identifying with matter, the soul recognizes itself as a pure spiritual intimately connected with God. In this way, the holy name delivers the soul from the bondage of matter.

A verse from *Hari-bhakti-vilāsa* suggests how to chant the holy name so it can begin transforming the soul and bestow the treasure it contains therein – love of God.

manaḥ saṁharaṇaṁśaucaṁ
maunaṁ mantrārtha-cintanam
avyagratvam anirvedo
japa-sampatti-hetavaḥ

'In order to become our wealth, the chanting of the holy name requires concentration (*manaḥ saṁharaṇam*). To focus our mind on the holy name,

> we need to purify it by observing the rules of external and internal purity (*śaucaṁ*). To purify the mind, we should avoid meaningless talk (*maunaṁ*). While chanting the holy name, we must meditate on its meaning (*mantrārtha-cintanam*). We should not chant while going somewhere or in-between other activities (*avyagratvam*). As we practice, we should patiently wait for the chanting to bear fruit (*anirvedam*).'
>
> *Hari-bhakti-vilāsa* 17.129

An integral part of spiritual practice is to reflect on the meaning of the holy name and its power to reveal the Lord. Queen Kuntī speaks her next verse to indicate this. Having humbly confessed to Krishna her inability to understand Him, she lists His names – all of which hold the seeds of love for God:

> ***kṛṣṇāya vāsudevāya***
> ***devakī-nandanāya ca***
> ***nanda-gopa-kumārāya***
> ***govindāya namo namaḥ***

> 'Let me therefore offer my respectful obeisances unto the Lord, who has become the son of Vasudeva, the pleasure of Devakī, the boy of Nanda and the other cowherd men of Vṛndāvana, and the enlivener of the cows and the senses.'
>
> *Śrīmad-Bhāgavatam* 1.8.21

Queen Kuntī begins with *Kṛṣṇaya*.[1] Gauḍīya Vaiṣṇavas consider the name 'Krishna' to be foremost of all the innumerable names of God, for it most fully describes God's qualities and nature. This statement may seem presumptuous to representatives of other religions. We will consider if we have

1 All names in this verse are in the dative case, 'I bow down to Krishna ...'

substantial reasons for making such statements. To do this, we need to analyze the meaning of the name from the points of view of *tattva* (philosophical principles) and *rasa*. The latter cannot be truly appreciated without understanding the former, thus we should always begin with the philosophical explanation.

Commenting on the *Brahma-saṁhitā* (5.1), Śrīla Jīva Gosvāmī gives a detailed philosophical analysis of the meaning of the name 'Krishna,' quoting from the *Mahābhārata* to explain the etymology:

kṛṣir bhū-vācakaḥ śabdo
ṇaś ca nirvṛti-vācakaḥ
tayor aikyaṁ paraṁ brahma
kṛṣṇa ity abhidhīyate [1]

'The word '*kṛṣ*' is the attractive feature of the Lord's existence, and '*ṇa*' means 'spiritual pleasure.' When the verb '*kṛṣ*' is added to '*ṇa*,' it becomes '*kṛṣṇa*,' which indicates the Absolute Truth.'

In Sanskrit, '*kṛṣṇa*' consists of two parts: '*kṛṣ*' and '*ṇa*.' The verbal root '*kṛṣ*' means 'to attract' or 'to subdue.' The first line of the verse states that the two roots '*kṛṣ*' (to attract) and *bhū* (to exist) are synonymous (*kṛṣir bhū-vācakaḥ*). Why? Because the underlying principle of existence is the great, all-predominating power that can only belong to God. In other words, '*kṛṣ*' indicates that Krishna is the cause of all that exists, and has absolute power over all that exists, holding the entire world in the orbit of His attraction.

In the second line of the verse, the syllable '*ṇa*' in the

1 *Mahābhārata*, *Udyoga-parva* 71.4; *Caitanya-caritāmṛta*, *Madhya-līlā*, 9.30. In the critical edition of the *Mahābhārata*, this verse is in *Udyoga-parva* 68.5.

word '*kṛṣṇa*' means '*nirvṛti*,' – 'spiritual pleasure' (literally 'the bliss that eclipses everything else'). Thus, joined together (*tayor aikyaṁ*), the syllables indicate the Absolute Truth which is 'the cause of all that is, which rules all that is and bestows bliss on all that is.'

Another possible meaning is 'one whose very existence consists of bliss.' Śrīla Jīva Gosvāmī also notes that the two parts of the word '*kṛṣṇa*' relate to each other as cause and effect. Therefore, a third meaning is 'one who is universally attractive *because* of the bliss contained within Him.'

Thus, the word '*kṛṣṇa*' describes the Supreme Absolute Truth (*paraṁ brahma*) in the fullest way because it refers to the infinite potency behind existence, which contains unlimited bliss and also bestows it. Judge for yourself how completely the two-syllables of '*kṛṣṇa*' describe God's nature. This is *tattva-vicāra*, the philosophical understanding of the meaning of the name 'Krishna.'

The *rasa-vicāra*, the aesthetic consideration of the nature of the Supreme Truth, sheds light on how Krishna bestows bliss on living beings. Gopal Guru Gosvāmī offers an explanation from this viewpoint:

ānandaika-sukha-svāmī
śyāmaḥ kamala-locanaḥ
gokulānandano nanda
nandanaḥ kṛṣṇa īryate

'Krishna is the name of a dark-skinned boy with
beautiful eyes resembling lotus petals. He is the
only one who can bestow supreme bliss. That boy is
Nanda Mahārāja's son, and He brings happiness to all
the inhabitants of Gokula.'

Bhaktivinoda Ṭhākura, *Bhajana-rahasya* 34

Krishna is more generous than anyone else in endowing sincere souls with His love, to bring them supreme bliss. His father's name, 'Nanda,' means joy, while Krishna is 'Nanda-nandana,' 'the joy of joy.' Śrīla Prabhupāda also explains why 'Krishna' denotes the highest form of God, in terms of *rasa*:

> *'Queen Kuntī specifically adores the incarnation or descent of Lord Kṛṣṇa above all other incarnations because in this particular incarnation He is more approachable.'*
> *Śrīmad-Bhāgavatam* 1.8.21, purport

Even in this world, politicians 'go out to the people' during election campaigns to demonstrate their accessibility. The one who proves to be most relatable usually wins. Likewise, God, the sum total of supreme bliss, comes to this world in various forms, so that living beings can share His happiness with Him. To some, He comes as the Burning Bush or Pillar of Fire, or to others in the form of the giant Kūrma turtle or Matsya fish. But are Kūrma or Matsya approachable? Can we go running or playing with Them? Is the form of Nṛsiṁhadeva approachable? Even Goddess Lakṣmī was scared to come forward, while the trembling demigods hid behind each other. What about Varāha? Paraśurāma? Even with Lord Rāmacandra, the most 'human-like' of all the *avatāras*, it is not so easy to develop a close relationship. Devotees nurture a relationship of service (*dāsya-rasa*) or respectful friendship (*gaurava-sakhya-rasa*).

Of all manifestations of God, only Krishna freely distributes His love. He is *akhila-rasāmṛta-mūrtiḥ*,[1] the most complete embodiment of all manifestations of love, and His unbelievable greatness lies in His unbelievable approachability.

1 *Bhakti-rasāmṛta-sindhu* 1.1.1.

While chanting Krishna's holy name, we can contemplate the philosophical meaning of His name and thereby purify our hearts by connecting with the infinite beauty and bliss of existence. Or, we can keep in mind the approachability of the dark-complexioned boy Krishna, who is willing to perfectly reciprocate with anyone's love. 'Krishna' contains all of God's infinite love for His living entities, which is why Gauḍīya Vaiṣṇavas consider it to be foremost.

The Seed of Love

By enumerating other names in 1.8.21, Queen Kuntī recalls Krishna's reciprocity with the love of various devotees. We will suggest possible reasons for her choices so that a glimmer of the unspoken sweetness might surface. *Kṛṣṇāya vāsudevāya*, she says:

> 'O Krishna, You are ready to give Yourself to everyone. But of all to whom You bestow Your love, my brother Vasudeva is the most fortunate, for You have become his son. Vasudeva simply asked for a son like You. But You said, "There is no other like Me so I will have to personally become your son." How wondrously you responded to his love.'

She goes on with *Devakī-nandanāya ca*:

> 'But Devakī was even more fortunate than Vasudeva. She loved You more than Vasudeva, so You agreed to enter her womb. What greater intimacy can one dream of – for eight months she carried You in her womb.'

The Lord Himself, the personified concentrated bliss, *ānanda-ghana-rūpa*, was there, present in her body! Can we imagine a greater fortune? No matter how hard Devakī tried to conceal her happiness from the vigilant eyes of Kaṁsa, she failed because she was so radiant. She could not believe her great fortune – that the blessed Lord, whose body is the resting place of the entire universe made up of all moving and non-moving living beings, was in her womb.

In the Tenth Canto, Devakī prayed to Krishna, who appeared as four-armed Viṣṇu:

> 'When the end of the world comes, the entire material cosmos, including all moving and non-moving creatures, enters Your transcendental body and rests there without any difficulties whatsoever. Now, that same transcendental body was born from my womb. Unable to believe this, people will simply laugh at me.'
>
> *Śrīmad-Bhāgavatam* 10.3.31

And then Queen Kuntī uses *Nanda-gopa-kumārāya*:

> 'And yet, Nanda Mahārāja loved You even more than Devakī did. Therefore, You were even more generous to him. You stayed in Devakī's womb for eight months, but You delighted Nanda Mahārāja, the simple cowherd, for many years. You grew up a little boy, a *kumāra* in his house. You bestowed upon him the happiness of taking care of You and playing with You.'

Raghupati Upādhyāya, the Vaiṣṇava poet, felt similar awe about Nanda Mahārāja:

śrutim apare smṛtim itare
bhāratam anye bhajantu bhava-bhītāḥ
aham iha nandaṁ vande
yasyālinde paraṁ brahma

> 'Those who are afraid of material existence worship the Vedic literature. Some worship *smṛti*, the corollaries to the Vedic literature, and others worship the *Mahābhārata*. As far as I am concerned, I worship Kṛṣṇa's father, Mahārāja Nanda, in whose courtyard the Supreme Personality of Godhead, the Absolute Truth, is playing.'
>
> *Caitanya-caritāmṛta*, *Madhya-līlā* 19.96

An ordinary child brings unbounded happiness to the parents. Therefore, it is difficult to imagine how deliriously happy Nanda Mahārāja was when Krishna, the master of infinite creation with all its beauties and opulence, crawled about in his garden as a small, helpless child!

Logically, we would expect Queen Kuntī to next mention Yaśodā's relationship with Krishna. But because of its exquisite nature, Queen Kuntī speaks about it separately in 1.8.31. She closes this prayer with *govindāya namo namaḥ*. Following the internal logic of this verse, where she has listed devotees of increasing love and intensity in sequence, we would expect the name of 'Govinda' to relate to a devotee whose love for Krishna is more intense than that of Nanda and Yaśodā. Those who have read the Tenth Canto know of these devotees. Out of reverence, Queen Kuntī does not mention any names, just as Śukadeva Gosvāmī did not dare utter their names – for who can truly fathom the intensity of their love? Besides, this subject cannot be discussed in public.

There is another explanation as to why Queen Kuntī chose to conclude with 'Govinda.' Krishna received this name after He passed from childhood (*kaumāra*) into His teens (*kaiśora*). Adolescence is the most magical time in one's life. When passing through this age, even ordinary people reflect a glimpse of divine beauty. If we analyze 'Govinda,' '*go*' here means 'senses' and '*vindati*' means 'to gain, to get.' Thus, '*Go-vinda*' means 'the one who captures all living beings' senses to Himself.' When Krishna turned adolescent, He captivated and appropriated the senses of all Vṛndāvana inhabitants with His incomparable beauty.

As a child, Krishna was the exclusive property of His parents. He enjoyed the love and adoration of Nanda, Yaśodā and other senior *gopīs*. As a *kaiśora*, the first thing He did was create a plausible pretext to gather everyone in one place, under the Govardhan Hill, to allow them to devour His beautiful form with their eyes.

For seven days, the besotted residents were oblivious of hunger or thirst. Krishna's marvelous beauty was their only food. A single glance at Krishna was sufficient to catapult the seer into love – with His beauty, strength, smile, wit, jokes, laughter, flute sounds, peacock feather, with everything He was. After this festival of love, Krishna was called Govinda. Remembering Govinda's generosity, Queen Kuntī glorifies this scene.

* * *

Anyone can begin their way to God. No matter how many material attachments and sins obstruct our paths, God wants to give Himself to us. The true greatness of God is in His approachability. The most approachable manifestation of God is His holy name. The entire *Śrīmad-Bhāgavatam* is about this: Krishna's approachability and the glories of His holy name. The scripture begins by glorifying that name:

āpannaḥ saṁsṛtiṁ ghorāṁ
yan-nāma vivaśo gṛṇan
tataḥ sadyo vimucyeta
yad bibheti svayaṁ bhayam

Śrīmad-Bhāgavatam 1.1.14

The verse states that anyone can break free from the terrible bonds of this world, from the jungle of *saṁsāra* if, even accidentally, they utter the holy name. One is at once liberated. Why? Because fear personified fears the holy name.

The scripture ends with a similar verse: *nāma-saṅkīrtanaṁ yasya sarva-pāpa praṇāśanam*[1] – glorifying Krishna, whose holy name is capable of destroying all sin. In the middle, the story of Ajāmila[2] is featured, which exemplifies the all-purifying potency of the holy name.

Yet, the essence of *Śrīmad-Bhāgavatam* is not simply to aid our liberation from sin and the terrible cycle of birth and death – but to teach us to love Krishna. Therefore, Queen Kuntī begins her prayer with God's names. All contain the seed of love for Him: *kṛṣṇāya vāsudevāya devakī-nandanāya ca nanda-gopa-kumārāya govindāya namo namaḥ*. In this prayer, she is not as much worshiping Krishna, as she is honoring the love that binds Him to His devotees. This is the true meaning of meditating on the Lord's holy name, as Śrīla Jīva Gosvāmī explains:

harir gopa-kṣauṇi-pati-mithunam anye ca vibudhā
na nah krūram citta mridulayitum isa lavam api
aho teṣām premā vilasati harau yas tu balavan
harer vā yas teṣu drutayati sa eva pratipadaṁ

'Neither Hari Himself, nor the king of the shepherd tribe Nanda, nor his faithful wife Yaśodā, nor any other inhabitant of Vraja could melt my icy heart.

1 I offer my respectful obeisances unto the Supreme Lord, Hari, the congregational chanting of whose holy names destroys all sinful reactions, and the offering of obeisances unto whom relieves all material suffering.' *Śrīmad-Bhāgavatam* 12.13.23.

2 Ajāmila was a disgraced *brāhmaṇa* who had fallen to a life of sin. Nonetheless, he was liberated after he uttered the holy name of Lord Nārāyaṇa on his deathbed.

It remained as cruel and cold as ever. But – lo and behold! As soon as I began contemplating the way the inhabitants of Vraja love Hari and the loving way He reciprocates, I felt my icy heart start to melt in the fire of their love!'

Gopāla-campū, *Pūrva* 1.81

CHAPTER 6

The Form that Quenches all Sorrows

Cascade of Mercy

Love always begins with the name of the beloved. Without a name, love is dead. Thus, from time immemorial, in all spiritual traditions, people chant the names of God. The wise know this as the only way to spiritualize their consciousness and enter the bliss of love contained within God's name.

Oddly enough, while recognizing the name of God, many spiritual traditions deny Him any form or image. The founders of these religions feared that worshiping a specific form of God would reduce Him to the level of the limited phenomena of this created world. However, if God has a name, then there must be a form contained within the name, and that form must be as spiritual as God's name.

Love, devoid of the image of the loved one, is just as unthinkable as love devoid of the beloved's name, for the two concepts 'love' and 'beauty' are inseparable. Sincere service to God's name dispels the dense fog that obscures our consciousness and reveals His transcendental image to us, disclosing His divine beauty. But this does not happen immediately.

In the meantime, what do we do with hearts not yet sufficiently purified to contemplate God's transcendental beauty? Our attempts to focus our consciousness on the sound of the holy name are obviously imperfect as the material world beckons and invites us from all around. How do we tear our eyes away from the beauty of this world? Especially for us, the Lord makes Himself available in the deity form (*arcā-vigraha*) for worship:

ya āśu hṛdaya-granthiṁ
nirjihīrṣuḥ parātmanaḥ
vidhinopacared devaṁ
tantroktena ca keśavam

'One who desires to quickly cut the knot of false ego, which binds the spirit soul, should worship the Supreme Lord, Keśava, by the regulations found in Vedic literatures such as the tantras.'
Śrīmad-Bhāgavatam 11.3.47

The *Tantra Śāstra* explains that for the benefit of all living entities, in accordance with their level of consciousness, Bhagavān, the Personality of Godhead, manifests Himself in five forms: *para*, *vyūha*, *vaibhava*, *antaryāmī* and *arcā*.

Para is Krishna Himself, of the spiritual world, who reveals Himself to the purest and most exalted living entities. To benefit the conditioned souls, He assumes the quadruple expansions (*vyūha*), who are involved in the manifestation of the material world. He also comes into this world in various avatars (*vaibhava*). He enters the hearts of all living beings as Paramātmā (*antaryāmī*). Finally, to make Himself available to the most ignorant, He manifests in the form of the *arcā-vigraha* so those blinded by attachment to matter can see Him, begin to serve Him, and meditate on His form. Thus, the Lord's mercy cascades into this world. Vaiṣṇavas are not afraid of worshiping the *arcā-vigraha* though it appears to be made of matter. They know that their desire to serve will induce God to enter that form, spiritualize it, and reciprocate through it. This is the topic of Queen Kuntī's next prayer.

Unearthly Beauty

namaḥ paṅkaja-nābhāya
namaḥ paṅkaja-māline
namaḥ paṅkaja-netrāya
namas te paṅkajāṅghraye

'My respectful obeisances are unto You, O Lord, whose abdomen is marked with a depression like

> a lotus flower, who is always decorated with garlands of lotus flowers, whose glance is as cool as the lotus and whose feet are engraved with lotuses.'
>
> *Śrīmad-Bhāgavatam* 1.8.22

Queen Kuntī compares each part of the Lord's body to a lotus flower, *paṅkaja*. The word '*paṅkaja*' means 'born from mud' because a lotus grows in mud. Despite this, it is a symbol of purity and beauty. Likewise, the *arcā-vigraha*, sculpted from wood, stone, or metal, has nothing to do with matter, for it personifies the unearthly beauty of God.

Another reason for Queen Kuntī to use this simile is to say that just as the lotus grows in water but is not wetted, Krishna descends to this world but remains transcendental to it. It is His transcendental form and not some material idol that Queen Kuntī worships here.

According to proper form, we are supposed to begin meditation on the Lord's form from His feet. However, Queen Kuntī begins from Krishna's navel: *paṅkaja-nābhāya* – 'Your navel is like a lotus,' so as not to confuse Krishna completely (she had already confused Him by her obeisance).

Poetry often carries layers of meanings and the commentator's task is to reveal the subtle shades of meaning otherwise missed by the inexperienced reader. Hence, Śrīla Prabhupāda offers another explanation for why Queen Kuntī begins her meditation on the Lord's form from his navel. Lord Viṣṇu is called *paṅkaja-nābha* since a lotus grows from His navel. The fourteen planetary systems rest within its stem. We live in one of them, *Bhū-maṇḍala*, at the center. The highest planetary system, *Satyaloka*, also shaped like a lotus, is where Lord Brahmā, the creator of this universe, resides. Queen Kuntī has already mentioned that the Lord is the original *puruṣa*, the original cause of everything; therefore, she begins her meditation from His navel, the source of the material universe. Śrīla Prabhupāda writes:

> *'Because such fallen souls cannot see anything beyond matter, the Lord condescends to enter into each and every one of the innumerable universes as the Garbhodakaśāyī Viṣṇu, who grows a lotus stem from the lotus-like depression in the center of His transcendental abdomen, and thus Brahmā, the first living being in the universe, is born. Therefore, the Lord is known as the Paṅkajanābhi. The Paṅkajanābhi Lord accepts the* arcā-vigraha *(His transcendental form) in different elements, namely a form within the mind, a form made of wood, a form made of earth, a form made of metal, a form made of jewel, a form made of paint, a form drawn on sand, etc.'*
>
> *Śrīmad-Bhāgavatam* 1.8.22, purport

Bhaktisiddhānta Sarasvatī explains that within the *arcā-vigraha*, the Supersoul, *antaryāmī*, dwells, which in turn is a manifestation of *vaibhava*, the Lord's *līlā-avatāras* who appear in this world. The *līlā-avatāras* emanate from *vyūha*, the fourfold expansion of the Lord, which emanates from Vasudeva, the transcendental Lord, who is the expansion of *svayaṁ-rūpa-tattva*, the original form of the Lord – Krishna in Goloka Vṛndāvana.[1] Therefore, by worshiping the *arcā-vigraha*, the aspiring devotee gets the opportunity to connect with the Supreme Lord Himself:

> *'Such persons, although they are unfit to enter into the spiritual affairs of the Lord, can see Him as the* arcā-vigraha*, who descends to the material world just to distribute favors to the fallen souls, including the above-mentioned women,* śūdras *and* dvija-bandhus*.'*
>
> *Śrīmad-Bhāgavatam* 1.8.22, purport

1 *Śrīmad-Bhāgavatam* 11.2.47, purport.

Queen Kuntī compares Krishna's eyes to a lotus flower – *paṅkaja-netrāya*, as if to say, 'My respectful obeisance unto You, O Lord, whose glance is as cool as the lotus.' On this, Śrīla Prabhupāda writes that when a person comes to the temple, looks at the Deities decorated with lotus flowers, catches the gaze of the Lord's lotus eyes, and immerses into the tranquil atmosphere of the temple, his agitated and feverish mind cools down.

Our minds are in a constant frenzy of passions, material desires, and emotions of stress, sorrow, resentment, and fear. Such a mind can never immerse in meditation or a sense of God's presence.

śokāmarṣādibhir bhāvair
ākrāntaṃ yasya mānasam
kathaṃ tatra mukundasya
sphūrti-sambhāvanā bhavet

'How can Lord Mukunda's image, even for a moment, appear in the heart of one whose mind is overwhelmed with anger, grief and other negative emotions?'

Padma Purāṇa. Quoted from *Bhakti-rasāmṛta-sindhu* 1.2.115

Śāstras also tell us how the lotus flower, like moonlight, camphor, and sandalwood paste, possesses an amazing ability to cool heat. Upon seeing a lotus, our mind spontaneously calms down and focuses. True meditation is only possible in a serene mind, uninflamed by sorrows and material desires. The fever within us subsides by itself as soon as we see the Lord's huge lotus eyes, compassionately gazing at us in the temple.

Love at First Sight

In the Eleventh Canto, Mahārāja Parīkṣit speaks of the miraculous effects of Krishna's transcendental form upon observers who have been fortunate enough to see Him:

> *pratyākraṣṭuṁ nayanam abalā yatra lagnaṁ na śekuḥ*
> *karṇāviṣṭaṁ na sarati tato yat satām ātma-lagnam*
> *yac-chrīr vācāṁ janayati ratiṁ kiṁ nu mānaṁ kavīnāṁ*
> *dṛṣṭvā jiṣṇor yudhi ratha-gataṁ yac ca tat-sāmyam īyuḥ*

> 'Once their eyes were fixed upon His transcendental form, women were unable to withdraw them, and once that form had entered the ears of the sages and become fixed in their hearts, it would never depart. What to speak of acquiring fame, the great poets who described the beauty of the Lord's form would have their words invested with transcendentally pleasing attraction. By seeing that form on Arjuna's chariot, all the warriors on the battlefield of Kurukṣetra attained the liberation of gaining a spiritual body similar to the Lord's.'
> *Śrīmad-Bhāgavatam* 11.30.3)

Being a direct manifestation of Krishna, the Deity in the temple can have the same effect on human consciousness. History has preserved amazing stories of people whose lives dramatically changed upon catching sight of the *arcā-vigraha.*

One such person was Dhanurdas. *Śūdra* by birth, wrestler by profession, he fell in love with a prostitute named Hemamba in his youth. Blinded and deafened by love, he saw nothing but her beautiful eyes, and never heard the condemning whispers behind his back as he walked through the town streets, carrying a silk umbrella over his beloved's head. Surprised by the sight, Rāmānuja asked a disciple to bring Dhanurdas to him.

'What is so impressive about that woman?' Rāmānuja asked. 'Shame, fear and even anger seemed to have abandoned your heart. The whole city is making fun of you, and you couldn't care less. Tell me your secret.'

'There is no secret. I have simply never seen anything more beautiful than her eyes in my life. Once I saw them, I couldn't look at anything else,' Dhanurdas said.

'What if I show you a set of eyes more beautiful? Will you stop serving her? Rāmānuja said with compassion.

'Oh yes! This woman's beauty has mesmerized me, but if someone else's beauty overshadows her image in my heart, I swear I'll serve the possessor of that beauty for the rest of my days,' Dhanurdas said passionately. 'I just don't think that is possible,' he added quickly.

That same day, in the evening, during *ārati*, Rāmānuja brought Dhanurdas to the Raṅganātha temple. Standing before the Deity, he said, 'O Dhanurdas, behold Raṅganātha, the master of the universe and consort of the goddess of fortune. He stands before you.'

Dhanurdas had visited the Raṅganātha temple many times before, but this day he felt like he was seeing the Deity for the first time. The world disappeared leaving nothing but Raṅganātha's huge, lotus-like eyes to penetrate his heart. Everything became a blur. Dhanurdas could not make out if the lotus eyes were looking from outside, or from within his heart. Time stood still. With his eyes, he drank Raṅganātha's beauty, revealed to him by the grace of the spiritual master. Admiration and delight overwhelmed him. His lips spontaneously whispered prayers while his body was seized with a sacred thrill. When he finally surfaced from his oblivion, he found his cloth wet through with tears. That day, he gave up everything and began serving Rāmānuja, who had revealed God's beauty to him.

* * *

Taj Khan, a devout Muslim from the village of Karoli, experienced a similar miracle at the temple where Sanātana Gosvāmī's Deity, Madana-Mohan resided. Taj Khan served as a messenger for the local *rāja* and spent the rest of his free time reading the Qur'an, which, as we know, forbids portraying God in any form, for 'Allah cannot be compared to anything.' (*Surah 'Ash-Shura,' Ayat* 11)

One day the *rāja* sent Taj Khan to Madana-Mohan temple with a letter for the priest (the *mahant*). Waiting for a reply, Taj Khan stood at the temple door. He could not enter because Muslims were forbidden. Out of curiosity, he looked through the lattice window into the temple room and his gaze accidentally fell upon the Madan-Mohan Deity. It seemed to Taj Khan that Madana-Mohan was looking straight at him. All the curses against idolaters in the Qur'an instantly vanished from his head. Waves of hitherto unknown happiness flooded his heart. Transfixed, he stood there gazing at Madana-Mohan, while Madana-Mohan gazed back.

Taj Khan woke to reality only when the *mahant* tapped him on the back. With difficulty, he tore his gaze away from the Deity and in half-oblivion, staggered like a drunken man back to the palace. In the evening, he went straight to the mosque to throw off his obsession. But wherever he was, the gaze of Madana-Mohan's lotus eyes followed him. No matter how hard he tried, he couldn't forget that look.

From that day, he seized every opportunity to run to the temple and secretly steal a glance of the Deity from afar. He abandoned the Qur'an and his daily prayers. His Muslim god-brothers turned away from him, considering him an apostate, while the *pūjārī*, suspicious of his tricks, threatened to beat the 'pagan' should he come near the temple. But who could ban Taj Khan from thinking of Madana-Mohan, crying in separation from Him, composing poetry and contemplating the Deity's image within his heart?

O how my heart yearns for thee!
Unthwarted by hunger, thirst or sleep.
Madana-mohana! Show yourself to me.
Each moment without your sight
Appears like an age to me.

Your sidelong glances thrill my heart.
Cast your glance but once at me.
Listen, son of Nanda, with a moonlike face,
Taja your servant stands begging by your gate,
For your sight and your grace.

Of course, Madana-Mohan answered his prayers, but now is not the right time or place to talk about what happened next.[1] We are simply interested to see how even fleeting contact with Krishna's image can change one's heart.

* * *

Some might doubt, 'Why has nothing like that happened to me? My heart still rages with passions and sorrows though I try to serve the Lord's form.' In answer, we should bear in mind that the main protagonist in all such stories is Krishna's causeless mercy. In our lives, it may not manifest as instantly and vividly as in the lives of Dhanurdas and Taj Khan, but there is no doubt that sincere service to the Deities gradually purifies the heart and helps us feel God's tangible participation in our lives. This is the next step on the path to Krishna, as Queen Kuntī will tell us.

1 This story is in a book by Śrīla Prabhupāda's Godbrother, O.B.L. Kapoor (Adikesava Dasa), Experiences in Bhakti: the Science Celestial.

CHAPTER 7

‘Send me Calamities Again and Again.’

Owls and Larks

Attaining God begins with serving His name. The holy name contains God's form and reveals it to those who are sincere. Worshiping God in the visible form of the Deity helps us to see Him in our hearts. Thereafter, His qualities are gradually revealed. *Caitanya-caritāmṛta*[1] describes Lord Caitanya's transcendental madness during the last period of His life. Chanting verses from scriptures, He would sometimes smell the aroma emanating from Krishna's body, relish the sweetness of His lips or hear His flute. This, too, is meditation on Krishna's qualities – when *Adhokṣaja*, God who is inaccessible by material senses, becomes *gocara*, the object of a devotee's direct experience.

Such meditation and such rewards are inaccessible to neophytes. However, the Lord bestows His topmost quality – His mercy – even upon beginners like you and me. In the following verses, Queen Kuntī indirectly shows which qualities we must possess to perceive Krishna's mercy. He showers mercy upon everyone, but only those with a pure heart can appreciate it.

Not everyone can recognize God's mercy and learn to admire God's qualities. Envy, which prevails in our hearts, prevents this. Some people feel such strong jealousy towards God, they cannot even acknowledge His existence. Appreciating His mercy is a far-off thing. Before we can grasp God's qualities, we must perform pious activities, such as study scriptures and perform austerities. Nārada Muni has said:

idaṁ hi puṁsas tapasaḥ śrutasya vā
sviṣṭasya sūktasya ca buddhi-dattayoḥ
avicyuto 'rthaḥ kavibhir nirūpito
yad-uttamaśloka-guṇānuvarṇanam

'Learned circles have positively concluded that the infallible purpose of the advancement of knowledge,

1 *Caitanya-caritāmṛta*, *Antya-līlā*, ch. 15-16.

> namely austerities, study of the Vedas, sacrifice, chanting of hymns and charity, culminates in the transcendental descriptions of the Lord, who is defined in choice poetry.'
> *Śrīmad-Bhāgavatam* 1.5.22

In other words, the ability to constantly praise the Lords' qualities (*guṇānuvarṇanam*) is the true goal and eternal outcome (*avicyutah arthaḥ*) of all forms of spiritual practice. This takes time to develop. As a rule, for us to glorify another's virtues, we can't just rely on mere hearsay – we need to experience these qualities to value and appreciate them. The closer the person is to us, the more they are part of our lives, and the easier it is for us to contemplate and speak of their qualities. To glorify Krishna's qualities, not formally, but from the heart, we must experience His participation in our lives.

We might object: 'Wait, everyone experiences the touch of the Supreme's mercy – God takes care of everyone.' True. The Lord is all-merciful, but we are ungrateful. When the sun rises, the lark sings, and the owl goes blind. Non-believers are like these owls. They like, prefer, insist on staying in the darkness of their atheism, denying the true evidence of the Lord, the Sun of eternal mercy.

> *dekhiyā nā dekhe yata abhaktera gaṇa*
> *ulūke nā dekhe yena sūryera kiraṇa*

> 'But faithless unbelievers do not see what is clearly evident, just as owls do not see the rays of the sun.'
> *Caitanya-caritāmṛta, Ādi-līlā* 3.86

Therefore, by speaking of Krishna's kindness, Queen Kuntī also touches upon the qualities we need in order to learn to appreciate that kindness.

Protector of the Unprotected

> ***yathā hṛṣīkeśa khalena devakī***
> ***kaṁsena ruddhāticiraṁ śucārpitā***
> ***vimocitāhaṁ ca sahātmajā vibho***
> ***tvayaiva nāthena muhur vipad-gaṇāt***

> 'O Hṛṣīkeśa, master of the senses and Lord of lords, You have released Your mother, Devakī, who was long imprisoned and distressed by the envious King Kaṁsa, and me and my children from a series of constant dangers.'
> *Śrīmad-Bhāgavatam* 1.8.23

Queen Kuntī compares Krishna's participation in her life to His participation in Devakī's life. We usually compare ourselves to others out of pride or envy. But Queen Kuntī is neither proud nor envious – she simply cherishes Krishna's mercy:

> 'O Master of the senses,' she says, 'You know my heart. It overflows with gratitude towards You. You saved me and all my children, while Devakī's six sons, Your brothers, were killed by Kaṁsa before her eyes. Why? I have only one answer: because I suffered more than her and needed Your protection more.'

This verse reveals an essential quality of pure devotees – their constant feeling of special connection with Krishna, of belonging to Him. Called *mamatā* in Sanskrit, this quality carries the elevated sentiment, 'Krishna is mine, He belongs to me.' Genuine service is impossible without *mamatā*. When picnicking together, each of Krishna's countless cowherd friends was confident that Krishna looked exclusively at him and ate only what he had shared. During the *rasā* dance, each *gopī* thought that Krishna danced exclusively with her. At dusk, at Ter-Kadamba, when Krishna herded the cows together by playing His flute, each cow was convinced that He exclusively called her. The feeling that such special mercy is undeserved to them makes Krishna even more beautiful in the eyes of His devotees.

Devakī's fate was most unfortunate. On her wedding day, her brother Kaṁsa almost killed her. Callously, he imprisoned her for a long time. Mercilessly, he killed her six sons one after the other in front of her. Devakī was in constant fear of him, especially while expecting Krishna's birth. After giving birth, she was separated from her son for twelve years. It was a terrible chain of events, but according to Viśvanātha Cakravartī Ṭhākura, Queen Kuntī seems to conclude, 'Still, Devakī did not suffer as much as I did.' Why did she feel this?

Devakī was waiting for the Lord to appear in her womb. In expectation of this, she hardly noticed her six children's death. Anticipating that the Lord Himself was going to enter her womb, she was happy, even in prison. Finally, after carrying Krishna under her heart, and then seeing Him born, she had nothing more to worry about. Even Kaṁsa repented and went on his knees to beg her forgiveness. When Krishna returned to Mathurā to kill Kaṁsa, all her suffering was over. Furthermore, throughout the hardship, Devakī had a protector – her husband, Vasudeva. He stood by her side, protecting, and comforting her. It is terrible that her children were all killed, but she still had a husband and could bear more children.

'I had no one but You, O *Nātha*.[1] You knew that You were my only protector, so You always came to save me,' implies Queen Kuntī. Krishna comes to those who need Him most. Therefore, He is *dīna-bandhu* – 'friend of the poor.' Śrīla Prabhupāda gives more insight:

> *'Krishna endows more favor to a devotee who is in greater dangers. Sometimes He puts His pure*

1 The word *nātha* means protector, lord, or husband.

> *devotees in such dangers because in that condition of helplessness the devotee becomes more attached to the Lord. The more the attachment is there for the Lord, the more success is there for the devotee.'*
> *Śrīmad-Bhāgavatam* 1.8.23, purport

Krishna is always ready to help us. He waits for the moment we realize how helpless we are and that no one but He can protect us.

The Certificate of Maturity in the School of Life

In 1.8.24, Queen Kuntī recalls how Krishna saved her family again and again:

> ***viṣān mahāgneḥ puruṣāda-darśanād***
> ***asat-sabhāyā vana-vāsa-kṛcchrataḥ***
> ***mṛdhe mṛdhe 'neka-mahārathāstrato***
> ***drauṇy-astrataś cāsma hare 'bhirakṣitāḥ***

> 'My dear Kṛṣṇa, Your Lordship has protected us from a poisoned cake, from a great fire, from cannibals, from the vicious assembly, from sufferings during our exile in the forest and from the battle where great generals fought. And now You have saved us from the weapon of Aśvatthāmā.'
> *Śrīmad-Bhāgavatam* 1.8.24

In the previous verse, Queen Kuntī consciously refers to Krishna as *vibhu* (omnipresent) to preface this verse and emphasize here that, 'O my omnipresent Lord! You were always with me, in every situation. It was You who saved us again and again!' As she sees her complicated life play out in her mind's eye, she recounts all the dangers that loomed over her and her sons.

When the Pāṇḍavas were still children and on a picnic, Duryodhana fed poisoned sweets to the ever-hungry Bhīma. To cover his tracks, the hateful prince threw Bhīma's stout body into the Yamunā. It was a miracle that Bhīma survived.

Later, Dhṛtarāṣṭra arranged for Queen Kuntī and her sons to stay in a summerhouse soaked in combustible resin. As one might expect, the place burst into flames. Again, by a miracle, the Pāṇḍavas escaped the fire and found their way to the forests through an underground passage. Wandering about in the wilderness, they met terrible cannibals – first the *rākṣasa* Hiḍimba, who wanted to devour them, then the gluttonous Bakāsura. Bhīma killed both.

Then in the *asat-sabhā* (an assembly of the vicious), the Kauravas cheated the Pāṇḍavas of their kingship and wealth in a game of dice. They had Draupadī dragged into the hall by her hair and tried to undress her in everyone's presence. Krishna intervened and protected chaste Draupadī.

During exile, the Pāṇḍavas met strife at every turn. Durvāsā Muni almost cursed them, a huge python almost devoured Bhīma, and Jayadratha tried to kidnap Draupadī. Every time, Krishna protected them.

The Pāṇḍavas grew stronger with victory over each ordeal. Thus, Krishna prepared them for the greatest test of their lives – the war at Kurukṣetra. During the eighteen days of battle, great warriors tried again and again to kill Queen Kuntī's sons, but Krishna stayed by their side and ensured not a hair fell from their heads.

Looking back, Queen Kuntī sees Krishna's hand behind every happening in her life and her heart overflows with gratitude. She could have viewed these events differently, because in all of them Krishna did not get directly involved. Other factors could easily be considered the saving grace: with antidote venom, the snakes in the Yamunā saved Bhīma from being poisoned; it was Vidura who warned Yudhiṣṭhira of a possible fire in Vāraṇāvata and advised the brothers to dig an underground passage in advance; Hiḍimba and Bakāsura were overpowered by Bhīma's might.

The same can be said about the happenings in the Kuru assembly. Yes, a miracle took place when Dushasana tried to strip Draupadī, but can it not be said that Draupadī was protected by her chastity? History is witness to the power of chaste women: the wife of a leper *brāhmaṇa* stopped the setting of the sun to save her husband, while Sītā's purity protected her from the encroachments of the unrestrainable demon, Rāvaṇa. Furthermore, was it not Yudhiṣṭhira's piety, Bhīma's strength, Arjuna's courage, the twins' wit, and Draupadī's loyalty that helped them survive their hardships in the forest? Moreover, Krishna could have taken part in the war, but He vowed not to take up arms. Only when Aśvatthāmā released six *brahmāstras* did Krishna personally intervene. But was that not too little too late? There was almost no one left to save.

There are two categories of people: the grateful and the blind. The former offer thanks to God in happiness and distress. Gratitude lives in their hearts and gradually turns into love. They treat all the events in their lives as occasions to remember Krishna. The latter are blinded by their happiness and distress. In victory, they ascribe all merit to themselves, and in defeat they curse their fate and sometimes God behind it. The pride that dwells in their hearts turns into envy and spite. A proud person can never be grateful, just as a grateful person can never be proud. The destiny of a grateful person is always full of great meaning – generations learn from their example. A proud person's fate is always 'a tale told by an idiot, full of sound and fury, signifying nothing.'[1]

1 William Shakespeare, Macbeth, Act V, Scene V.

Both categories undergo training at the same school of life, and their teacher is one – God. However, some agree to become His disciples, while others are confident that they can do without Him.

Krishna's Two Promises

Does this mean that God is biased? Does He favor some and dislike others? No, He teaches the grateful and the blind, and most importantly, uses their examples to teach a third party – us. We will retell two consecutive events, one of ingratitude and pride, and the other of gratitude and humility, to contrast the qualities.

* * *

When the duel between Bhīma and Duryodhana was over, the surviving warriors of the Pāṇḍava army began celebrating victory. They beat their drums, laughed through tears, embraced each other, and praised Bhīma's feat. Krishna raised His hands to cool down their fervor.

When all hushed, He said, 'Yes, Duryodhana is defeated. He knew no shame. He was foolish, stubborn, and greedy. Now this scoundrel is reaping the fruits of his crimes. Yet he is a king. There is no good in mocking him. Let us leave him with his conscience. He does not deserve our thoughts. Fortune has smiled upon us – this prince and all his sycophants are destroyed. We have nothing more to do here.'

Hearing these words, Duryodhana gasped with indignation. Raising himself on his elbows and glaring at Krishna, he hissed, 'How dare You call it luck, O son of the slaves of Kaṁsa? Do You think I did not see You prompting Bhīma to strike me below the belt? Do You think I did not know that it was You who taught the Pāṇḍavas how to kill Bhīṣma, Droṇa, Karṇa and Bhūriśravā? If not for You, my enemies would have never been able to defeat me!'

Duryodhana collapsed thereafter. Krishna gazed at him with compassion and said, 'O son of Gāndhārī, your own atrocities killed you and your brothers. Have you forgotten, O fool, how I asked you to return the kingdom to the Pāṇḍavas? Out of greed, you refused. You should have been killed the moment you insulted innocent Draupadī by trying to undress her. Do you remember what I promised her? "The Himalayas may crumble to sand, the sky may fall to the ground, the ocean may dry up, sooner than I break My word. I promise you that all who have offended you will fall bleeding to the ground!" Duryodhana, you deserve your end – I have nothing to do with it.'

'You can say what You like, Krishna!' said Duryodhana, languishing in the dust. 'I have lived a glorious life. I studied the *Vedas*. I gave donations. I performed sacrifices. Like a father, I took care of my subjects. I was a good king. I ruled a vast kingdom that stretched from sea to sea. I stepped on the heads of my adversaries. Friends loved me, and enemies hated me. Great kings honored me, and great warriors bowed before me. No one could defeat me in a fair fight. I have lived a happy life, and now the Heavens await me! Is there anyone on Earth more fortunate than me?'

At that moment, even the *gandharvas* and *apsarās* could not refrain from glorifying Duryodhana. They showered flowers upon him. An enraptured audience often applauds the feats of such 'heroes,' but such boasting never fools Krishna. He knows the words come from an embittered and spiteful heart.

Leaving Duryodhana to his tortured death, the Pāṇḍavas rode with Krishna to the desolate camp of the defeated enemies to take the spoils. Arjuna was about to step off his chariot when Krishna ordered him to take the *Gāṇḍīva* bow and two quivers of arrows with him. Arjuna was puzzled because there was no one left to fight. He obeyed anyway, though Krishna made no further explanation. As Arjuna dismounted, Krishna quickly jumped down too. In the same moment, for no obvious reason, the chariot burst into flames and within seconds Arjuna's famed chariot was a pile of smoking ashes.

'What happened, O Krishna?' said Arjuna in astonishment.

'For eighteen days, your chariot has been the prime target for our enemies, replied Krishna. 'Arrows charged with powerful mantras should have destroyed it long ago. My presence has been protecting it.'

Affectionately placing his arm around Arjuna, Krishna addressed the Pāṇḍavas, 'When I arrived at Mahārāja Virāṭa's palace just before the war, Arjuna greeted Me with words I will never forget. He said, "O Keśava, You are my brother and my best friend. Truly, You are dearer to me than anyone else in this world. I dedicate my life to You. No one else can protect me." In reply, I said, "I promise you, O Pārtha, not a single hair will fall from your head!" I have kept My word!'

Tears of gratitude and love welled in the Pāṇḍavas' eyes. They knew that Krishna always keeps His word: *kaunteya pratijānīhi na me bhaktaḥ praṇaśyati* – 'O son of Kuntī, declare it boldly that My devotee never perishes.' (*Bhagavad-gītā* 9.31)

Gratitude as a Sādhana

God is behind everything. In the case of His devotees, He personally fulfills their desires, personally disrupts their plans, and personally takes care of them, helping them to come to Him faster. They usually live a hard life, but the gratitude in their hearts grinds away all the suffering they have endured, transforming it into love for God.

However, those possessed by pride, like Duryodhana, rely on their own strength. God is of little interest to them, for they do not want to be obliged to anyone. In reciprocation, God turns away from them and leaves them in the care of the impassive law of *karma*. For a while, fortune may seem to smile upon them, but as their pride swells, they near their inevitable end. The law of karma works in a specific way: whatever we are most proud of – our beauty, abilities, strength, wealth, or learning – turns into the source of our suffering. The proud make plans for happiness, which are doomed to collapse, leaving them to curse destiny and God for their lives. Thus, pride turns their suffering into anger.

The third category of people, those in-between, like you and I, are the majority. In many ways, we are like Duryodhana. Like him, we rejoice in our victories and grieve in our defeats. Like him, we like to brag about our accomplishments in public, while inside we accumulate the poison of resentment against others, against life, against God. Like him, our hearts cherish the hope for happiness in this world. We find it difficult to imagine how we could be happy with nothing else but Krishna.

Yet, one quality distinguishes us from Duryodhana: we are wise enough to see that there is no point in fighting with Krishna. We willingly bow our heads before Him. In that alone, we resemble the Pāṇḍavas and Queen Kuntī.

So, what are we supposed to do with hearts torn apart and unable to find peace in anything? How can we feel gratitude towards God and appreciate His participation in our fate? This is especially difficult because He is unlikely to come to us and tell us how He has cared for us all this time.

The only thing we can do is make gratitude our *sādhana* – chanting God's holy name, contemplating the beauty of His form, and trying to see how His mercy has manifested itself in everything, even the worst adversities of our lives. When this *sādhana* has sufficiently purified our hearts, we will be able to follow in Queen Kuntī's footsteps and utter her next prayer in an unwavering voice.

Teacher of the Entire World

Queen Kuntī says:

> ***vipadaḥ santu tāḥ śaśvat***
> ***tatra tatra jagad-guro***
> ***bhavato darśanaṁ yat syād***
> ***apunar bhava-darśanam***

> 'I wish that all those calamities would happen again and again so that we could see You again and again, for seeing You means that we will no longer see repeated births and deaths.'
>
> *Śrīmad-Bhāgavatam* 1.8.25

In an extraordinary way, she uses the word '*vipadām*,' which means 'danger,' 'suffering,' 'misery' or 'poverty' and inverts it to mean '*sampadam*,' which denotes 'wealth,' 'treasure,' 'opulence.' Queen Kuntī says, 'O teacher of the entire world! All the dangers and trials (*vipadāṁ*) that You have been sending me have turned into my wealth (*sampadam*). Therefore, keep sending them incessantly to me (*śaśvat*).'

What are we to make of this prayer? It appears to defy common sense. Which sane person would ask God to send more dangers into their life? It is difficult for us to sincerely thank Him for the problems He has already sent us. Often, when we try, we are not convincing, as exemplified in Mikhail Lermontov's bitter and ironic poem:

> I am grateful to you for everything.
> For passions' long torments,
> For bitterness of tears and poison of kiss,
> For vengeance of enemies and slander of friends,
> For the passion of my heart, wasted in the desert,
> For all with which I have been deceived.
> Grant only one wish, that from now on
> I will not be grateful to you much longer.[1]

With such an expression of gratitude for life's difficulties, it is better to remain silent. History has preserved the courageous words of Pope Leo I, which come closer to Queen Kuntī's sentiments. The Pope addressed Attila, the ruthless leader of the Huns who had come to invade Rome, with 'Hail, Attila, the scourge of God!' According to legend, Attila was flattered and pacified by these words and turned back with his army. Thus, Rome was saved from invasion.

Pope Leo I was grateful for the grace though he did not ask God for more tests. Still, his courage is rare. Most people do not want anything bad to happen to them. As the saying goes, 'while fish swim deeper to find better food, man seeks better opportunities to enjoy' – we want to stay in our comfort zone and avoid undergoing any tests or misfortunes. Hardly anyone sees mercy in their hardships.

So, what was wrong with Queen Kuntī? Does she defy common sense? If we ponder the prayer, we will see a higher common sense behind it. In it, Queen Kuntī shares her experience of happiness though we will find it difficult to grasp because we have no such experience.

1 Mikhail Lermontov, Gratitude. Translation by Sergei Zagny.

The goal of *all* human efforts is one – to achieve happiness and avoid suffering. We all desire it but have different understandings of *what* will make us happy. Our understanding rests on either experience or faith (that certain things will bring happiness), which is ultimately the same because we cannot get experience without having some preliminary faith.

Everyone has experience of material happiness; this is why we strive for it. The problems come because material happiness is neither unobstructed nor eternal. Moreover, can we call the dubious experience of material enjoyment happiness anyway? Can happiness be reduced to the relief people feel when they scratch the itch? Is happiness possible in a world defined as a place of misery by its creator – *duḥkhālayam aśāśvatam?*[1] Śrīla Prabhupāda reiterates the point:

> 'This material world is certified by the Lord in the *Bhagavad-gītā* as a dangerous place full of calamities. Less intelligent persons prepare plans to adjust to those calamities without knowing that the nature of this place is itself full of calamities.'
>
> *Śrīmad-Bhāgavatam* 1.8.25

Therefore, from time immemorial, intelligent people have searched for an alternative happiness which is cloudless and eternal. Scriptures speak of it: *raso vai saḥ rasaṁ hy evāyaṁ labdhvānandī bhavat* – 'The Lord is the reservoir of eternal bliss. When one reaches Him, he is filled with spiritual bliss.' (*Taittirīya Upaniṣad* 2.7.1)

Although many set off on a quest for that happiness, few find it. 'Many are called, but few are chosen.'[2] Why? What prevents us from gaining unobstructed, pure spiritual happiness?

1 *Bhagavad-gītā* 8.15.

2 The Gospel of Matthew, 20:16.

The answer is disappointingly simple: *our persistent hope for material happiness.* Since it rests on actual experience of some kind of happiness, it is difficult to relinquish. It is a hope that dies last and prevents us from concentrating on the search for God. Śukadeva Gosvāmī describes our unfortunate predicament:

kvacit sakṛd avagata-viṣaya-vaitathyaḥ svayaṁ
parābhidhyānena
vibhraṁśita-smṛtis tayaiva marīci-toya-prāyāṁs tān
evābhidhāvati

'The conditioned soul sometimes personally appreciates the futility of sense enjoyment in the material world, and he sometimes considers material enjoyment to be full of miseries. However, due to his strong bodily conception, his memory is destroyed, and again and again he runs after material enjoyment, just as an animal runs after a mirage in the desert.'

Śrīmad-Bhāgavatam 5.14.10

Stubbornly, we go on chasing the mirage of material happiness until we die of thirst. The hope for material happiness deters us from focusing on the spiritual quest and robs our consciousness of its memory of God. Krishna warns:

bhogaiśvarya-prasaktānāṁ
tayāpahṛta-cetasām
vyavasāyātmikā buddhiḥ
samādhau na vidhīyate

'In the minds of those who are too attached to sense enjoyment and material opulence, and who are bewildered by such things, the resolute determination for devotional service to the Supreme Lord does not take place.'

Bhagavad-gītā 2.44

Bearing these truths in her heart, Queen Kuntī pleads to Krishna, 'The adversities and dangers sent by You, O teacher of the world, have become my greatest treasure, for they help me relinquish the illusion of material happiness and strive only for You, without distraction.'

Cure for Blindness

Commenting on 1.8.25, Viśvanātha Cakravartī Ṭhākura compares the suffering that God sends us to *añjana*, an Ayurvedic ointment applied to the eyes to eliminate cataracts. Just as *añjana* causes a burning sensation before it restores clear vision, suffering causes discomfit before it brings restoration.

If we unpack the metaphor further, we can say that the experiences of material pleasures obscure our vision like cataracts and prevent us from seeing the true nature of this world, and from seeing God and feeling His mercy.

In other words, the adversities that come to us should be perceived as a cure sent by the Lord. This is why Queen Kuntī calls Him *jagad-guru*, the spiritual master of the entire world. Krishna sends us difficulties because He knows that we are sick and in need of healing. When people realize they are seriously sick, they are willing to take the most bitter and burning medicines to get better. Our misfortune is that we do not realize that we are sick, and like foolish children begrudge God for prescribing bitter medicines to heal us. Our disease is forgetfulness of God. Its symptom is fear, which permeates our existence:

bhayaṁ dvitīyābhiniveśataḥ syād
īśād apetasya viparyayo 'smṛtiḥ
tan-māyayāto budha ābhajet taṁ
bhaktyaikayeśaṁ guru-devatātmā

> 'Fear arises when a living entity misidentifies himself as the material body because of absorption in the external, illusory energy of the Lord. When the living entity thus turns away from the Supreme Lord, he also forgets his own constitutional position as a servant of the Lord. This bewildering, fearful condition is effected by the potency of illusion, called māyā. Therefore, an intelligent person should engage unflinchingly in the unalloyed devotional service of the Lord, under the guidance of a bona fide spiritual master, whom he should accept as his worshipable deity and as his very life and soul.'
>
> *Śrīmad-Bhāgavatam* 11.2.37

In our foolish attempt to be an autonomous, pleasure-filled sovereign, we have long inhabited the material realm within a succession of material bodies that we have identified as 'myself' each time. The only way we have survived such a painful, long-standing separation from God, who is integral to our sense of completeness, wholeness, and happiness, is by forgetting that He exists. The disease of forgetfulness perverts our memory and clouds it.

The unfortunate result of losing awareness of our Lord, who is our protector, master, and friend, is a harrowing, all-consuming, existential fear that grips us to our core. It beats underneath all our activities, motivations, and surface fears, and is the source of all our insecurities and miseries.

If the disease and the root cause of all our sufferings is forgetfulness of God, then to heal from the symptoms and disease, we must learn gradually to remember God always. In remembrance of Him, we are ourselves. Therefore, everything that helps us remember Him is good, and everything that obstructs that remembrance causes harm. This is how a person striving for God regards the events of their life. Śrīla Prabhupāda writes:

> *'Generally, the distressed, the needy, the intelligent and the inquisitive, who have performed some pious activities, worship or begin to worship the Lord. Others, who are thriving on misdeeds only, regardless of status, cannot approach the Supreme due to being misled by the illusory energy. Therefore,* ***for a pious person****, if there is some calamity there is no other alternative than to take shelter of the lotus feet of the Lord. Constantly remembering the lotus feet of the Lord means preparing for liberation from birth and death. Therefore, even though there are so-called calamities, they are welcome because they give us an opportunity to remember the Lord, which means liberation.'*
>
> *Śrīmad-Bhāgavatam* 1.8.25, purport

But, alas, we do not easily ingest the bitter cure of suffering. As Śrīla Prabhupāda says, it takes a stock of piety (as bolded above). Some of us emerge from the crucible of suffering with purified, humbled, rejuvenated hearts that are softer and more receptive to the suffering of others. Others grow embittered and cruel after undergoing the intensity. What quality enables us to gratefully accept trials as medicine?

Krishna describes those who turn to Him in difficult situations as magnanimous (*udārāḥ*).[1] Magnanimity, in this context, is the opposite to the petty-mindedness that causes us to foster grudges and resentments, and thus aggravate the disease of forgetfulness. Magnanimity is the quality of a grateful, generous, and forgiving heart. To be magnanimous and not embittered, we need to have accrued a stock of piety (*sukṛti*).

But what kind of piety makes people magnanimous? What kind of piety is lacking in those unable to pass the tests sent by

1 *Bhagavad-gītā* 7.18.

God without holding grudges? Trials, difficulties, and dangerous situations will come upon us, whether we ask for them or not. This is why we should be prepared in advance for them.

In the above purport, when Śrīla Prabhupāda writes about the piety of those who are in distress, who are in need, who are intelligent, and who are inquisitive, he is referring to the *Bhagavad-gītā*.[1] Śrīla Jīva Gosvāmī elaborates that piety here means faith in the path of *bhakti*, arising from the association with exalted Vaiṣṇavas. 'But if everything comes down to mere faith,' an attentive reader may object, 'then all believers should pass the test. But they do not.'

Faith varies from person to person, we answer. According to Śrīla Jīva Gosvāmī, true faith is the ability to recognize Krishna behind everything that happens in the material world and simultaneously understand that the shortcomings of the material world do not affect Him.

What this means is that Krishna is not influenced by the dualities of material pains and pleasures. He isn't biased, cruel, or judgemental. He harbors no resentment, anger, or vengeful feelings. He never makes mistakes. He observes our choices and activities, and no matter how much we err, stumble or misuse ourselves and others, He never stops loving us and seeking our benefit.

Krishna is the Absolute and the source of unending love. Everything He sends to us is His grace. In every circumstance, He has arranged the possibility of our growth, betterment, and upliftment. He is our well-wishing protector, always. If we understand that He is free from imperfections, and that everything

1 *Bhagavad-gītā* 7.16, 'O best among the Bhāratas, four kinds of pious men begin to render devotional service unto Me – the distressed, the desirer of wealth, the inquisitive, and he who is searching for knowledge of the Absolute.'

He does is a perfect expression of love, then we will not foster grudges and resentment. Firm faith in the infallibility and benevolence of God is the characteristic of those with noble hearts, and therefore, Krishna calls them magnanimous. To remain grateful to God in times of success is a sign of humility. To remain grateful in times of calamities is the sign of unshakeable faith.

One who lacks such faith cannot see God behind everything, or worse, accuses Him of injustice and cruelty. A mystic of recent times addressed this issue in a letter of consolation and guidance, written as God's conversation with a soul, 'This was from Me ... know that, it was from Me.' Though the mystic came centuries after Queen Kuntī and belonged to a completely different spiritual tradition and culture, he articulates the same credo of faith that will help us to endure the most demanding situations in our lives and derive from them the invaluable lessons of love.

'Have you ever thought that everything that concerns you, concerns Me, also? You are precious in my eyes and I love you; for this reason, it is a special joy for Me to train you. When temptations and the opponent [the evil one] come upon you like a river, I want you to know that This was from Me.

'I am your God, the circumstances of your life are in My hands; you did not end up in your position by chance; this is precisely the position I have appointed for you. Weren't you asking Me to teach you humility? And there - I placed you precisely in the 'school' where they teach this lesson. Your environment, and those who are around you, are performing My will. Do you have financial difficulties and can just barely survive? Know that This was from Me.

'You made plans and have your own goals; you brought them to Me to bless them. But I want you to leave it all to Me, to direct and guide the circumstances of your life by My hand, because you are the orphan, not the protagonist. Unexpected failures found you and despair overcame your heart, but know that This was from Me.

'But I want to teach you the most deep thoughts and My lessons, so that you may serve Me. I want to teach you that you are nothing without Me. Some of my best children are those who, cut off from an active life, learn to use the weapon of ceaseless prayer… In everything I, your Lord, will be your guide and teacher. Remember always that every difficulty you come across, every offensive word, every slander and criticism, every obstacle to your works, which could cause frustration and disappointment, This is from Me.

'Know and remember always, no matter where you are, that whatsoever hurts will be dulled as soon as you learn in all things, to look at Me. Everything has been sent to you by Me, for the perfection of your soul. All these things were from Me.'[1]

The Lord's Justice and Mercy

The formula of faith is confidence in the Lord's justice (in His absolute impartiality) and hope in His mercy: *vaiṣamya-nair-ghṛṇye na*,[2] derived from the philosophy of inconceivable simultaneous oneness and difference of God and His creation. Constant reflection on the Lord's justice and His mercy is that very *sādhana* of gratitude mentioned above. Lord Brahmā's famed prayer captures the mood:

1 St. Seraphim Vyritsa, Russian Orthodox saint known for clairvoyance and healing, 1866-1949. His letter to a bishop, 'This was from Me.'

2 *Vaiṣamya-nairghṛṇye na sāpekṣatvāt tathā hi darśayati* – 'The Lord is impartial and not cruel, for the pleasures and pains experienced by living entities are the result of their karma, as the scriptures show.' *Vedānta-sūtra* 2.1.34.

tat te 'nukampāṁ su-samīkṣamāṇo
bhuñjāna evātma-kṛtaṁ vipākam
hṛd-vāg-vapurbhir vidadhan namas te
jīveta yo mukti-pade sa dāya-bhāk

'My dear Lord, one who earnestly waits for You to bestow Your causeless mercy upon him, all the while patiently suffering the reactions of his past misdeeds and offering You respectful obeisances with his heart, words and body, is surely eligible for liberation, for it has become his rightful claim.'

Śrīmad-Bhāgavatam 10.14.8

This *sādhana* allows one to gradually regain sight and receive the Lord's *darsana* (*bhavato darśanaṁ yat syād*). One who tries to feel the Lord's mercy and justice every day of his life, will be prepared for trials when they come. Duryodhana could not comprehend Krishna's mercy and justice, and therefore spewed curses at the time of dying. Queen Kuntī and the Pāṇḍavas realized these qualities and thus were able to thank Him, endlessly seeing Him in all calamities.

When a person receives Krishna's *darśana*, the terrible mirage of material suffering dissipates on its own. Śrīla Prabhupāda explains:

'The spirit soul is transcendental to all material calamities; therefore, the so-called calamities are called false. A man may see a tiger swallowing him in a dream, and he may cry for this calamity. Actually, there is no tiger and there is no suffering; it is simply a case of dreams. In the same way, all calamities of life are said to be dreams. If someone is lucky enough to get in contact with the Lord by devotional service, it is all gain. Contact with the Lord by any one of the

> *nine devotional services is always a forward step on the path going back to Godhead.'*
> *Śrīmad-Bhāgavatam* 1.8.25, purport

We might feel that it is impossible for us to see our pains, struggles, and woes as a dream. It is a tall order because the sufferings seem so tangible. This is because we are so deeply identified with our bodies, corollary roles, and connections. But the supreme power of devotional service will gradually transform our vision and feeling. One day we'll be able to repeat Queen Kuntī's words as our own. Meantime, we utter them with admiration, wonder and appreciation, which will help purify us on our way:

> 'O Krishna, teacher of the entire world. You generously sent difficulties and trials into my life. They have turned into my greatest treasure, for they have freed me from the illusory hopes of material happiness and allowed me to focus on You. They have healed me from blindness and helped me to see You behind everything. The veil has fallen from my eyes, my heart has cleansed, and the mirage of material existence has vanished. I have learned to see and feel You behind all the events of this world. From now, I am not afraid of repeated birth and death. I am truly happy. Therefore, I ask You: please send me those tests again and again!'

In this way, contact with the Lord, the source of eternal bliss, helps us achieve the two major goals of life: absolute happiness and freedom from suffering. It is this experience that Queen Kuntī shares with us.

The Causes of Blindness

After establishing that the dangers she has endured are her exclusive treasures that have brought her closer to Krishna, Queen Kuntī in her next prayer speaks about the dangers of accumulating any other kind of treasure:

> ***janmaiśvarya-śruta-śrībhir***
> ***edhamāna-madaḥ pumān***
> ***naivārhaty abhidhātuṁ vai***
> ***tvām akiñcana-gocaram***

> 'My Lord, Your Lordship can easily be approached, but only by those who are materially exhausted. One who is on the path of [material] progress, trying to improve himself with respectable parentage, great opulence, high education and bodily beauty, cannot approach You with sincere feeling.'
>
> *Śrīmad-Bhāgavatam* 1.8.26

She glorifies the dangers sent to her as her wealth,[1] and now condemns ordinary wealth by pointing out the dangers hidden within it. She defies the conventional views of people of this world and turns them upside down.

We usually seek shelter in:
janma – high birth
aiśvarya – wealth, strength, might, power
śruta – scholarship, knowledge, education, erudition
śrī – beauty, brilliance, the power that beauty gives.

Śrīla Prabhupāda calls these the four pillars of material progress. All people aspire for them because of the illusion of

1 In Sanskrit the word 'danger' (*vipatti*) and 'wealth' (*sampatti*) are derived from the same root. The difference is only in applied prefixes.

security that they create. To some extent, our parentage, wealth, scholarship, and beauty dissipate our fears, but they also affect human consciousness in the same way as drugs or wine. Śrīla Prabhupāda reflects on how these drive society along a blind path:

> *'All materialistic men are mad after possessing all these material opulences, and this is known as the advancement of material civilization. But the result is that by possessing all these material assets one becomes artificially puffed up, intoxicated by such temporary possessions.'*
>
> *Śrīmad-Bhāgavatam* 1.8.26, purport

Queen Kuntī diagnoses the effect as *edhamāna-madaḥ*. In Sanskrit, the verb root *mad* has several meanings: 'to rejoice,' 'to intoxicate,' 'to drive mad,' 'to evoke pride,' and 'to cast into grief or poverty.' In other words, poverty and grief are inseparable companions of drunken joy. Therefore, noble birth, wealth, good education, and beauty increase (*edhamāna*) material happiness but also enhance pride, drive a person crazy, and make us spiritually destitute and aggrieved.

In this world, dangers and suffering are sobering, while material success and prosperity are intoxicating. Likewise, dangers help us regain sight and see the Lord, whereas the wine of material success blinds us. This philosophical truth rings true in the biological sense too. The effects of alcohol on vision are well known. Prolonged consumption brings atrophy of the optic nerve; in the most severe cases of alcohol poisoning, one may go completely blind. The same happens to those of us hopelessly intoxicated by our wealth. Narada Muni reiterated this when he cursed the naked and intoxicated demigods Nalakuvera and Manigriva for their insolence.

asataḥ śrī-madāndhasya

dāridryaṁ param añjanam
ātmaupamyena bhūtāni
daridraḥ param īkṣate

'Atheistic fools and rascals who are very much proud of wealth, fail to see things as they are. Therefore, returning them to poverty is the proper ointment for their eyes so they may see things as they are. At least a poverty-stricken man can realize how painful poverty is, and therefore he will not want others to be in a painful condition like his own.'

Śrīmad-Bhāgavatam 10.10.13

How does material success blind us? An analogy illustrates the answer: if we take a piece of clear glass and look through it, we can see the world. But if that same glass was painted with a layer of silver, what would we see? Ourselves. Transparent glass becomes a mirror.

When we look at the world through the prism of a mind purified by gratitude to the Lord, we see reality and God behind it. But when we look through the prism of our wealth and possessions, (*janmaiśvarya-śruta-śrī*) – a thin layer of silver – we see nothing but ourselves everywhere. Such self-involved people do not live in the real sense. They only admire themselves.

Poverty in Spirit

This focus on the self and the habit of relying on our personal strength and grandeur do not allow (*na evarhati*) us to cry out to Krishna for help (*tvām abhidhātum vai*). The word '*abhidhātum*' means 'to express fully, exhaustively.' Our cries vary in intensity and seriousness. Therefore, Krishna reserves the right not to respond to every call. He expects complete sincerity from us and only then manifests Himself in His name.

When Duḥśāsana tried to undress Draupadī in public, she first sought protection from her husbands and family elders. She did not call for Krishna. When she realized that no one could help her, she prayed to Krishna so piteously and tearfully that thirteen years later, Krishna still recalled the moment:

> *ṛṇam etat pravṛiddham me*
> *hridayān nāpasarpati*
> *yad govindeti cukrośa*
> *kṛṣnā mām dūra vāsinam*

> 'Her eyes full of tears, Draupadī cried out to Me: "O, Govinda!" At that time, I was far from Hastināpura. But her cry made Me her debtor and ever since My debt to her has been growing. This feeling does not leave My heart.'
>
> *Mahābhārata, Udyoga-parva* 58.21

Queen Kuntī concludes verse 1.8.26 by calling Krishna *akiñcana-gocaram*. '*Go*' means 'eyes or other senses,' and '*go-caram*' means 'that which the senses can reach.' She means to say:

'O Krishna, to see You, to hear You, to feel Your touch, to feel Your kindness and sweetness, to feel Your participation in one's life – in a word, to truly understand You, one must be no less than akiñcana, that is, a person who regards nothing in this world as their own. From all others, You are hidden by the thick veil of māyā.'

Although, '*akiñcana*' means 'poor' or 'destitute,' what is meant here is not economic poverty, but the biblical 'poverty in spirit'[1] – a heartfelt contrition over one's inner poverty, fallen condition and helplessness. This is the essential definition

1 'Blessed are the poor in spirit, for theirs is the kingdom of heaven' (Gospel of Matthew, 5: 3). Unlike in modern usage, 'the poor in spirit' refers to humble people.

of humility. Queen Kuntī came from a noble family. She was endowed with unfading beauty and was one of the most influential and educated women of her time. Her sons received immeasurable bounty. Mahārāja Yudhiṣṭhira received everything from Krishna – an exquisitely beautiful and blessed wife, a vast prosperous kingdom, and limitless riches. Krishna arranged Arjuna's marriage to His own sister, Subhadrā, who embodies His internal energy. Nevertheless, Queen Kuntī and her sons always remained *akiñcanas*, beggars, never considering any opulence to be their own. Śrīla Prabhupāda illustrates this principle with the example of a bank clerk:

> *'The cashier may count millions of dollars for his employer, but he does not claim a cent for himself. Similarly, one has to realize that nothing in the world belongs to any individual person, but that everything belongs to the Supreme Lord.'*
>
> *Bhagavad-gītā* 3.30, purport

Humility Defined

Defining humility (*dainya*), Śrīla Sanātana Gosvāmī states:

> *yenāsādhāraṇāśaktā-*
> *dhama-buddhiḥ sadātmani*
> *sarvotkarṣānvite 'pi syād*
> *budhais tad dainyam iṣyate*

> 'Wise people define the humble person as one who considers himself fallen and absolutely unfit, even though in fact he is endowed with all perfections.'
>
> *Bṛhad-bhāgavatāmṛta* 2.5.222

According to this definition, we could say that humility is synonymous to honesty. An honest bank teller never thinks that the money he manages belongs to him. If, by some misunderstanding, he appropriates something for himself, prison awaits him. Likewise, an honest person understands that all their virtues, strengths and talents come from above. God entrusts us with a particle of His energy and sees how we use it. If we prove honest to Him, we will be entrusted with more. Furthermore, Krishna may entrust us with His most valuable treasure, a particle of His internal energy, the energy of love, *hlādinī-śakti*.

However, if we try to appropriate the talents and abilities given to us, squander them, or like misers who bury treasure in the ground, hide them away or neglect them, then the same fate as the thieving clerk awaits us – prison.

The entire material realm is a vast penal colony for thievish souls. Therefore, true humility is extremely rare here. The Lord has specifically created this colony to help us get free from the proclivity to steal. Reasonable people understand this and try to consciously overcome this tendency. Sanātana Gosvāmī writes:

> *yayā vācehayā dainyaṁ*
> *matyā ca sthairyam eti tat*
> *tāṁ yatnena bhajed vidvāṁs*
> *tad-viruddhāni varjayet*

> 'An educated person (vidvan) must make conscious efforts so that his speech, behavior and thoughts help him to establish himself in humility and carefully avoid anything that prevents this.'
>
> *Bṛhad-bhāgavatāmṛta* 2.5.223

In Christianity, this practice of self-observation is called sobriety and is practiced in Hesychasm – a contemplative monastic tradition of Eastern Catholicism and Eastern Orthodoxy. Practitioners continuously chant the Jesus Prayer in their minds with great focus and a watchful attention on the mind's thoughts.

They understand that without sobriety their chanting of God's holy name is fruitless: God does not take seriously the prayers of a torrid and impassioned mind.

Those intoxicated by material opulence must sober up if they want to see the Lord's merciful smile. Those who want to be perpetually intoxicated, seek to increase their so-called opulence (in verse 1.8.26, *edhamāna* conveys this sense of constant expansion) and will eventually have to suffer a painful hangover. Interestingly, in his commentary on the *Mahābhārata*, Śrīpad Madhvācārya quoted a *Ṛg Veda* verse where God is called *edhamāna-dviṭ* – 'the one who cuts pride or greed.'

> *śṛṇve vīra ugram-ugraṁ damāyann*
> *anyam anyamatinenīyamānaḥ*
> *edhamānadviḷ ubhayasya rājā*
> *coṣkūyate viśa indro manuṣyān*

> 'The Lord in the form of half lion, half man, Nṛsiṁha, is famous for His incomparable prowess! Again and again, He pacifies the villainous demons, casting them into the darkness of hell. Those who are good-natured, He diligently helps advance on the path to the light, leading to salvation of the soul. Those who strive to aggrandizement beyond all measure are put in their place (edhamāna-dviṭ) by the strict but just Lord.'
>
> *Ṛg Veda* 6.47.16. Quoted from *Mahābhārata-tātparya-nirṇaya* 1.100

Queen *Kuntī* urges us on a journey toward a true experience with the Lord. From 1.8.23-1.8.26, she has mentioned, directly or indirectly, several qualities required for this. At first glance, these seem to be an array of qualities: chastity, hope for Krishna's special mercy, gratitude, patience, willingness to accept lessons from God, the teacher of the world, and, finally, simple honesty, or the unwillingness to appropriate that which does not belong to us. In reality, these are all facets of the same quality – humility.

Humility is like a digestive enzyme. It helps us to assimilate all the lessons that the Lord generously sends into our lives. As undigested food turns into poison, so lessons that have not been learned turn into resentment, envy, and anger. However, those same lessons can turn into a source of happiness and wholeness should the enzyme of humility help us digest them. This is how humility brings about love of God. Sanātana Gosvāmī goes even further to say that humility is both the cause of *prema* and its effect:

paripākeṇa dainyasya
premājasraṁ vitanyate
parasparaṁ tayor itthaṁ
kārya-kāraṇatekṣyate

'When humility is fully ripe, love infinitely floods the heart. Therefore, humility and love are always the cause and effect of each other.'

Bṛhad-bhāgavatāmṛta 2.5.225

In this way, humility and love nourish each other and facilitate each other's growth. In naming the facets of humility, Queen Kuntī identifies the initial manifestations of love. As the process of spiritual practice matures our humility to its most profound, we acquire the greatest wealth – love of God, where God Himself becomes the devotee's proerty. This is the subject of her next verse.

The Wealth of the Poor and the Poverty of the Rich

namo 'kiñcana-vittāya
nivṛtta-guṇa-vṛttaye
ātmārāmāya śāntāya
kaivalya-pataye namaḥ

'My obeisance unto You, who are the property of the materially impoverished. You have nothing to do with the actions and reactions of the material modes of nature. You are self-satisfied, and therefore You are most gentle, and master of the monists.'

Śrīmad-Bhāgavatam 1.8.27

In this verse, Queen Kuntī sums up the previous four verses (where she has charted Krishna's help and protection for her and the wider family) by addressing Krishna with various epithets that describe how He reveals Himself in His relationships with pure devotees and reciprocates their love. These are '*akiñcana-vittāya*,' '*nivṛtta-guṇa-vṛttaye*,' '*ātmārāmāya*,' '*śāntāya*,' '*kaivalya-pataye*.'

We will highlight points from the wonderful commentary by Śrīla Prabhupāda which brings out the nuanced meanings and beauty of Queen Kuntī's words. Śrīla Prabhupāda begins by deepening the discussion on *akiñcana*, which means 'one who has no material possessions.' For us to give up our possessions is painful because we have tied up our sense of identity so tightly to these. In the purport, he says, 'A living being is finished as soon as there is nothing to possess. Therefore, a living being cannot be, in the real sense of the term, a renouncer.' It is difficult if not impossible to become *akiñcana* in the material world. One would feel 'finished', i.e. dead, redundant, empty. The desire to acquire and take possession of everything we lay our eyes on is constant and unconscious. The yearning is almost irresistible because it is inherent to the soul. We yearn because of our sense of incompleteness. The *Bṛhad-āraṇyaka Upaniṣad* elaborates:

> *tasmād api etarhi ekākī kāmayate*
> *jāyā me syād jāyā me syāt*
> *atha prajāyeyātha vittaṁ me syād*
> *atha prajāyeya atha vittam me syāt*
> *atha karma kurvīyeti |*
> *atha karma kurvīya iti*
> *sa yāvad apy eteṣāmekaikaṁ na prāpnoty*
> *sa yāvat api eteṣām ekaikam na prāpnoti*
> *akṛtsna eva tāvan manyate*

> 'In the beginning man was alone, only one. He desired, "Let there be a wife for me that I may have offspring and let there be wealth for me that I may offer sacrifices." Verily, this is the essential desire – for one to have a partner. Furthermore, the lonely person wishes, "Let there be a wife for me that I may have offspring and let there be wealth for me that I may offer sacrifices." So long as he does not obtain either of these things, he thinks he is incomplete.'
>
> *Bṛhad-āraṇyaka Upaniṣad* 1.4.17

The s*cripture analyzes the* psychological causes of karma – the powerful impulse for action that is well known to all of us. It states that we are moved to act because of the sense of incompleteness, lack of self-sufficiency and inadequacy (*akṛitsnata*) inherent to all conditioned souls as soon as we sever our connection to God. These feelings embed insecurity and fear in the heart, which turn into an insatiable loneliness, which in turn gives rise to our primary desire: the hope to rid our incompleteness by marrying (*jāyā me syāt*).

This ushers in the second desire: to produce offspring and to go on living through one's children (*atha prajāyeya*). A third desire to have possessions in this world (*atha vittam me syāt*) naturally follows. To support a spouse and children, one needs a house, some livestock, land, and money (*vittam*). Money is also required for the performance of sacrificial rites or for distributing charity (*atha karma kurvīyeti*). Reasonable people understand that without this they will not be able to secure a happy future in this life or the next – which becomes the fourth desire. As long as these desires remain unfulfilled, we continue to feel like failures (*sa yāvat api eteṣām ekaikam na prāpnoti akṛtsna eva tāvan manyate*).

Ironically, when these desires are fulfilled, the feeling of incompleteness does not go away. In striving to fulfill these goals, our consciousness externalizes, and the soul endlessly wanders the world in pursuit of (unattainable) happiness.

The attempts to accomplish these four desires are called 'progress' in material civilization, and people naively believe that such progress is *artha*, something important and valuable. But from the perspective of *akiñcana*, all this progress is *anartha*:

> *'Advancement of material vision or material civilization is a great stumbling block for spiritual advancement. Such material advancement entangles the living being in the bondage of a material body followed by all sorts of material miseries. Such material advancement is called* anartha*, or things not wanted. Actually, this is so. In the present context of material advancement, one uses lipstick at a cost of fifty cents, and there are so many unwanted things which are all products of the material conception of life. By diverting attention to so many unwanted things, human energy is spoiled without achievement*

of spiritual realization, the prime necessity of human life. The attempt to reach the moon is another example of spoiling energy because even if the moon is reached, the problems of life will not be solved.'

Śrīmad-Bhāgavatam 1.8.27, purport

Material civilization whittles down to the petty realization of these four material desires, starting with lust (symbolized by lipstick) and ending with the attempts to get to the moon and other higher planets to secure a better future. All this activity is *anartha*, because it delivers a bad infinity: in this world, a happy life of completeness means a spouse, which means children, which requires money and property, which are obtained by performing rituals – karma. Any karma generates new desires, which further entangles the tiny, embodied living entity even more in desires, actions, and consequences, and therefore suffering. Rotating in a cycle of karma, we die like silkworms in cocoons. Without ever realizing our eternal spiritual natures, we take new births according to our karmic destinies. This cycle continues perpetually.

Reasonable people try to solve the problem of incompleteness in a different way: they direct their desires toward attaining God, understanding that nothing but restoration of their connection with God, the Complete Whole, will help them regain their lost integrity.

For such individuals, the entire world with its perishable treasures is nothing more than a heap of rubbish. They set off on a quest for imperishable treasure, God, and for that purpose become *akiñcana*, a beggar. Fulfilling the devotee's quest, God becomes their wealth. Therefore, He is called *akiñcana-vitta* (the beggar's treasure).

'Similarly, a devotee renounces the material world not for nothing but for something tangible in spiritual

value... The devotees are generally without material prosperity, but they have a very secret treasure-house in the lotus feet of the Lord.'
Śrīmad-Bhāgavatam 1.8.27, purport

Just as a miser carefully hides wealth in a cache, an *akiñcana* devotee hides their treasure deep in their heart. In a prayer to Krishna, Bilvamaṅgala Ṭhākura writes:

kārāgṛhe vasa sadā hṛdaye madīye
mad-bhakti-pāśa-dṛḍha-bandhana-niścalaḥ san
tvāṁ kṛṣṇa he! pralaya-koṭi-śatāntare 'pi
sarvasva-caura! hṛdayān nahi mocayāmi

'Now I have bound You with the rope of love and put You in the prison house of my heart! Stay there, stay there, stay there! You cannot free Yourself from this tight bondage! O Krishna! You have robbed me of everything I had – my material assets, my name, my fame, my beauty, my reputation, my kith and kin, my heart and mind! The proper punishment for You is to remain forever and ever in the prison house of my heart, bound up tightly in the rope of love! If crores of *pralayas* come, still I won't release You! Never will you escape! This is suitable punishment for such a great thief as You!'
Śrī Caurāgragaṇya-Puruṣāṣṭakam 8

Love of God is our only true wealth that no one can steal from us. Any outward wealth diminishes; it is impossible to preserve. In fact, it is our *sense of ownership*, not the property as such, that holds us back on the path of spiritual progress. Śrīla Prabhupāda retells the story of Śrīla Sanātana Gosvāmī who kept a touchstone in a rubbish heap as if it had no significance:

'This specific example is given for the neophyte devotees just to convince them that material

> *hankerings and spiritual advancement go ill together. Unless one is able to see everything as spiritual in relation with the Supreme Lord, one must always distinguish between spirit and matter. A spiritual master like Śrīla Sanātana Gosvāmī, although personally able to see everything as spiritual, set this example for us only because we have no such spiritual vision.'*
>
> *Śrīmad-Bhāgavatam* 1.8.27, purport

Mithilā Burns

A true devotee may possess immense wealth (have a spouse, children, and property) but still go on considering themselves a beggar. History has preserved Mahārāja Janaka's words regarding his 'poverty.'

> *anantaṁ bata me vittaṁ*
> *yasya me nāsti kiñcana*
> *mithilāyāṁ pradīptāyāṁ*
> *na me kiñcit pradahyate*

> 'Indeed, my treasures are untold, but nothing here is mine. Even if all Mithilā burns to ashes, nothing of my own burns.'
>
> *Mahābhārata, Śānti-parva* 17.18

The line has become proverbial, spoken under the following circumstances.

One day, upon Mahārāja Janaka's invitation, Śukadeva Gosvāmī visited Mithilā. He was offered a seat of honor, after which he began instructing Mahārāja Janaka and the numerous *brāhmaṇa* sages always gathered in great numbers in the court of the generous king. All the while, however, Śukadeva Gosvāmī addressed the king as if no one else was around. Eventually, the conceited sages, offended by Śukadeva Gosvāmī's 'disregard', considered that the guest was trying to curry favor with the king to receive a generous reward. Śukadeva Gosvāmī was amused and pained. The sages' silent resentful thoughts were clearly audible to him. To glorify Mahārāja Janaka and protect the sages from unnecessary offenses, he created a mirage.

Suddenly, thick acrid smoke filled the palace, leaving no air to breathe. Rushing to the windows, the sages saw Mithilā city engulfed in flames. Palaces, citizens' homes, *āśramas* and sages' solitary huts were on fire. Flames were now spreading towards Mahārāja Janaka's vast palace. Panic-stricken, the sages fled in all directions to save their meager belongings.

'My deer skin! My loincloth! My only cloth! My *kamaṇḍalū*!' they cried out.

Only Mahārāja Janaka was unmoved and placid. He uttered, 'Even if all Mithilā burns to ashes, nothing of mine burns,' as if inviting Śukadeva Gosvāmī to go on speaking.

After some moments, the mirage dispelled, and the scattered sages began returning to their seats, heads downcast. They realized there was no fire, except the fire of material desires, which still burned in their hearts. They were too ashamed to look at each other in the eyes. Settling down, they saw Śukadeva Gosvāmī still instructing Mahārāja Janaka. Both were deeply engaged in unperturbed discussion.

* * *

Krishna gives everything to His devotees who have given up their sense of possession, just as He gave everything to Sudāmā *brāhmaṇa*. He states:

ye dārāgāra-putrāpta-
prāṇān vittam imaṁ param
hitvā māṁ śaraṇaṁ yātāḥ
kathaṁ tāṁs tyaktum utsahe

'Since pure devotees give up their homes, wives, children, relatives, riches and even their lives simply to serve Me, without any desire for material improvement in this life or in the next, how can I give up such devotees at any time?'
Śrīmad-Bhāgavatam 9.4.65

The wealth that is sometimes at a devotee's disposal should not be confused with the wealth of ordinary people. For the latter, wealth is generated by the three modes of material nature, and therefore becomes an insurmountable obstacle on their spiritual paths. Krishna gives devotees their wealth. The modes of material nature and the reactions of material activities have nothing to do with it. Devotees cease to be affected by these forces and come out of the reach of the law of karma.

Thus, in 1.8.27, Queen Kuntī addresses Krishna as *nivṛtta-guṇa-vṛtti* – one who stops the action of the three modes of material nature, and in this way frees His devotees from the stock of their karma. Śrīla Prabhupāda writes,

'The material disease is due to hankering after and lording it over material nature. This hankering is due to an interaction of the three modes of nature, and neither the Lord nor the devotees have attachment for such false enjoyment. Therefore, the Lord and the devotees are called nivṛtta-guṇa-vṛtti. The perfect nivṛtta-guṇa-vṛtti is the Supreme Lord because He never becomes attracted by the modes of material nature, whereas the living beings have such a tendency... Because the Lord is the property

of the devotees, and the devotees are the property of the Lord reciprocally, the devotees are certainly transcendental to the modes of material nature.'

Śrīmad-Bhāgavatam 1.8.27, purport

The bond between Krishna and His pure devotees has nothing to do with material attachments of this world that induce nothing but suffering. By employing *nivṛtta-guṇa-vṛtti*, Queen Kuntī accentuates Krishna's transcendental affection for His unalloyed devotees, as noted in Canto Ten, '*Bhagavān bhakta-bhaktimān*'[1] – 'Bhagavān becomes a devotee of His devotees.' To all others, the Lord is impartial – He is *ātmārāma*, which is Queen Kuntī's next epithet. On this, Śrīla Prabhupāda says:

'The unalloyed devotees and the Lord are transcendentally attached to one another. For others, the Lord has nothing to reciprocate, and therefore He is called ātmārāma, self-satisfied.'

Śrīmad-Bhāgavatam 1.8.27, purport

In *Teachings of Queen Kuntī*, Śrīla Prabhupāda includes a further shade of meaning. It is not just Krishna who is *ātmārāma*, but his devotees also become *ātmārāmas* in fellowship with him, the supreme *ātmā*.

'O Krishna, at that time, one becomes happy in Your fellowship. You are happy in Yourself, and one who surrenders to You becomes happy, as You are.'

Teachings of Queen Kuntī, ch 10

Although Śrīla Prabhupāda offers no explanation to Queen Kuntī's next epithet, *śāntā* (peaceful), Viśvanātha Cakravartī writes that in this context it means the Lord easily forgives His pure devotees' offenses and remains calm and peaceful, despite the misconduct.

1 *Śrīmad-Bhāgavatam* 10.86.59.

The final epithet is *kaivalya-pati*, which Śrīla Prabhupāda translates as 'master of the monists,' as *kaivalya* usually denotes impersonal liberation. In the purport (for 1.8.27), he writes that Krishna is '*the master of all monists who seek to merge into the existence of the Lord. Such monists merge within the personal effulgence of the Lord called the brahma-jyoti.*'

However, the word *kaivalya* also means 'purity.' Therefore, Śrīla Jīva Gosvāmī translates this word as 'pure knowledge of the Lord.'[1] This epithet can also mean that Krishna is the master of those who know Him, have connected so deeply to Him, that their hearts are pure and they have the opportunity to see Him face to face.

If we string these epithets together, Queen Kuntī's verse describes Krishna's mercy from two different perspectives. The first:

'O Krishna, You are closely tied to Your devotees, who have nothing but You. You reciprocate their feelings – for You there is no one dearer than them. You liberate them from the influence of the three modes of material nature and elevate them to Your spiritual platform, turning them into *ātmārāmas*. Even if they sometimes slip, You do not attach much importance to their mistakes. If a devotee turns to You to fulfill his material desires, You remain unperturbed – such requests do not move Your heart. However, if a devotee desires liberation, You grant it. I offer my obeisance unto You again and again.'

The second:

'O Krishna, everyone knows that You fulfill all desires, but You are especially kind to Your pure devotees who have given up everything in this world for Your sake. You bestow upon them all riches. However, those riches do not affect them. Why?

1 *Prīti-sandarbha, Anuccheda* 1.

Because they always associate with You, an *ātmārāma*, and thus they become as self-satisfied as You. Peace and tranquillity descend into their hearts, for You are always peaceful. In the end, they receive from You the greatest reward – the opportunity to eternally associate with You and personally serve You. I offer my obeisance to You again and again.'

CHAPTER 8

The Activities of the Inactive

Four Misconceptions

From the next verse (1.8.28) Queen Kuntī talks about the Lord's pastimes in this world, explaining their pure spiritual nature. Śrīla Prabhupāda cautions us, *'The devotees enter into the transcendental pastimes of the Lord, which are never to be misunderstood as material.'* In fact, this section of Queen Kuntī's prayers serve as a valuable explanation of an important verse from the *Bhagavad-gītā.*

janma karma ca me divyam
evaṁ yo vetti tattvataḥ
tyaktvā dehaṁ punar janma
naiti mām eti so 'rjuna

'One who knows the transcendental nature of My appearance and activities does not, upon leaving the body, take his birth again in this material world, but attains My eternal abode, O Arjuna.'

Bhagavad-gītā 4.9

At first it seems that Krishna's *līlās* are easy to understand. They have been described in detail in *Purāṇas* and *Itihāsas.* Vyāsadeva, Śukadeva Gosvāmī and other great sages have explained them, and *ācāryas* thereafter have expounded on them more. Nevertheless, there is a reason that Krishna stipulates: *evaṁ yo vetti tattvataḥ* – 'Only one who has perfectly comprehended the nature of My activities will never take birth in this world again.' To truly understand the Lord's activities, we first must feel His participation in our lives. From 1.8.28-1.8.31, Queen Kuntī, who is a direct witness and participant in the Lord's *līlās*, gives reasons why ordinary people find it so difficult to grasp the meaning of His pastimes.

Most people reject accounts of the Lord's activities in *Purāṇas* and *Itihāsas* as myths. The main reason is that they have difficulty in reconciling God's mercy and the existence of evil and pain in a world that He has created. Such people do not believe in God at all and try to improve the world themselves or have doubts about His mercy.

Some who do believe in God and are able to reconcile the existence of evil with His mercy, reject *Purāṇic* stories because they cannot believe that God can personally come to Earth. Primitive realism prevents them from doing so; it seems to them that by coming here in a human-like form, the Lord becomes part of the duality of this world and loses His transcendence.

Those souls who can accept that the Lord comes into this world are rare, but they also find it difficult to understand why He comes in various strange forms, such as a fish, an animal, a half-man and half-lion, etc. Queen Kuntī has already noted that when the Lord appears on stage as an actor, disguised as a character, it is difficult for the audience to recognize Him. Often, people consider *līlās* to be primitive zoomorphism or anthropomorphism and that the narrations are fiction.

Those who can accept God's various incarnations cannot understand His pastimes in the form of Krishna, where the Lord's sweetness and beauty completely overshadow His power. To understand perfectly means to start admiring and loving. An ignorant person standing in front of a brilliant artist's painting sees nothing more than a crudely painted canvas and resents that someone has spoiled a nice cloth that could have been utilized in the household. A layperson will judge the merits of the painting by how 'realistic' the depicted people or objects are. A person of education may observe the magical world with nonchalance, condemning the artist for excessive imagination. An expert in painting will note the composition, play of chiaroscuro and symbolism. But only a true connoisseur, being delighted, will feel the emotions that guided the artist's brush in creating the piece of art.

God's sole motivation is love – love that is boundless. It is no wonder our imperfect minds cannot understand His motives. Often, in trying to comprehend the Lord's activities, people impose restrictions on His love.

'A loving God could not have created this world because there is too much evil here,' atheists say.

'The Absolute Truth cannot have a form or interfere with the affairs of this world,' the impersonalists and deists claim.

'God is a person. He can love, but, being the highest intellect, He cannot violate the laws of logic,' rationalist theologians argue.

'God can do everything except one thing – He can never forget that He is the Supreme,'[1] say those who bow before God's omnipotence.

Only those who believe in the infinity of God's love and strive to share that love can accept Him *as He is* and understand God's motivations to come into our world. An ordinary person's motives are not easy to understand. What to speak about God? Therefore, we first need to serve God's name, then bow before His beauty, and then feel His presence in our lives. This will give us some experience and touch of God's love, and this in turn (not dry logic) helps us understand God's driving motives to come into this world and perform His pastimes.

In the next few verses, Queen Kuntī will refute the four common misconceptions: God is unjust, God is not all-powerful, God is not all-merciful, living entities have no free will.

1 'Wherefore, He cannot do some things for the very reason that He is omnipotent.' Aurelius Augustine, The City of God, Bk 5, ch. 10.

Incorruptible Judge

manye tvāṁ kālam īśānam
anādi-nidhanaṁ vibhum
samaṁ carantaṁ sarvatra
bhūtānāṁ yan mithaḥ kaliḥ

'My Lord, I consider Your Lordship to be eternal time, the supreme controller, without beginning and end, the all-pervasive one. In distributing Your mercy, You are equal to everyone. The dissensions between living beings are due to social intercourse.'

Śrīmad-Bhāgavatam 1.8.28

God exists, and He is just. Queen Kuntī, is a witness of the great war in which millions of soldiers died, including her grandchildren. We must take her as an authority because she speaks from deep personal realization and experience. These are not the careless reflections of an ordinary person. She begins 1.8.28 with *'manye tvāṁ'* – 'I know,' and goes on, 'that You are eternal time (*kāla*), the controller of the world (*īśānam*).' By looking at some definitions we can gain a deeper sense of what she means with these words.

Kālaṁ comes from the Sanskrit '*kāl*,' 'to measure.' *kālayati sarvam iti kālam*[1] – 'Time is what measures everything and puts an end to everything.' About Himself, Krishna says in *Bhagavad-gītā* 10.30: *kālaḥ kalayatām aham* – 'Among subduers I am time.' Another definition of time is *saṅkalayati kālayati vā bhūtānīti kālaḥ* – 'Time impartially measures all the merits and demerits and rewards everyone justly.'

Therefore, Queen Kuntī characterizes God as *īśvara*, the incorruptible ruler of this world. Since He is time, time has no

1 From *Vacaspatyam*, Sanskrit dictionary by Pandit Taranatha Tarkavachaspati.

power over Him (*anādi-nidhanaṁ*). Śrīla Prabhupāda elaborates:

> *'Another name of the Paramātmā feature of the Lord is kāla, or eternal time. Eternal time is the witness of all our actions, good and bad, and thus resultant reactions are destined by Him. It is no use saying that we do not know why and for what we are suffering. We may forget the misdeed for which we may suffer at this present moment, but we must remember that Paramātmā is our constant companion, and therefore He knows everything, past, present and future. And because the Paramātmā feature of Lord Kṛṣṇa destines all actions and reactions, He is the supreme controller also. Without His sanction not a blade of grass can move.'*
>
> *Śrīmad-Bhāgavatam* 1.8.28, purport

Chanakya Pandit also reflects on the overwhelming power of time:

> *kālaḥ pacati bhūtāni*
> *kālaḥ saṁharate prajāḥ*
> *kālaḥ supteṣu jāgarti*
> *kālo hi duratikramaḥ*

> 'Time helps all living entities to ripen, and time brings death to them. Time alone stays awake when all the rest are asleep. Truly, time is insurmountable.'
>
> *Cāṇakya-nīti-darpaṇa* 6.7

Eternal time rules over everything – its power has neither beginning nor end (*anādi-nidhanaṁ*), therefore it is *vibhum* – the greatest, the all-pervading and all-encompassing. It is impossible to hide anywhere from omnipresent time because it *carantaṁ sarvatra* – 'goes everywhere.' Impartial time strikes everyone, bringing everyone the fruits of their karma:

āyuḥ karma ca vittaṁ ca
vidyā nidhanam eva ca
pañcaitāni hi sṛjyante
garbhasthasyaiva dehinaḥ

'One's lifespan, profession, wealth, education and cause of death – these five things are predetermined even before one's birth.'
Cāṇakya-nīti-darpaṇa 4.1

When one speaks of the inevitability of time, the ancient story of the dove and Garuḍa is often remembered.

Once Yamarāja, lord of the realm of the dead, visited Lord Rāma in Ayodhyā. He saw a dove perched on the palace gates and smiled to himself. A smile from the God of Death hardly bodes well.

'What does your smile mean?' the pigeon asked in a trembling voice.

'My smile always means one thing – death will soon strike you.'

Yamarāja strode on, leaving the petrified dove in a panic. Just then, Lord Viṣṇu's giant eagle, Garuḍa, flew up to the palace. The dove implored, 'You are the lord of birds, our king. Please protect me!'

Garuḍa listened to the story and promised, 'I will take you to Lokāloka where no one will touch you.'

The delighted pigeon fluttered onto Garuḍa's back and together they flew to Lokāloka, a giant mountain situated at the boundary of inhabited worlds. With a sense of accomplishment, Garuḍa returned to Ayodhyā just as Yamarāja was leaving the palace. Seeing the great bird panting, Yamarāja said, 'Why are you breathing so heavily?'

Garuḍa explained that he had saved a poor pigeon from death by flying it to Lokāloka. Hearing this, a broad smile of satisfaction spread across Yamarāja's face. Now, it was Garuḍa's turn to be alarmed.

'Why are you smiling?' he asked.

'That pigeon has already been eaten by a cat. When I saw it squatting on the palace gates, I was astonished because I knew it was destined to die today hundreds of thousands of miles from Ayodhyā. I smiled then because it became clear to me that someone would help this pigeon meet his death where he was destined to die – he himself would not be able to get there for years. Truly, fate is inevitable, and even I never tire of being surprised.'

God's Omnipotence and the Soul's Freedom

In 1.8.28, Queen Kuntī calls Krishna '*vibhu*,' which means omnipotent and omnipresent. But how can God's omnipotence and omnipresence reconcile with the freedom of a living being? Are our choices free if God already knows what we are going to do? If our lives are predestined, how can we exercise freedom?

It seems that we are puppets in the hands of a cruel puppeteer. We hear that not a blade of grass can move without God's permission! Therefore, He is to blame for our miseries. Perhaps, He delights in our torments? Russian poet, Nickolai Gumilev, expressed these thoughts:

All of us — righteous and sinners,
Born in prison, raised at the altar,
All of us are funny actors
In the theater of the Creator…

God leaning forward is watching,
He is caught up in the drama…
Pity if Cain is crying,
Hamlet will have blissful moments!

That goes against His intentions!
To avoid deviations,
God will entrust the production
Into Pain's hands, a deaf titan.

Now the pain's shooting higher
Cunningly webbing and freely,
Those who choose to retire,
Are castigated severely.

Tortures grow out of proportion
Fear and dismay – even greater;
What if continues His celebration
In the theater of the Creator.[1]

Similar doubts have visited all thinkers, from biblical Job to F. M. Dostoevsky,[2] making it imperative for us to know

1 N. S. Gumilev, 'Theatre'. Translated by Maya Jouravel.

2 The Book of Job 21:7, 'Wherefore do the wicked live, become old, yea, are mighty in power?' The Book of Job 24:12, 'Men groan from out of the city, and the soul of the wounded crieth out: yet God layeth not folly to them.'
Dostoevsky, The Brothers Karamazov: 'Tell me why it is those poor mothers stand there? Why are people poor? Why is the babe poor? Why is the steppe barren? Why don't they hug each other and kiss? Why don't they sing songs of joy? Why are they so dark from black misery? Why don't they feed the babe?

Queen Kuntī's defense of God, paid for by her entire difficult life. Living beings do have freedom, she says. How so? Because God is just: *samaṁ carantaṁ sarvatra* – He harbors neither attachment nor enmity towards anyone.

If God had not endowed us with freedom, then there would be no need of His justice. It would make no sense to award consequences to choices and actions controlled or dictated by divinity. Queen Kuntī describes Krishna as *samaṁ*, which means 'You are absolutely fair. You simply award everyone what they deserve.' Everything that comes to us is supreme justice. Śrīla Prabhupāda explains:

> *'The living beings are given as much freedom as they deserve, and misuse of that freedom is the cause of suffering. The devotees of the Lord do not misuse their freedom, and therefore they are the good sons of the Lord. Others, who misuse freedom, are put into miseries destined by the eternal kāla. The kāla offers the conditioned souls both happiness and miseries. It is all predestined by eternal time.'*
>
> *Śrīmad-Bhāgavatam* 1.8.28, purport

When we blame others or fate for our suffering, we effectively accuse God of injustice. He is always ready to forgive us, but are we ready to forgive Him for sending us troubles? Are we ready to accept that He can do anything?

By definition, *Vibhu*, the almighty God, the universal mind, can neither be cruel or unjust, for these qualities would indicate His weakness, incompleteness, and imperfection. Moreover, the fact that we operate with the concepts of justice and injustice implies the objective existence of absolute justice, that is, God. The existence of any relative truth depends on the Absolute.

Writer and Christian apologist, C.S. Lewis made a brilliant argument in favor of the existence of a just God: 'My argument against God was that the universe seemed so cruel and unjust. But how had I got this idea of just and unjust? A man does not call a line crooked unless he has some idea of a straight line. What was I comparing this universe with when I called it unjust? If the whole show was bad and senseless from A to Z, so to speak, why did I, who was supposed to be part of the show, find myself in such violent reaction against it? A man feels wet when he falls into water, because man is not a water animal: a fish would not feel wet. Of course, I could have given up my idea of justice by saying it was nothing but a private idea of my own. But if I did that, then my argument against God collapsed too – for the argument depended on saying that the world was really unjust, not simply that it did not happen to please my private fancies.'[1]

The Source of Evil

If we understand God to be truly omnipotent and just, then the natural question to follow is why there's so much suffering and evil in this world. From the atheists' perspective, this is the strongest argument against the existence of an 'all-good God.' Charles Darwin said, 'This very old argument from the existence of suffering against the existence of an intelligent first cause seems to me a strong one; whereas, as just remarked, the presence of much suffering agrees well with the view that all organic beings have been developed through variation and natural selection.'[2]

Queen Kuntī provides another explanation in 1.8.28: that suffering exists in this world precisely because God has made

1 C.S. Lewis, Mere Christianity, Book II, The Rival Conceptions of God.

2 Charles Darwin, Religious Beliefs, The Autobiography of Charles Darwin 1809-1882.

living beings free. *Bhūtānāṁ yan mithaḥ kaliḥ* – 'People quarrel with each other and cause suffering to each other.' The Vedic aphorism cited earlier – 'The Lord is impartial and not cruel, for the pleasures and pains experienced by the living beings are the result of their karma, as shown by the scriptures'[1] captures the same idea.

According to this understanding, humans cause *kaliḥ*, which means 'strife,' 'dissension,' 'wars.' Why do we quarrel and inflict endless suffering to one another? Because of pride and envy, which manifests as the desire to compete for the limited resources of material nature. J.P. Sartre articulated this desire most frankly: 'The other robs me of my space; the other's existence is an unacceptable scandal.'

We bring about our own suffering and will have to endure it until we stop trying to lord over material nature. God has nothing to do with it. Pain breeds pain: the pain we inflict upon others inevitably returns to us. This world is a snowball of pain. All human suffering is the result of our rebellion against God's sovereignty. To illustrate this, Bhaktisiddhānta Sarasvatī told a sad parable about a man's fight with the sky.

Once upon a time there was a man who despised others and considered all to be insignificant compared to himself. One day he decided that the sky had grown too self-important and too proud of its power.

'The sky pours down hurricanes, torrential rains, lightning, hail, and at the slightest problem rumbles thunder. It deserves a good lesson, so it stops boasting of its power,' he thought. 'I must smash the sky with my fists!'

He began boxing with the sky to subdue it. He jumped up,

1 *Vaiṣamya-nairghṛṇye na sāpekṣatvāt tathā hi darśayati*, *Vedānta-sūtra* 2.1.34.

swung his fists about and sputtered curses. But no matter how hard he tried, the sky remained as unperturbed and merciful as ever, while he grew weary in the fruitless battle. Finally, all strength left him. Drained, he collapsed to the ground, hurting all over. Still, lying there, he went on accusing heaven of injustice.[1]

* * *

All attempts to take revenge upon God end likewise. Still, we do not give up. The endless futile attempts by all kinds of social reformers to make humanity happy betray their resentment towards God's 'failed' attempt to create a perfect world. Furthermore, most amazing is that those who deep down despise others undertake these improvements. Resentment towards God, pride, and hate band together. German philosopher, Nietzsche, unwittingly corroborated this truth in his writings.

'There are days when a feeling comes to me that is darker than the darkest melancholy – contempt for man. And to dispel all doubts about who and what I despise, I will say frankly: I despise the man of today, with whom I am fatally connected, as a contemporary.'[2]

'Indeed, at hearing the news that 'the old god is dead,' we philosophers and 'free spirits' feel illuminated by a new dawn; our hearts overflow with gratitude, amazement, forebodings, expectation – finally the horizon seems clear again, even if not bright.'[3]

1 Battle with the Sky, in *Upākhyāne Upadeśa* (Instructive Stories).

2 F. Nietzsche, Beyond Good and Evil.

3 F. Nietzsche, Gay Science.

'Ye Be Not Judged ...'

Queen Kuntī begins 1.8.28 with the word *manye* – 'I consider,' 'I see,' to invite us to look at the world through her eyes; eyes of one who bows before the Lord. This is the only freedom we have. We can either survey the world with judgmental eyes and see nothing but suffering, or we can take efforts to start seeing this world as a place where everyone '*creates their own destiny under the supervision of the Supreme Lord,*'[1] who is imperturbable and just.

If we 'see' with judgemental eyes, we will have to reject God and try to personally reinstate justice in this 'unjust world.' History records man's numerous attempts to find someone to blame and make the world 'fairer' – from the bloody French revolution to the Russian one. All ended the same way – resulting in yet more suffering, injustice, and pain. One motivated by pain inflicts nothing but more pain on others. Nevertheless, we do not give up our attempts to 'restore justice.'

Our tendency to seek 'justice,' assert 'good,' and fight 'evil' (according to our personal understanding) is too deeply rooted in our hearts to be easily removed. This is how *rāga* and *dveṣa*, affection and aversion, manifest. Voluntarily or involuntarily, we constantly play the role of a judge – we 'improve' the environment, we condemn social order, we judge others near and far, and ultimately pass judgment on God.

Marina Tsvetaeva, a prominent Russian poet of the early twentieth century, wrote a poem while living through turbulent Russian history that expresses the passionate grief and resentment we are discussing:

> black mountain
> blocks the earth's light.

1 Śrīla Prabhupāda, *Śrīmad-Bhāgavatam* 1.8.28, purport.

Time–time–time
to give back to God his ticket.

I refuse to – be. In
the madhouse of the inhumans
I refuse to – live. To swim

on the current of human spines.
I don't need holes in my ears,
no need for seeing eyes.
I refuse to swim on the current of human spines.
To your mad world – one answer: I refuse.[1]

The habit of judgment grows in our hearts from the soil of ignorance – based on misunderstanding our nature, the nature of this world, and the nature of God. Ignorance breeds pride, and pride breeds confidence in one's own righteousness and the habit of judging and looking for the guilty.

Queen Kuntī explains that when we look at the world from this lens, we cannot comprehend the way eternal time and God, who are behind all the events of our lives, operate. We will never accept or grasp the valuable lessons God wants us to learn. He sends us what we deserve – in exactly the way that can help us, heal us, and transform us. Failing to grasp this, we blame others for our misfortunes and reject God. Thus, our habit of judgment deprives us of the opportunity to understand, perceive, and love God. By holding on to our relative 'good' and 'evil,' we deny ourselves the opportunity to attain the Absolute Good.

Whether we are aware of it or not, we are in a state of permanent war with God, rather like the proud man from the parable. When we envy or blame someone, it means that we do not understand the Lord's justice and impartiality, and,

1 Marina Tsvetaeva, 'Black Mountain', from 'Poems to the Czechoslovakia,' 9 May 1939. Translated by Ilya Kaminsky and Jean Valentine.

therefore, we continue multiplying pain and evil in this world by creating resentment and fighting with others – *bhūtānāṁ yan mithaḥ kaliḥ*.

It is of little importance whether our accusations are fair or not because by pointing at the guilty, we blame ourselves: when our index finger points at someone, the other three fingers point back to ourselves. On this, Mahārāja Parīkṣit formulates an essential principle on which the law of karma rests:

> *yad adharma-kṛtaḥ sthānaṁ*
> *sūcakasyāpi tad bhavet*

> 'The destination intended for the perpetrator of irreligious acts is also intended for one who identifies the perpetrator.'
>
> *Śrīmad-Bhāgavatam* 1.17.22

We can acknowledge someone else's wrongdoing, but that is different from flinging blame at them. We often judge others to justify ourselves, 'Under those circumstances, I could not have acted otherwise.' The hardest thing in this world is to take full responsibility for ourselves and what happens to us, and thus break the vicious circle of karma, mutual accusation, pain, resentment and claims for justice.

It is important to say that taking full responsibility does not mean condemning ourselves. Hating ourselves or some quality that we have is no different from hating others because we continue being the judge. Cruel self-judgment and soul-draining guilt are yet more manifestations of pride. As the saying goes, self-deprecation is worse than pride because self-deprecation makes us even more self-centered than pride.

Taking responsibility means to recognize the Lord's justice, mercy, and thank Him for all the invaluable lessons He has taught us. It is the prerogative of God in His form as time to judge us, and we need only to graciously acknowledge His right to do so.

* * *

Once a *sādhu* on his deathbed in Vṛndāvana summoned his disciples and said, 'Soon I will be judged in the court of Yamarāja. He will summon Chitragupta, his scribe, who will take out a thick book that lists all my actions and thoughts.

In a droning voice, as befits court clerks, Chitragupta will read aloud the episodes of my life, one after another. After the first episode, I will ask for the right to respond. I will tell Yamarāja that I could not have acted otherwise in the situation, and that I had compelling reasons to behave that way. I will explain everything. I will tell him how I was wronged and hurt, and how I simply responded to that pain.

Hearing me, Yamarāja will nod his head favorably. Encouraged by his reaction, I will carefully listen as Chitragupta reads on. After the next event, I will again explain everything and see Yamarāja sympathetically nod. Episode by episode, I will prove that I simply could not have acted otherwise. Increasingly reassured by my own rightness, I will shed tears of self-pity. I will be so convincing that I will believe that I could not have acted otherwise.

At the end, all will be silent, and Yamarāja will ask, "Have you said everything?" I will answer, "Yes," and await his verdict. Finally, Yamarāja will conclude, "All this is fine. I have one last question: if nothing depended on you, then why were you so proud?" I will have nothing to say to that and have to admit my guilt.'

* * *

There is scope to justify our actions by circumstances, upbringing, environmental influences, and pain caused by others. So, what are we being judged for? It is not for the actions (which may be predetermined by our past), but for *our state of mind, our attitude towards others and the world* when we commit our acts.

Glorifying Krishna's impartiality, Queen Kuntī speaks of the greatest, ultimate humility that we must attain by asking and remembering, 'Who am I?' An infinitesimal particle of spirit, one ten-thousandth part of the tip of a hair, imagining myself to be the center of the universe and trying to make the entire world revolve around me. When we acknowledge this truth, extraordinary joy and bliss will descend upon our soul, the veil will fall from our eyes, and we will see the Lord's smiling face.

Let us repeat once again: the only freedom we have is the freedom to choose what kind of a world we are going to live in: one ruled by injustice and absurdity, or one where everyone '*creates their own destiny under the supervision of the Supreme Lord.*' (*Śrīmad-Bhāgavatam* 1.8.28, purport)

God does not interfere or play any role in the lives of those who try to establish their own 'justice.' He leaves them to the judgment of impartial time. But He comes personally to the rescue of those who choose Him. This is the theme of the next verse.

Three Reasons why Krishna's Pastimes are Incomprehensible

na veda kaścid bhagavaṁś cikīrṣitaṁ
tavehamānasya nṛṇāṁ viḍambanam
na yasya kaścid dayito 'sti karhicid
dveṣyaś ca yasmin viṣamā matir nṛṇām

'O Lord, no one can understand Your transcendental pastimes, which appear to be human and so are misleading. You have no specific object of favor, nor do You have any object of envy. People only imagine that You are partial.'

Śrīmad-Bhāgavatam 1.8.29

In the previous verse, Queen Kuntī addressed Krishna as impassive time that sorts everything out (*kālam*), and as creator and ruler of this world (*īśānam*) who from time immemorial rewards each of us according to our deserving (*anādi-nidhanaṁ vibhum*). Believers usually think of God in this way – as an impartial, omnipotent judge who punishes and rewards.

However, here, in 1.8.29, Queen Kuntī refers to Him as Bhagavān – the Personality of Godhead, who possesses unlimited energies, of which the foremost is mercy and compassion. To understand God in this light is much more difficult, which is why Vyāsadeva says:

kālaḥ pacati bhūtāni
sarvāṇy evātmanātmani
yasmiṁs tu pacyate kālas
taṁ na vedeha kaścanan

'All living beings are under the rule of time, and time brings death (pacati) to all that live. However, no one

knows He who puts an end (pacyate) to time itself.'
Mahābhārata, Śānti-parva 239.25

The word '*pacati*' means 'digests.' Its first usage in the verse means time 'digests' us and brings us death. In the second occurrence, it means that God 'digests' time and puts an end to it for the devotee.

We often confuse impartiality for indifference. God is just, but not indifferent. How can someone who is the embodiment of love be content by exercising mere impartiality? God is a person, not an impersonal law. His *kṛpā-śakti*, the energy of compassion, gives rise to His prime quality – He is *bhakta-vatsala*,[1] He loves His devotees. This quality predominates over all His other qualities just as an emperor rules his subjects. Driven by this quality, the Lord takes on a human-like form to come to the aid of His devotees. Therefore, understanding His deeds is much more difficult than comprehending the impartiality of time.

Why is it so difficult to comprehend the activities of the Personality of Godhead? Queen Kuntī answers this question in the second line: *tavehamānasya nṛṇāṁ viḍambanam*. Viśvanātha Cakravartī Ṭhākura brings to light its meanings:

'Because your intentions (*īhamānasya*) can mislead (*viḍambanam*) anyone, even those who are well versed in the scriptures (*nṛṇāṁ*).'

No one can understand God's actual intentions, the motives of His actions. Why would Rāma need the help of the monkeys? Why would He kill Bali by hiding and shooting an arrow in the monkey warrior's back? Why would He send innocent Sītā Devī to the forest? And when He comes as Krishna, at night He dances

1 *Mādhurya-kaḍambinī* 8.7.

with other people's wives. Why? He loves the inhabitants of Vraja, but why does he leave them for good? The questions go on. No one can fully comprehend the Lord's motives and discern the supreme purport and supreme love in His actions.

'Because as Rāma and Krishna, Your activities resemble those of an ordinary person's activities. You pretend (*viḍambanam*) to be an ordinary person (*nṛṇāṁ*).'

Rāma cries and laments when Rāvaṇa steals Sītā Devī. Krishna sucks Yaśodā's breast, crawls around Nanda Mahārāja's yard, and rolls in cow dung. Who can understand why God does these things (*īhamānasya*). Śrīla Prabhupāda reminds us:

> *'His pastimes appear to be exactly like that of a human being, but actually they are transcendental and without any tinge of material contamination.'*
>
> *Śrīmad-Bhāgavatam* 1.8.29, purport

Because, coming into this world, You dazzle everyone (*anye narā viḍambitā*) with Your beauty and splendor. It is as if You mock the ignorant just like the sun mocks fireflies. Ordinary people cannot grasp Your beauty and Your wondrous deeds, which are far beyond the ordinary. Fools laugh at You when You come in the guise of an ordinary person, and You laugh at them.'

Like child's play, Rāma killed fourteen thousand *rākṣasas* with a blade of grass. When Duryodhana wanted to foolishly take Krishna captive, Krishna burst into laughter and showed His universal form. But seeing it, Duryodhana still could not recognize God.

God in the False Mirror of the Human Mind

In the last words of 1.8.29, Queen Kuntī underscores that ordinary people see the world through their partialities (*viṣamā matir nṛṇām*). When they think of Krishna's *līlās*, they think He is also partial. Such is human mentality – we see in the world only a reflection of our minds (*matiḥ*). The envious see envious people everywhere, the noble see nobility, the sick see pain, the deceitful suspect everyone else of lies, the hypocritical accuse others of hypocrisy, the lusty declare the history of the world to be one of unquenched lust, and the true saint sees nothing but kindness in others.

* * *

Once there was a young man. Confronted by relentless cruelty and evil in life, he concluded that the world is unjust.

'I must change the world at all costs,' he thought. Filled with determination, he set off on a quest for like-minded people. Soon he met a *sādhu* he knew, who asked, 'What's the matter with you? You are not yourself!'

The young man told him about his resolution.

'Good idea, I have also been thinking of changing the world. Let's go together. We need companions. Let's ask anyone we meet their opinion of the world and quickly find others who will help us change it.'

They set off. After a while, they met a man in love.

'What do you think of the world?' the *sādhu* asked.

'Oh, it is wonderful and amazing!' exclaimed the young lover. 'There is so much love, tenderness and beauty in it!'

'Perhaps this is not our best first recruit,' said the *sādhu*. His companion agreed, marveling at the naivety and foolishness of the lover.

Along the way, they met a merchant whose reply to the same question was, 'This world is full of cunning people! Everyone is out to deceive the other. We must be on guard! Likely, you want to cheat me too. Be off on your way!'

Onward, the *sādhu* and young man met a potter, blacksmith, and cowherd. Each said something that deemed them unsuitable. Finally, they met a peasant working in a field.

When asked if he would like to join them, he reproachfully said, 'Do you think I have nothing else to do? I need to plough my field, sow wheat, and harvest. Everything is just in my world. I get as much as I work.'

The young man, who had set out to fix the world, was baffled. The *sādhu* said, 'My friend, we must part ways. Go wherever you want, but first tell me, do you still think it's all about changing the world?'

* * *

The anecdote illustrates Queen Kuntī's point – we are biased by nature (*viṣamā matir nṛṇām*). Our bent of mind prevents us from understanding Krishna's activities. Verse 1.8.29 simultaneously addresses both elements: Krishna's extraordinary *līlās* and the block that obstructs us from comprehending them. Just as pride, which manifests in our attempts to judge and blame others, prevents us from understanding the Lord's justice, so the habit of dividing the world into friends and enemies makes us doubt that God, who comes to this world for the benefit of His devotees, can be impartial.

To divide people as our own or other, is the first lesson taught by Shanda and Amarka in Hiranyakasipu's *gurukula*. It is the habit of an ungodly nature. Material love (*rāga*) always breeds material hatred (*dveṣa*); these are two sides of the same coin. In the material world, loving someone means siding with them and opposing those whom they consider to be enemies. We think that out of love for some people, we need to hate others. The enemies of our friends must become our enemies. This is a flaw inherent in the limited thinking of individuals of this world.

To 'shield' God from this deficiency, philosophers and theologians have created all kinds of sterile concepts of the Absolute Truth, free from personal qualities. Over the centuries, they have depersonalized God in various ways.

Agnostics claim that God is incomprehensible, a strictly sealed secret, with no possibility of human contact. According to deists, God is like a watchmaker who creates the giant mechanism of this world with its laws, winds it up and then no longer interferes in its affairs. Impersonalist philosophers of all stripes believe that God, the Person, coming to this world in the form of *avatāras*, is as illusory as the material world itself. From their point of view, if God responds to believers' prayers, then He can no longer claim the right of being the Absolute Truth, which is unchanging and immovable. These are various attempts to deprive God of His energies and His personhood.

Such philosophers see God through the prism of their own biases, says Queen Kuntī. We could amalgamate their flawed rationale in the following way: 'When your personal God comes into this world, He takes a human-like form. But how can one who acts here remain transcendental to the modes of material nature? Moreover, He Himself admits that He comes here to protect devotees and kill demons: *paritrāṇāya sādhūnāṁ/vināśāya ca duṣkṛtām.*[1] This means He discriminates against some groups and favors others. All this explicitly proves that He is either not God at all, or, at best, a lower, material, anthropomorphic hypostasis of the transcendental Absolute – 'God' of cattlemen and housemaids.'

Dhṛtarāṣṭra, blind in all senses of the word, is the epitome of such thinkers. He believed in God but could not fully believe that Krishna is God. His reasoning, 'Did Krishna favor the Pāṇḍavas? Of course! Was He an enemy of Duryodhana? Of course. Did He take sides in the Kurukṣetra war? He did! When required, He broke His promise not to accept arms. He rejoiced when Karṇa released his deadly weapon at Ghaṭotkaca and was seriously alarmed when Bhīṣma promised to kill all the Pāṇḍavas. He particularly loved the Pāṇḍavas and hated others. In a word, He behaved like an ordinary person who has friends and enemies. Therefore, He is partial and doesn't even consider it necessary to conceal His partiality. How can He be God?'

Although Dhṛtarāṣṭra's father Vyāsadeva, his advisor Sañjaya, and his beloved brother Vidura, repeatedly advised him that Krishna is God, he could never fully believe it. An agnostic will not recognize God even if God stood before him. On the eve of the great war, Dhṛtarāṣṭra was offered the gift of sight by his father, but he preferred to remain blind. He did not want to give up the innate blindness of material attachments that induced him to divide the world into 'mine' and 'not mine,' and prevented him from understanding the personal nature of God. That is why he received *sāyujya-mukti* at the end of his life where he merged with the Lord's effulgence rather than being awarded residence in the Lord's abode.

1 'To deliver the pious and to annihilate the miscreants, as well as to reestablish the principles of religion, I Myself appear, millennium after millennium.' *Bhagavad-gītā* 4.8.

Since most of us are driven by material attachments, it is not surprising that we find it so hard to grasp God's personal nature. Upon hearing that Krishna is especially kind to His devotees, we end up thinking that devotional service is a way to buy God's favor. But what kind of God (and His mercy) is bought and sold? Śrīla Prabhupāda admonishes, '*Foolish people think that devotional service is flattering the Lord to get special mercy.*' (*Śrīmad-Bhāgavatam* 1.8.29, purport)

Devotional service has nothing to do with flattery. Duryodhana, accustomed to buying friends and allies, tried his best to flatter Krishna when He came to Hastināpura as the Pāṇḍavas' ambassador. The foolish prince employed professional singers to extoll Krishna's exploits, dancers to entertain, and chefs to prepare the finest cuisines. But, Krishna did not even glance in their direction. Instead, He went directly to Vidura's modest abode, where Vidura's wife, Parasvi, confused with delight, fed Him banana peels. Krishna is incorruptible. It is in Parasvi's banana peel that Krishna's partiality seems to lie.

The Quintessence of Bliss

Krishna cannot be partial if only because Vyāsadeva, Śukadeva Gosvāmī and hundreds of other sages, who severely condemn material attachments, worship Him as God. An aphorism from the *Nīti Śāstra* reads:

> *ayaṁ nijaḥ paro veti*
> *gaṇanā laghu-cetasām*
> *udāra-caritānāṁ tu*
> *vasudhaiva kuṭumbakam*

> 'Only petty people always divide the world into friends and foes. Those with a big heart consider the entire world to be one family.'
> *Hitopadeśa* 1.71

Krishna praises His devotees for treating enemies and friends alike: *samaḥ śatrau ca mitre ca.*[1] What to speak of Him then? What do we make of His activities?

When accusing Krishna of favoritism, biased people simply project their material consciousness onto God. Ordinary people seek happiness outside themselves because of inner emptiness, a sense of lack. We tend to ascribe our own motives to others. Therefore, when God comes to the material world to help His devotees, it appears to us that He does this because He or His devotees also lack something.

In truth, neither Krishna nor His pure devotees ever seek external happiness. They have no interest in happiness generated by the modes of material nature. They know that dead matter can never make the soul happy. Krishna does not need Duryodhana's delicious food. Even beginner devotees lose their taste for gross material pleasures; great devotees and the Lord are far beyond such trifling pursuits.

By definition, God is self-satisfied. He is *ātmārāma.* The relationship between Krishna and His pure devotees is a manifestation of Krishna's internal potency, His *svarūpa-śakti*. The quintessence of this is *hlādinī-śakti*, the energy of bliss, and the quintessence of this is *bhakti*, or *rati*, the energy of love and devotion, eternally living in the heart of both Bhagavān and the *bhakta.*

Therefore, the relationship is an exchange of Krishna's internal energy, bringing bliss to both. It was this precious inner energy of spiritual love that Krishna gratefully accepted when Parasvi held out a banana peel to Him.

By bringing joy to His devotees and deriving happiness from their love, Krishna simply interacts with His own energy

1 *Bhagavad-gītā* 12.18.

of bliss, which is non-different from Himself. Thus, He remains *ātmārāma*, self-satisfied. The pastimes of the Lord and His pure devotees are always motivated by the wholeness of pure love. That is why Śrīla Prabhupāda says these are 'without any tinge of material contamination.' Krishna serves His devotees, and the devotees serve Him, not for the sake of bliss, but *out* of bliss. That is the nature of pure love, which has nothing to do with petty material attachments.

Finite material pleasures cannot satisfy the soul's infinite thirst for bliss. Just as salty water only increases thirst, so material pleasures only poison the soul and make it even greedier. Infinite spiritual bliss cannot but make one infinitely generous. When the Lord comes to the material world, He is motivated by the desire to share His bliss with others. Brahmā relishes this truth in his ardent and repentant prayers to Krishna after he misunderstands the Lord's pastimes:

prapañcaṁ niṣprapañco 'pi
viḍambayasi bhū-tale
prapanna-janatānanda-
sandohaṁ prathituṁ prabho

'My dear Master, although You have nothing to do with material existence, You come to this earth and imitate material life just to expand the varieties of ecstatic enjoyment for Your surrendered devotees.'
Śrīmad-Bhāgavatam 10.14.37

The incident when Durvāsā Muni cursed and offended Ambarīṣa Mahārāja brings further depth to the discussion. Replying to Durvāsā Muni's desperate prayers for protection, Lord Nārāyaṇa explained the reason for His 'special favor' towards Mahārāja Ambarīṣa: His spiritual bliss is incomplete if it is not shared with His devotees:

nāham ātmānam āśāse
mad-bhaktaiḥ sādhubhir vinā
śriyaṁ cātyantikīṁ brahman
yeṣāṁ gatir ahaṁ parā

'O best of the brāhmaṇas, without saintly persons for whom I am the only destination, I do not desire to enjoy My transcendental bliss and My supreme opulences.'

Śrīmad-Bhāgavatam 9.4.64

The Desire Tree

'Alright,' an opponent might concede, 'but we still have questions. Why, when coming to the material world, does Krishna share spiritual bliss only with devotees and not others? Moreover, He kills demons. Why? Is it really to please His bloodthirsty devotees?'

Let's answer the second question first. To destroy demons, God certainly does not need to personally descend. Demons can very well kill each other. It is their nature to compete and fight. God has also established the law of karma, which impartially sums up all our actions and implements balance. Krishna meant it when He told the dying Duryodhana, 'You deserve your end – I have nothing to do with it.' In the *Padma Purāṇa*, Lord Viṣṇu states:

muhūrtenāpi saṁhartuṁ
śakto yadyapi dānavān
mad-bhāktānāṁ vinodārthaṁ
karomi vividhāḥ kriyāḥ

'O Brahmā, I can destroy all demons in an instant. In this world I act [not for that purpose but] only for the pleasure of My bhaktas.'

Quoted from *Paramātma-sandarbha*, *Anuccheda* 93

In other words, the Lord comes to Earth to increase His devotees' love. Along the way, He destroys the demons, restores the shaken foundations of religion, inspires faith in the innocent, and cleanses this world of contamination. These are merely by-products of His presence.

On this, Śrīla Jīva Gosvāmī gives an interesting analogy.[1] Sometimes devotees who gather to sing and dance in praise of God, invite professional musicians to play with them. Their goal is to please Krishna with devotional chanting and dancing. Simultaneously, the activity purifies and benefits the immediate atmosphere, the entire world, and the invited professionals have a spiritual experience even though they have no idea of *bhakti*.

But why does God share His spiritual happiness only with His devotees and not with everyone? Simple – He's willing to share with everyone, but only devotees accept His gift. A great pianist may want as many people as possible to experience the happiness he derives from music, but can everyone appreciate the melodies? Therefore, Prahlāda Mahārāja sums up Krishna's impartiality by comparing Him to a desire tree (*kalpataru*):

citraṁ tavehitam aho 'mita-yoga-māyā-
līlā-visṛṣṭa-bhuvanasya viśāradasya
sarvātmanaḥ samadṛśo 'viṣamaḥ svabhāvo
bhakta-priyo yad asi kalpataru-svabhāvaḥ

'O my Lord, Your pastimes are all wonderfully performed by Your inconceivable spiritual energy; and by her perverted reflection, the material energy, You have created all the universes. As the Supersoul

1 *Paramātma-sandarbha, Anuccheda* 93.

> of all living entities, You are aware of everything, and therefore You are certainly equal toward everyone. Nonetheless, You favor Your devotees. This is not partiality, however, for Your characteristic is just like that of a desire tree, which yields everything according to one's desire (*kalpataru-svabhāvaḥ*).'
>
> *Śrīmad-Bhāgavatam* 8.23.8

Anyone can turn to Krishna, just as anyone can turn to a *desire tree*. Krishna fulfilled the desires of Duryodhana and Arjuna when they both came to ask for help. Duryodhana chose Krishna's army while Arjuna chose Krishna. Non-devotees are simply unable to appreciate spiritual bliss – they do not want it and therefore do not receive it.

Thus, true impartiality outwardly manifests as partiality. This is the nature of divine impartiality. In 1.8.29, Queen Kuntī says, 'Actually, You have no particular attachment or dislike for anyone. You bestow Your mercy equally upon all; however, it is devotees who want to accept it, while demons do not.'

Śrīla Prabhupāda uses part of an analogy from Viśvanātha Cakravartī Ṭhākura to reinforce the point, *'This does not mean that the sun is partial in distributing its rays. The sunrays are open to everyone, but the capacities of the receptacles differ.'* (*Śrīmad-Bhāgavatam* 1.8.29, purport)

Our dispositions and receptivity determine what bliss we can receive from God. Śrīla Prabhupāda explained that there are four types of relationships God can have with living beings. We will illustrate these with four analogies, comparing God to the sun each time.

Absorbing the Sunrays of Mercy

Scriptures speak of a *sūrya-kānta* stone (also called *sūrya-maṇi*) which absorbs sun rays. By accumulating solar energy, it also becomes a source of heat and light. Thus, the sun comes into contact with a *sūrya-kānta* and makes it like itself. This is the first type of dealing between a living being and God, where a pure devotee absorbs God's mercy, accumulates it, and distributes it further on, like the *sūrya-kānta*. We see true saints emanate a glow. The haloes painted around their heads in pictures illustrate the light of spiritual energy accumulated within them. Their love and compassion for others is a reflection of the love and compassion of the Lord, which is a manifestation of His internal potency of *bhakti*.

In the second type of interaction, the living being is like the *cakravāka* bird, a type of duck. The drake and duck are in love and inseparable during the day. At sundown, they are forced to part and spend the night yearning for each other. When the sun rises, they rejoice not because it is sunrise but because it brings their reunion. They remember the sun again only when it sets. The same is true for those whose devotion to God is fueled by mixed motives. They remember God when they find themselves in an inconvenient situation. If their faith is sincere, the Lord answers their prayers, and they rejoice. However, they do not remain interested in God's mercy for long. Śrīla Prabhupāda says:

> *'Suffering men, needy men, inquisitive persons, or philosophers make temporary connections with the Lord to serve a particular purpose. When the purpose is served, there is no more relation with the Lord. A suffering man, if he is pious at all, prays to the Lord for his recovery. But as soon as the recovery is over, in most cases the suffering man no longer cares to keep any connection with the Lord. The mercy of the*

Lord is open for him, but he is reluctant to receive it. That is the difference between a pure devotee and a mixed devotee.'

Śrīmad-Bhāgavatam 1.8.29, purport

The third dynamic compares the living being to the blind. Those without sight can never benefit from the sun because they cannot see it. They aren't concerned if it is there or not; their night is eternal. This is the lot of moral atheists, agnostics, and impersonalists who do not care about the Lord. They choose to live in darkness.

Finally, the fourth dynamic characterizes living beings as owls and thieves. Bright sunlight blinds owls. It also deprives thieves of the opportunity to continue stealing to feed their families. The sun is seen as an interference for both. This is how *asuras*, militant atheists, see God who obstructs them from executing their plans. They curse or mock Him when He incarnates in a human-like form and contemptuously label it as anthropomorphism.

* * *

We have tried to resolve the problem of understanding God's activities: He answers His devotees' prayers and kills demons, while remaining impartial and self-satisfied. If, for some reason, these explanations do not convince readers, then in *Paramātma-sandarbha*[1] Śrīla Jīva Gosvāmī has offered an alternative understanding: God may well show favor to His devotees, for that is His nature. A desire tree fulfills the wishes of those who

1 In the *Paramātma-sandarbha*, *Anuccheda* 93, Śrīla Jīva Gosvāmī gave an alternative explanation for *Śrīmad-Bhāgavatam* 8.23.8 (quoted above), based on Sanskrit rules. Two opposing meanings are possible: 'You are impartial by nature' (*aviṣamaḥ svabhāva*) and 'You are partial by nature' (*viṣamaḥ svabhāvaḥ*).

have taken shelter of it and is not obliged to fulfill the desires of those who don't want to come near it. Śrīla Prabhupāda elaborates upon this:

> *'The Lord makes distinctions according to the mentality of the living being, but otherwise He is equal to everyone. Like a desire tree, the Lord fulfills the desires of one who takes shelter of Him, but one who does not take such shelter is distinct from the surrendered soul. One who takes shelter at the lotus feet of the Lord is favored by the Lord, regardless of whether such a person is a demon or a demigod.'*
>
> *Śrīmad-Bhāgavatam* 8.23.8, purport

This aspect of God's nature does not interfere with His flawless impartiality – that is why He is God – He *defies* the laws of linear logic. His inconceivable power (*cintya-aiśvarya*) allows Him to combine partiality and impartiality and turns His seeming partiality into an adornment. In the next verse, Queen Kuntī describes how this quality manifests in God's pastimes.

The Miracle is God

janma karma ca viśvātmann
ajasyākartur ātmanaḥ
tiryaṅ-nṝṣiṣu yādaḥsu
tad atyanta-viḍambanam

> 'Of course it is bewildering, O soul of the universe, that You work, though You are inactive, and that You take birth, though You are the vital force and the unborn. You Yourself descend amongst animals, men, sages and aquatics. Verily, this is bewildering.'
>
> *Śrīmad-Bhāgavatam* 1.8.30

Queen Kuntī explains why it is so difficult to fathom the Lord's birth and activities in this material world. The price to understand them is high because the reward is just as high – Krishna says that whoever understands the mystery of His birth and activities will break free from the cycle of births and deaths:

> *janma karma ca me divyam*
> *evaṁ yo vetti tattvataḥ*
> *tyaktvā dehaṁ punar janma*
> *naiti mām eti so 'rjuna*

> 'One who knows the transcendental nature of My appearance and activities does not, upon leaving the body, take his birth again in this material world, but attains My eternal abode, O Arjuna.'
>
> *Bhagavad-gītā* 4.9

It is difficult to understand the birth of He who is unborn (*ajasya janma*) and about the activities of He who is inactive (*akartuh karma*). If we could somehow accept that the unborn takes birth and the inactive seems to act, then there is still the baffling and marvelous fact that God doesn't just take human form (*nṛṇāṁ*) but also descends upon Earth as animals (*tiryak*) and aquatics (*yādaḥsu*) such as a fish and turtle!

Appearing in a human form bewilders people (*viḍambanam*) but coming as lower animals goes beyond all reason (*atyanta-viḍambanam*). The human mind fails; short-circuits. By taking these forms, Bhagavān seems to deliberately belittle Himself. Try telling someone on the street that God comes into this world as a huge boar or turtle and watch their reaction.

The most amazing thing, Viśvanātha Cakravartī writes, is that when Krishna assumed the form of an animal, He behaved exactly like that animal. A boar has poor sight and compensates with well-developed hearing and sense of smell, so when the omniscient Lord assumed the form of Varāhadeva, He searched for planet Earth by sniffing and grunting around. When Hiraṇyākṣa saw Lord Boar holding Earth on His tusks, he burst into laughter and mocked, 'Hark, amphibious creature!'

Therefore, Queen Kuntī uses '*atyanta-viḍambanam*' to stress, 'Indeed, when You want to deceive people, no one can compare with You in doing so!' Those who know the truth are dedicated to Him and never laugh at Him, whatever guise He takes. Reverently, they offer prayers and admire His omnipotence.[1]

* * *

How can we understand that the unborn takes birth? *Māyāvādī* philosophers assert that the unborn cannot take birth and the inactive does not act. In their view, God's *janma* and karma are merely an illusion, a mirage, *māyā*. As proof, they cite Krishna's own words:

ajo 'pi sann avyayātmā
bhūtānām īśvaro 'pi san
prakṛtiṁ svām adhiṣṭhāya
sambhavāmy ātma-māyayā

> 'Although I am unborn and My transcendental body never deteriorates, and although I am the Lord of all living entities, I still appear in every millennium in My original transcendental form.'
>
> *Bhagavad-gītā* 4.6

However, if the unborn has never taken birth, and the inactive

1 'When the great sages and thinkers who are residents of Janaloka, Tapoloka and Satyaloka heard the tumultuous voice of Lord Boar, which was the all-auspicious sound of the all-merciful Lord, they chanted auspicious chants from the three Vedas.' *Śrīmad-Bhāgavatam* 3.13.25.

has never acted, then the only thing that could be said about Him is that nothing can be said about Him. Discussing God's 'illusory activities' would be like retelling a trifling TV series or gossiping. Why would great self-satisfied sages like Śukadeva Gosvāmī enjoy hearing about these 'material pastimes of *māyā*'? Being *ātmārāmas*, they cannot be attracted by anything material. Sūta Gosvāmī clearly says *ittham-bhūta-guṇo hariḥ* – Krishna's transcendental qualities are so attractive that they lure even the great *ātmārāmas* out of balance. (*Śrīmad-Bhāgavatam* 1.7.10)

Another possibility could be that God does take birth. Therefore, He has a beginning and an end. But then He cannot be God. By definition, God cannot have an end. He is eternal. Therefore, the only valid way to resolve this contradiction is to recognize the existence of God's logically incomprehensible energy (*acintya-śakti*) which reconciles all contradictions. This power is also called *avitarkya* or *tarka-asaham*, which means 'not subject to the laws of linear logic.'

One could reasonably counterargue that the introduction of such a concept is simply a verbal evasion, an escape from the problem. C.S. Lewis, a proponent of rational theology makes such a case, 'It is no more possible for God than for the weakest of His creatures to carry out both of two mutually exclusive alternatives; not because His power meets an obstacle, but because nonsense remains nonsense even when we talk it about God.'[1] For such people, the birth of the unborn and the activity of the inactive are meaningless combinations of words that prove nothing.

This echoes the well-known paradox that atheist logicians utilize in their attempts to refute the existence of an omnipotent God. 'Can God create a rock that He Himself cannot lift?' they

1 C. S. Lewis, The Problem of Pain. (New York: Simon & Schuster, 1996).

ask. Either He cannot create such a stone, or He cannot lift it. Both 'logical' answers deny God's omnipotence. Rational theologians (followers of Aristotelian logic) resolve the problem by defining omnipotence as the unlimited ability to create *the possible*. In their opinion, God is not deprived of his omnipotence by being unable to do something obviously impossible. This position is not much different from the famed assertion by the ludicrous character in Chekhov's story who insisted, 'This cannot be, because this just can never be.'[1]

Trying to bring God under the laws of reason means to reduce Him to our level. By taking this position, we impose endless restrictions on Him. Reason that does not know the limits of its application, turns into a vice. For some inexplicable reason, philosophers of rationalism think God is obliged to act according to material laws of logic and reason. Even monarchs of this world are exempt from prosecution and not obliged to obey the laws they have established for their subjects. By denying the existence of God's incomprehensible, illogical, mystical energy, rationalists simply betray their own disbelief. Śrīla Prabhupāda often retold a story to illustrate this.

* * *

Wandering around the world, Nārada Muni once met a learned *brāhmaṇa*. Hearing that Nārada Muni would visit the Lord, the overjoyed *brāhmaṇa* said, 'Dear Muni, when you go to see the Lord, please ask Him when I will attain liberation.'

Nārada Muni agreed and went on his way until he met a cobbler sitting under a tree mending shoes. The enthusiastic shoemaker made the same request, 'O Dev, people say you see the Lord every now and then. Please ask Him when I might be liberated.'

1 A. Chekhov, A Letter to a Learned Neighbour, 1880.

After reaching Vaikuṇṭha and bowing before Lord Nārāyaṇa, Nārada Muni humbly inquired on behalf of the *brāhmaṇa* and shoemaker.

Lord Nārāyaṇa replied, 'The shoemaker will come back to Me as soon as he leaves his body but the *brāhmaṇa* will have to stay in the material world for millions of lifetimes.'

'How is this possible?' said Nārada Muni, surprised. 'The shoemaker hardly reads or writes. His occupation is impure while the *brāhmaṇa* studies the *Vedas* and observes all scriptural rules.'

'You will understand for yourself. Go back to them and when they ask, tell them I was threading an elephant through the eye of a needle.'

Back on Earth, Nārada saw the *brāhmaṇa* giving a scriptural discourse to his disciples.

'Well, what happened? Did you meet the Lord? Did you ask when I will see Him?' said the learned man.

'The Lord said you will not see Him even after millions of lifetimes.'

'What!' The *brāhmaṇa* was indignant. 'That's ridiculous. Obviously, you don't know who I am. People submit themselves to my knowledge. I don't believe you saw Lord Nārāyaṇa. If you did, then tell me what He was doing?'

'He was pulling an elephant through the eye of a needle.'

'Ha ha ha... such nonsense! Now everything is clear to me. You are not Nārada Muni but an impostor. Go fool someone else!'

Nārada Muni proceeded to the shoemaker who was still under the banyan tree, mending shoes.

'Did you ask the wonderful Lord when I might see Him?' said the cobbler.

'As soon as this life is over.'

The shoemaker burst into tears of gratitude. 'Tell me more about the Lord. What was He doing when you were there?'

'He was pulling an elephant through the eye of a needle.'

The shoemaker clapped his hands in rapture. 'Oh, how incredible my Lord is!'

Nārada Muni mused. 'Do you really believe that the Lord can pull an elephant through the eye of a needle?'

'Why not? Of course, I do!'

The humble man picked up a tiny banyan seed from the ground. 'I have been sitting under this tree all my life. Fruit, full of seeds, falls from it every day, and each tiny seed contains within itself another banyan tree. If the Lord can fit a huge tree into a tiny seed, then why can't He thread an elephant through the eye of a needle?'

* * *

The *brāhmaṇa* and shoemaker both possessed intelligence, but the latter knew how to use it to support his faith in the incomprehensible Lord. Meanwhile, the *brāhmaṇa* put intelligence and (inadequate) logic above faith and God. Faith in Bhagavān's incomprehensible energy, which can act against the laws of logic, is true spiritual faith. It allows us to understand Him and get closer to Him. Rational belief in God is a symptom of the materialism inherent in all humans.

Another name for Bhagavān's *acintya-śakti* is *aghaṭa-ghaṭana-patīyasī-śakti*[1] – the energy that allows Him to accomplish the impossible, and instantly and completely reconcile irreconcilable contradictions and merge incompatible qualities. Without faith in this energy, it is impossible to comprehend His *līlās*, which mock the human mind.

Although the word *acintya* means 'incomprehensible' in its literal sense, what is meant here is not the absolute incomprehensibility of God and His activities – but their incomprehensibility *by means* of the linear material logic we usually employ to comprehend the material world. Spiritual reality is understood through faith in the words of the revealed scriptures: *śrutes tu śabda-mūlatvāt*[2] – 'Since God is the root from which all Vedic scriptures (*śruti*) have grown, the supreme inconceivable Truth can be comprehended through the revealed scriptures.' Thus, Śrīla Jīva Gosvāmī defined *acintya-śakti* as *tarkalabhyam sastraika gamyam*[3] – 'potency that can be grasped not through logic but only through scriptures.'

Such faith is not blind but rests on rational grounds. Any reasonable person can understand that each sphere of life has its own laws. For example, the objects of quantum mechanics simultaneously possess the properties of a wave and a particle, which goes beyond the limits of ordinary logic. And just as laws operating in the quantum world differ from laws operating in the mechanical world, laws operating in spiritual reality differ from the material plane. This is why those people connected to spiritual reality can perform miracles. A miracle is simply the intervention of a higher power, adhering to different laws,

1 This term is first used by Śrīdhara Svāmī in his commentary on *Bhagavad-gītā* (9.5). This is how Śrīla Jīva Gosvāmī defines *acintya-śakti* in his *Tattva-sandarbha, Anuccheda* 43: *durghaṭa-ghaṭanā-patīyasyā svābhāvika-tad-acintya-śaktyā.*

2 *Vedānta-sūtra* 2.1.27.

3 *Sarva-saṁvādinī*, commentary on *Paramātma-sandarbha*, chapter 57.

acting in our reality. When a king visits a prison, he does not go there to obey the prison laws but to break them and release prisoners before their term is over. Similarly, when Bhagavān comes here and exhibits His *līlās*, He disregards the laws of material reality. Those hardened in their rationality are baffled each time this miracle happens. Russian poet and Nobel Laureate, Boris Pasternak, expressed the idea beautifully in a poem:

> 'But a miracle is a miracle – and the miracle is God.
> When we are in confusion, then in the midst of our straggling
> It overtakes us and, on the instant, confounds us.[1]

The goal of spiritual practice is to go beyond our sad, rational, karmic predestination and move from the world of selfish causality to the world of causeless love. Only to help us do this does Bhagavān reveal His *līlās* to us. But if we try to apply linear material logic while hearing the narrations, then we deprive ourselves of the opportunity to comprehend and love Him, and thus get free from the prison of reason. Should a prisoner mistake the visiting king as a guard, he can never take advantage of the royal mercy available to him.

To fall in love with the Lord and attain His mercy, we must cast aside our logic and perceive how the Unborn takes birth and remains unborn, and how the Inactive acts and simultaneously remains inactive. Sometimes, ordinary people have understood this. Ivan Turgenev, a prominent nineteenth century Russian writer and poet wrote:

> 'Whatever a man prays for, he prays for a miracle.
> Every prayer reduces to this: 'Great God, grant that twice two be not four.'
> Only such a prayer is a real prayer from person to person.

1 Boris Pasternak, 'Miracle'. From Doctor Zhivago, 1958).

To pray to the cosmic spirit, to the higher being, to the Kantian, Hegelian, quintessential, formless God is impossible and unthinkable.
But can a personal, living, imaged God make twice two not be four?
Every believer is bound to answer, he can, and is bound to persuade himself of it.'[1]

The only sting comes in the last sentence – because it is not a question of forcibly convincing ourselves of something the mind refuses to believe, but of reflecting upon God's illogical *līlās* to open our minds and share in the living miracle of God's love.

* * *

According to *Bhagavad-gītā*, the Absolute Truth is Puruṣottama, the Supreme Personality, and not just some impersonal pure Universal Intelligence. By definition, the impersonal aspect of the Absolute Truth has no attributes, while personality has qualities and energies: *parāsya śaktir vividhaiva śrūyate* – 'His potencies are immeasurable, as confirmed in the *Vedas*.'[2] *Viṣṇu Purāṇa* defines the personal feature of Absolute Truth, Bhagavān:

jñāna-śakti-balaiśvarya-vīrya-tejāṁsy aśeṣataḥ
bhagavac-chabda-vācyāni vinā heyair guṇādibhiḥ[3]

'The word Bhagavān means 'a person possessing omniscience (*jñāna – strength of mind*), infinitely

1 Ivan Turgenev, 'Prayer', Poems in Prose, 1881.

2 *Śvetāśvatara Upaniṣad* 6.8.

3 The translation of these attributes is according to explanation by Śrīla Jīva Gosvāmī in *Bhagavat-sandarbha*, *Anuccheda* 1.

powerful senses (*śakti*), an infinitely mighty body (*bala*), power (*aiśvarya*), incomprehensible potency (*vīrya – acintya-śakti*), dazzling beauty (*teja*) and complete freedom from base qualities.'

Viṣṇu Purāṇa 6.5.79

Drawing together our discussion of 1.8.27-1.8.30, Queen Kuntī addresses the human difficulty in understanding the manifestations of the Personality of Godhead. The more personal these manifestations are, the harder it is to understand them. She explains that the prime potency of the Personality of Godhead is the potency of His love. For most people, it manifests in the form of just retribution for their actions – the law of karma. But for those who seek a relationship with Him, it manifests as His personal intervention in their lives. His love is suprarational, it works wonders and is not subject to the laws of linear logic. Most striking is how this love overpowers Bhagavān Himself. God, seized with love, can forget His omnipotence – as shown in the next verse where Queen Kuntī illustrates how 'weak' and 'vulnerable' God can become as He submits to the love of His devotees. To understand *all* of His activities, one must try to comprehend the overwhelming force of His love.

The Omnipotence of Love

gopy ādade tvayi kṛtāgasi dāma tāvad
yā te daśāśru-kalilāñjana-sambhramākṣam
vaktraṁ ninīya bhaya-bhāvanayā sthitasya
sā māṁ vimohayati bhīr api yad bibheti

'My dear Kṛṣṇa, Yaśodā took up a rope to bind You when You committed an offense, and Your perturbed eyes overflooded with tears, which washed the mascara from Your eyes. And You were afraid,

> though fear personified is afraid of You. This sight is bewildering to me.'
>
> *Śrīmad-Bhāgavatam* 1.8.31

Having previously discussed the general human incapacity to fully understand Krishna's activities, in this verse Queen Kuntī confesses that some of Krishna's actions are incomprehensible even to her. Bhagavān's inner potency, His *yogamāyā*, can accomplish the impossible (*aghaṭana ghaṭana patīyasī śakti*), but it works the most amazing miracle in Vṛndāvana, where, in response to the devotees' pure love, it causes God to forget His omnipotence.

Being a relative of Nanda Mahārāja, Queen Kuntī sometimes visited Vṛndāvana. She recalls once on *Dīpāvalī*, when it is customary to visit relatives and exchange gifts and sweets, she witnessed the *dāma-bandhana-līlā*. Śrīla Prabhupāda describes the pastime:

> *'The Lord, in His naturally childish playful activities, used to spoil the stocked butter of mother Yaśodā by breaking the pots and distributing the contents to His friends and playmates, including the celebrated monkeys of Vṛndāvana, who took advantage of the Lord's munificence. Mother Yaśodā saw this, and out of her pure love she wanted to make a show of punishment for her transcendental child. She took a rope and threatened the Lord that she would tie Him up, as is generally done in the ordinary household. Seeing the rope in the hands of mother Yaśodā, the Lord bowed down His head and began to weep just like a child, and tears rolled down His cheeks, washing off the black ointment smeared about His beautiful eyes. This picture of the Lord is adored by Kuntīdevī because she is conscious of the Lord's supreme position. He is feared often by fear personified, yet He is afraid of His mother, who*

> *wanted to punish Him just in an ordinary manner.'*
> *Śrīmad-Bhāgavatam* 1.8.31, purport

Some might ask, 'What is so special about this *līlā*? God has come as a fish, a boar, and now as an ordinary child. That is no big deal. Queen Kuntī has already established that God descends on Earth to play various roles, like an actor on stage. So why is His role as an ordinary child more special than the rest? Isn't He pretending to be a child, just as He pretended to be a fish and boar? Earlier, Queen Kuntī called it pretence – *viḍambanam*.'

If this were so, then Queen Kuntī, observing from her neutral position of *aiśvarya-jñāna*, would have recognized Krishna's 'acting.' Instead, she uses the words *bhaya-bhāvanayā* – 'Krishna was scared.' He was not pretending to be scared, He *felt* real fear. Seeking help, His eyes darted side to side (*sambhramākṣam*). Recalling this moment with delight, she confesses that she cannot fathom how God, who is feared by death itself, is afraid of a mere cowherd woman.

The sole purpose to write the *Śrīmad-Bhāgavatam* is to glorify the Vraja inhabitants. In the First Canto, Queen Kuntī is first to do this. Bhīṣmadeva glorifies the power of *vraja-prema* in the next chapter. In the Tenth Canto, Krishna sends Uddhava, the great scriptural scholar, to Vraja, to confirm with all his authority that there is nothing higher and more powerful than this love in all creation, and that it conquers God Himself.

Those who try to comprehend God intellectually can never understand how almighty God can be deprived of His omnipotence. For those who have grasped the suprarational logic of the revealed scriptures, these extraordinary circumstances, under which Krishna agreed to be bound by Mother Yaśodā, only prove that Krishna is almighty God. Out of all different manifestations of God, only He can forget about His omnipotence to such an extent.

Let us go back to the paradox of God's omnipotence. Advocates of rational theology resolve it by redefining the concept. They restrict divine omnipotence to the limits of what is logically acceptable. 'In order for God to be unable to lift the stone He has created,' they say, 'that stone must be equal to Him, that is, it must be infinite. Of course, God cannot create such a stone, because there is nothing equivalent to God by definition.'

'If we speak of Lord Nārāyaṇa in Vaikuṇṭha,' we would reply, 'we could agree with this resolution. However, Krishna, the original Nārāyaṇa, may allow Himself to resolve it differently. His omnipotence is in *being able* to forget His omnipotence by submitting to pure spiritual love that equals His own. God's love is as infinite as He is, and He may well invest that infinite love in another person's heart. His submission to His own love in the pure heart of a devotee does not in any way diminish His omnipotence.'

'Wait!' the dissatisfied rationalists say. 'How does this not diminish His omnipotence? In just this *līlā*, the Lord, who is supposed to be self-satisfied and imperturbable, feels hungry, gets angry when He's not fed, then breaks a pot in frustration, and finally goes off to steal butter. Later, God, who is feared by fear personified, sees the stick in His mother's hand and runs away terror-stricken. Worse, he is not fast enough to get away. He is easily caught and has no choice but to cry for fear. The simple mother ties up almighty God to a clay mortar with a ribbon she pulls from her hair, and He is unable to break free. By insisting that Krishna is God, you contradict yourselves. You just cited *Viṣṇu Purāṇa* which says God cannot possess base qualities (*vinā heyair guṇādibhiḥ*) and then celebrate a God prone to stealing, getting hungry, angry, frustrated, and fearful. What kind of God is this? He cannot be called perfect.'

Our answer, 'It is true. God is certainly free from all vices and imperfections. But isn't mercy the topmost of all virtues?

Whatever merits one may have, if he is devoid of mercy, his qualities bring joy to no one. Virtue is only a virtue when it brings happiness to others. Is it not so? Can we call the beauty of a callous person beauty? If one's heart is cruel, does his mind, power, or impartiality remain virtuous, or do they not turn into vices? Who needs such beauty, intelligence, and power? Lacking kindness and mercy is the greatest vice. Mercy makes Krishna all-attractive. It gives rise to all other virtues and removes all imperfections.

yathā tvaṁ kṛpayā bhūtyā
tejasā mahimaujasā
juṣṭa īśa guṇaiḥ sarvais
tato 'si bhagavān prabhuḥ[1]

'O my Lord, You are the center of causeless mercy, therefore You are the Supreme Personality of Godhead, the object of everyone's worship, possessing all opulences – valor, opulence, fame, power, etc.'

Śrīmad-Bhāgavatam 6.19.5

'Furthermore, just as mercy gives rise to all merits and virtue, it can also obscure them temporarily. A father is not deprived of his strength when he allows his child to ride on his back and command him. For a while, he simply submits to his child out of love. In the pastime, shortly after shedding tears, Krishna effortlessly knocks down the age-old yamala-arjuna trees while being tied up and sets Kuvera's two sons free.

'When any virtue takes the position of serving mercy, it reaches perfection. Bhagavān is already infinitely omnipotent, but when His omnipotence serves His mercy, it reaches super-

1 The translation is made in accordance with Viśvanātha Cakravartī's commentary on this verse and Śrīla Jīva Gosvāmī 's commentary on verse 10.9.19 in *Laghu-vaiṣṇava-toṣaṇī*.

excellent perfection. Śrīla Jīva Gosvāmī has commented that this entire *līlā* is a manifestation of Bhagavān's mercy towards Yaśodā Devī. He became a playful child to reciprocate her love. Forgetting His omnipotence, He revealed His mercy to its utmost. As manifestations of His love, the emotions of annoyance, anger and fear became His adornments.'

'All right,' our persistent opponents object, 'We can accept that God employs His inner energy to obscure His knowledge of His omnipotence so that He can perfectly reciprocate His devotee's love, and that this "ignorance" becomes His adornment. But in doing so He gets scared, annoyed, and angry, and in this way suffers. Our own experience tells us that these emotions are unpleasant and destructive. Who wouldn't be humiliated if they were forcibly tied up to a mortar? Saint Augustine says, "God is called omnipotent on account of His doing what He wills, not on account of His suffering what He wills not; for if that should befall Him, He would by no means be omnipotent."[1] Is it not that these emotions being experienced by Bhagavān diminish His greatness?'

'Not at all,' we answer. 'The iron shackles around the legs of a prisoner and the gold chain around a rich man's neck are both chains, but far from the same. Yes, the bondage of material ignorance enslaves us and makes us suffer. Material emotions of fear and distress are not enjoyable, but when the Lord is bound with the bonds of a devotee's love, the same emotions become a source of great bliss for Him. His so-called fear, annoyance and anger are nothing more than aromas of bliss that He experiences when He voluntarily surrenders to His devotees' love. A bee, imprisoned within the petals of a closed lotus, endlessly enjoys its nectar.'[2] In this regard, Śrīla Prabhupāda writes,

1 Aurelius Augustine, The City of God, Book 5, chapter 10. Originally published 5th Century AD.

2 The arguments in this paragraph are from *Rāga-vartma-candrikā*, part 2.

'Generally, the Lord is worshiped by the devotees in a reverential attitude, but the Lord is meticulously pleased when the devotee, out of pure affection and love, considers the Lord to be less important than himself. The Lord's pastimes in the original abode of Goloka Vṛndāvana are exchanged in that spirit. The friends of Kṛṣṇa consider Him one of them. They do not consider Him to be of reverential importance. The parents of the Lord (who are all pure devotees) consider Him a child only. The Lord accepts the chastisements of the parents more cheerfully than the prayers of the Vedic hymns.' (*Śrīmad-Bhāgavatam* 1.8.31, purport)

'My Lord can do Anything!'

Cold reasoning is an inappropriate tool for attaining revelation. The reality reflected in revelation is infinite, while reason utterly limits it. 'This cannot be, because this just can never be!' it insists. To understand Bhagavān's pastimes requires rapturous faith: 'God can do anything!' Though even this is not enough to enter the *līlās*.

In preceding verses, Queen Kuntī has already identified humility as the key to realizing Bhagavān. The devotee must become *akiñcana*, that is, give up pride and the sense of ownership. This includes pride in one's intelligence. When such humility is perfected, it enables one to enter the kingdom of God and participate in His pastimes.

Pride, or false ego, has two sides, *ahantā* and *mamatā*, 'I' and 'mine.' For those immersed in matter, the greatest importance lies in a sense of ownership, i.e., 'what is mine,' as consciousness identifies and defines itself through the material objects of this world. But as one elevates their consciousness, these affiliations with gross matter weaken and the feeling of ownership fades, giving way to the prevalence of an inner 'I.'

Those who have somewhat developed their consciousness are less attached to matter but still attached to their unique 'I.' Writers, artists, and philosophers can fall into this category. They still identify with matter, though on the subtler level of their mind and intellect.

By evolving the consciousness further, we gradually transform this material ego into a spiritual 'self.' In doing so, we pass through the 'zero point' of impersonal liberation where there is no ego whatsoever. We become ready to leave the reflected tree of the material world. Returning to eternal reality, the soul realizes, 'I am an eternal servant of God' – *kṛṣṇera nitya-dāsa.*[1] It abandons all futile attempts to become happy independently of God.

At the same time, consciousness that is freed from identification with matter, at the beginning is still largely focused on itself, albeit in connection with God. By persistent meditation on its eternal relationship with God and rendering service to Him and His eternal companions, the soul gradually develops an affectionate attachment (*mamatā*), 'Krishna is my Lord and my master.' The spiritual 'I' generates the spiritual 'mine.' When this *mamatā* becomes undivided, when the soul wants to possess nothing but Krishna, it reaches the pinnacle of spiritual evolution. At this stage, the soul's concentration on God becomes unbroken and with the rope of *mamata*, the soul binds God to its heart:

ananya-mamatā viṣṇau
mamatā prema-saṅgatā
bhaktir ity ucyate bhīṣma-
prahlādoddhava-nāradaiḥ

'When one develops an unflinching sense of ownership or possessiveness in relation to Lord

1 *Caitanya-caritāmṛta, Madhya-līlā* 20.108.

> Viṣṇu, or, in other words, when one thinks Viṣṇu and no one else to be the only object of love, such an awakening is called bhakti by exalted persons like Bhīṣma, Prahlāda, Uddhava and Nārada.'
>
> *Nārada-pañcarātra.*
> Quoted from *Caitanya-caritāmṛta, Madhya-līlā* 23.8.

Explaining the nature of the Lord's activities in these last verses, Queen Kuntī simultaneously glorifies those who have given up their possessions in this world, and made Krishna their own, 'Krishna is mine!' She marvels at the invincibility of their love and invites us to marvel with her. She wants to show us that the true goal of all human endeavors is undivided love for God. She herself pleads for it later. In the next five verses, from 1.8.32, she illuminates how Krishna's main reason to come to this world is to give us the opportunity to attain such unflagging attachment.

CHAPTER 9

The Birth of the Unborn

What is True Dharma?

Having described Bhagavān's activities (His karma), Queen Kuntī now starts explaining the reasons for His birth in this world (His *janma*). We need to understand why He personally comes to Earth, so that nothing can keep us here, and our desire to love Krishna and go back to Him becomes sincere and perfect.

The previous chapter may raise a doubt in the attentive reader, 'You said God must invest His love into one's heart. Everything depends on Him. Therefore, if I have no love or affection for Him, it simply means that He does not want me to love Him. Perhaps He wants me to go on suffering in the material world and He loves only a chosen few. He does not care about everyone else.' Anticipating this objection, Queen Kuntī makes it clear for whom Krishna comes to this world:

kecid āhur ajaṁ jātaṁ
puṇya-ślokasya kīrtaye
yadoḥ priyasyānvavāye
malayasyeva candanam

> 'Some say that the Unborn is born for the glorification of pious kings, and others say that He is born to please King Yadu, one of Your dearest devotees. You appear in his family as sandalwood appears in the Malaya hills.'
>
> *Śrīmad-Bhāgavatam* 1.8.32

Queen Kuntī begins with the words '*kecid āhuḥ*,' 'some say' to distance herself from the opinions. She does this because she is about to present an array of reasons for Krishna's descent. They are all meaningful in themselves, but she will conclude with the most important reason at the end.

Why do people give different explanations for Krishna's descent? Śrīla Prabhupāda clarifies:

> *'But still there are different opinions as to why He takes His birth. That is also declared in the* Bhagavad-gītā. *He appears by His own internal potency to reestablish the principles of religion [dharma] and to protect the pious [righteous] and to annihilate the impious. That is the mission of the appearance of the Unborn.'*
>
> Śrīmad-Bhāgavatam 1.8.32, purport

Sages describe the reasons for Krishna's descent in their own ways because their conceptions of dharma and righteousness vary. Some say the Unborn takes birth to glorify great pious kings (*puṇya-ślokasya*). Viśvanātha Cakravartī cites a verse from the *Padma Purāṇa*[1] to show that Mahārāja Nala and Mahārāja Yudhiṣṭhira are the intended kings for the epithet, though Śrīla Prabhupāda explains, *'Mahārāja Nala was also celebrated as a great pious king, but he had no connection with Lord Krishna. Therefore, Mahārāja Yudhiṣṭhira is meant here to be glorified by Lord Krishna.'* (*Śrīmad-Bhāgavatam* 1.8.32, purport)

A righteous king helps his subjects follow dharma and thus become happy. The trouble is that even demoniac rulers hide behind dharma. Jarāsandha, Dhṛtarāṣṭra and even Duryodhana called themselves 'protectors of dharma.' Therefore, the Lord comes to this world to proclaim His opinion of a true protector of religion. Queen Kuntī gives this as her first reason. Śrīla Prabhupāda writes:

> *'Lord Śrī Krishna certainly wanted to establish the kingdom of the Pāṇḍavas for the good of all in the world. When there is a pious king ruling over the world, the people are happy. When the ruler is*

1 *'puṇya śloko nalo raja munay-sloko yudhiṣṭhiraḥ,' Padma Purāṇa* 1.49.6.

impious, the people are unhappy. In the Age of Kali in most cases the rulers are impious, and therefore the citizens are also continuously unhappy. But in the case of democracy, the impious citizens themselves elect their representative to rule over them, and therefore they cannot blame anyone for their unhappiness.'

Śrīmad-Bhāgavatam 1.8.32, purport

Queen Kuntī lists another reason for the Lord's descent – His desire to glorify Mahārāja Yadu. Ever since Krishna's birth in Mahārāja Yadu's dynasty (the *Yadu-vaṁśa*), their names have become inextricably linked, and Mahārāja Yadu is associated with Krishna's splendor and greatness.

Of all lineages, why did Krishna choose this one? Mahārāja Yadu refused to follow lower material dharma for the sake of upholding his highest *dharmic* duty. He chose to incur his father's wrath rather than give up the opportunity to dedicate his life to attaining his spiritual goal. Therefore, Mahārāja Parīkṣit glorified Mahārāja Yadu: *yadoś ca dharma-śīlasya/nitarāṁ muni-sattama* – 'O best of munis, you have also described the descendants of Yadu, who were very pious and strictly adherent to religious principles.' (*Śrīmad-Bhāgavatam* 10.1.2)

Again and again, Krishna teaches us how to make the difficult choice of giving up our lower duties for the sake of higher ones. Deciding between material morality and spiritual duty is much harder than choosing between righteousness and sin. Krishna took birth in the Yadu dynasty to forever sanctify Mahārāja Yadu's choice.

In the next verses (1.8.33-34), Queen Kuntī cites two other possibilities for the Lord's descent:

apare vasudevasya
devakyāṁ yācito 'bhyagāt

ajas tvam asya kṣemāya
vadhāya ca sura-dviṣām

'Others say that since both Vasudeva and Devakī prayed for You, You have taken Your birth as their son. Undoubtedly You are unborn, yet You take Your birth for their welfare and to kill those who are envious of the demigods.'

bhārāvatāraṇāyānye
bhuvo nāva ivodadhau
sīdantyā bhūri-bhāreṇa
jāto hy ātma-bhuvārthitaḥ

'Others say that the world, being overburdened like a boat at sea, is much aggrieved, and that Brahmā, who is Your son, prayed for You, and so You have appeared to diminish the trouble.'

Śrīmad-Bhāgavatam 1.8.33-34

All these dharmic reasons for Krishna to descend to Earth are significant. He comes to establish true dharma through righteous kings – this was important. He comes to give acclaim to the dharmic principle of renouncing material enjoyment for devotional service, as exemplified by Mahārāja Yadu. This was more important. He comes to immortalize the devotion of Vasudeva and Devakī who chose to serve the Lord under the threat of death. This was a still higher reason.

Much higher than these is the dharma of compassion. Hearing the prayers of Lord Brahmā, the greatest of the demigods, the Lord comes to lay the road to salvation for all people of this world. At that time, the world was ruled by incredibly powerful demons who had performed severe austerities and possessed such extraordinary strength and mystical power that Lord Brahmā, the creator of the world, was rendered powerless.

'Please, come. I am helpless on my own!' he prayed. Feeling compassion for all living beings subjugated by the demoniac forces, Krishna responded.

From this, Queen Kuntī reaches the most profound reason for the Lord's descent in the next verse:

bhave 'smin kliśyamānānām
avidyā-kāma-karmabhiḥ
śravaṇa-smaraṇārhāṇi
kariṣyann iti kecana

'And yet others say that You appeared for the sake of rejuvenating the devotional service of hearing, remembering, worshiping and so on in order that the conditioned souls suffering from material pangs might take advantage and gain liberation.'

Śrīmad-Bhāgavatam 1.8.35

The Lord's compassion extends far beyond our imagination. 'The Lord is more merciful to the suffering living beings than they can expect,' says Śrīla Prabhupāda in the purport to this verse. Krishna doesn't just help those living entities present in the material world at the time of His coming but paves the way to liberation for all conditioned souls suffering due to ignorance, for the rest of time. Ignorance (*avidyā*) generates endless desires within the soul to enjoy (*kāma*). These keep the soul shackled to karma and force it to suffer (*kliśyamānānām*). Śrīla Prabhupāda explains the *karmic* mechanism of enslavement in a remarkable way:

'A living being cannot help but render service because he is constitutionally made for that purpose. The only function of the living being is to render service to the Lord. The Lord is great, and living beings are subordinate to Him. Therefore, the duty of the living being is just to serve Him only. Unfortunately the

illusioned living beings, out of misunderstanding only, become servants of the senses by material desire. This desire is called avidyā, or nescience. And out of such desire the living being makes different plans for material enjoyment centered about a perverted sex life. He therefore becomes entangled in the chain of birth and death by transmigrating into different bodies on different planets under the direction of the Supreme Lord. Unless, therefore, one is beyond the boundary of this nescience, one cannot get free from the threefold miseries of material life. That is the law of nature.'

Śrīmad-Bhāgavatam 1.8.35, purport

The chain is vicious because ignorance triggers desires, which generate karma (selfish activity), which deepens ignorance, which generates new desires. The conditioned soul perpetually rotates in the circle of karma like a squirrel in a wheel. Krishna comes to this world to break the cycle. He displays His *līlās* of pure love to all conditioned living beings to awaken in them the spirit of service long extinguished under the influence of matter. When we hear or remember Krishna's narrations, we catch a glimpse of the Lord's pure love, which dispels the darkness of ignorance in our hearts and brings back to us the memory of our original nature. The Lord's *līlās* set us free from prison by eradicating our ignorance, material desires and even karma that has already begun bearing fruit.

ānanda-cinmaya-rasātmatayā manaḥsu
yaḥ prāṇināṁ pratiphalan smaratām upetya
līlāyitena bhuvanāni jayaty ajasram-
govindam ādi-puruṣaṁ tam ahaṁ bhajāmi

'I worship Govinda, the primeval Lord, whose glory ever triumphantly dominates the mundane world by the activity of His own pastimes, being reflected in the mind of recollecting souls as the transcendental entity of ever-blissful cognitive rasa.'

Brahma-saṁhitā 5.42

Thus, after presenting a long chain of reasons for Krishna's descent, Queen Kuntī concludes that Krishna has come for us – you and me. She summarizes her reflections on the ultimate reason and meaning of the Lord's activities and birth in the next verse.

The Science of Hearing

At the start of her prayers, in 1.8.20, Queen Kuntī reflected that, 'You [Krishna] come here to give people the science of devotional service, *bhakti-yoga*,' which begins with hearing and chanting the holy name of the Lord. In 1.8.36, she reaches full circle back to this idea and concludes by describing the fullest manifestation of *bhakti-yoga* and the two amazing fruits it bears – seeing Krishna and escaping death:

śṛṇvanti gāyanti gṛṇanty abhīkṣṇaśaḥ
smaranti nandanti tavehitaṁ janāḥ
ta eva paśyanty acireṇa tāvakaṁ
bhava-pravāhoparamaṁ padāmbujam

'O Kṛṣṇa, those who continuously hear, chant and repeat Your transcendental activities, or take pleasure in others' doing so, certainly see Your lotus feet, which alone can stop the repetition of birth and death.'

Śrīmad-Bhāgavatam 1.8.36

The verse glorifies *Śrīmad-Bhāgavatam* for giving us the chance to hear about Krishna's activities, cherish them, constantly think upon them, and thus experience true happiness. The word '*ihitaṁ*' (*tavehitaṁ* in the verse) refers to 'Your deeds,' but can also denote 'desires' and 'intentions,' which extends the overall meaning – that *Śrīmad-Bhāgavatam* not only allows us to learn about God's activities but understand His intentions and desires.

Queen Kuntī explains that those who listen to *Śrīmad-Bhāgavatam* 'very soon (*acireṇa*) begin to see Your lotus feet, that is, to personally serve You.' Intentionally, she does not speak of Krishna but of His feet because the purpose of hearing *Śrīmad-Bhāgavatam* is not to see God, but to love Him.

All Vedic scriptures state that spiritual practice should give one a true experience of connection with God; the experience of seeing Him: *Ātmā vā are draṣṭavyaḥ*.[1] Some misguided seekers say, 'Show me God and I will believe in Him,' when actually we must first believe in God to become qualified to see Him. God reserves the right to hide Himself from those who do not believe in Him: *nāhaṁ prakāśaḥ sarvasya/yoga-māyā-samāvṛtaḥ* – 'I am never manifest to the foolish and unintelligent. For them, I am covered by My internal potency, and therefore they do not know that I am unborn and infallible.' (*Bhagavad-gītā* 7.25)

Others believe in God but are in no haste to start loving Him. 'How can we love someone whom we have never seen?' they say. Another mistaken expectation. First, we need to love God, and only then can we see Him: *premāñjana-cchurita-bhakti-vilocanena/santaḥ sadaiva hṛdayeṣu vilokayanti* – 'Only those whose eyes are anointed with the balm of love for the Supreme Lord can constantly see Him.' (*Brahma-saṁhitā* 5.38)

To believe in God and love Him, we must hear narrations about Him, from the lips of those who love Him. *Ātmā vā are draṣṭavyaḥ śrotavyo mantavyo nididhyāsitavyaḥ* – 'You must

1 *Bṛhad-āraṇyaka Upaniṣad* 4.5.6.

see the Lord. To do this, you have to hear about Him, think about Him and fully concentrate your consciousness on Him.' (*Bṛhad-āraṇyaka Upaniṣad* 4.5.6)

Otherwise, even if God stood before us, we wouldn't be able to discern Him. Devotional service, beginning with hearing stories about Krishna, is the only way to truly see and love Him. Śrīla Prabhupāda explains:

> *'The Supreme Lord Śrī Kṛṣṇa cannot be seen by our present conditional vision. In order to see Him, one has to change his present vision by developing a different condition of life full of spontaneous love of Godhead. When Śrī Kṛṣṇa was personally present on the face of the globe, not everyone could see Him as the Supreme Personality of Godhead. Materialists like Rāvaṇa, Hiraṇyakaśipu, Kaṁsa, Jarāsandha and Śiśupāla were highly qualified personalities by acquisition of material assets, but they were unable to appreciate the presence of the Lord. Therefore, even though the Lord may be present before our eyes, it is not possible to see Him unless we have the necessary vision. This necessary qualification is developed by the process of devotional service only, beginning with hearing about the Lord from the right sources. The* Bhagavad-gītā *is one of the popular literatures which are generally heard, chanted, repeated, etc., by the people in general, but in spite of such hearing, etc., sometimes it is experienced that the performer of such devotional service does not see the Lord face to face. The reason is that the first item,* śravaṇa, *is very important. If hearing is from the right sources, it acts very quickly. Generally people hear from unauthorized persons. Such unauthorized persons may be very learned by academic qualifications, but because they do not follow the principles of*

devotional service, hearing from them becomes a sheer waste of time. Sometimes the texts are interpreted fashionably to suit their own purposes. Therefore, first one should select a competent and bona fide speaker and then hear from him. ***When the hearing process is perfect and complete, the other processes become automatically perfect in their own way.'***

Śrīmad-Bhāgavatam 1.8.36, purport

We have stressed the last sentence because of its importance. *Bhakti* begins by hearing narrations of Krishna, but the process needs to be perfect for us to see Krishna. Hearing from the right source, in the right way, gradually changes our perception of the world. Presently, we see in this world only what we want to see.

eka eva padārthas tu
tridhā bhavati vīkṣitaḥ
kuṇapaṁ kaminī māṁsaṁ
yogibhiḥ kāmibhiḥ śvabhiḥ

'Three different beings will look at the same object and see three different things. Looking at a beautiful girl, the yogi sees in front of him a vessel of excrement, blood, bones and urine. A young man sees in her the object of his desires, and a hungry dog – an appetizing piece of meat.'

Cāṇakya-nīti-darpaṇaḥ 14.16

While we nourish the predatory desire to enjoy matter, we will be unable to see God. He will simply not fit within our perspective of the world. But if we listen with faith and due respect to a pure person speaking about the Lord, their words will gradually reshape our mind – the medium through which we look at the world – and we will begin to see God where we used to see matter. Śrīla Jīva Gosvāmī reiterates this, 'In the process of hearing, a person gains a certain spiritual experience.'[1]

By hearing from a great Vaiṣṇava, we receive a flicker of their experience and begin to see the world through their eyes. Their words are a lifebuoy thrown to us as we drown in the ocean of material existence. Faith enables us to clasp tight to the lifebuoy and swim to shore.

For such a miraculous rescue, the qualities and caliber of the speaker must be proper. Śrīla Prabhupāda explains how they must not tint Krishna's words with their own misinterpretations or distort meanings for the sake of being trendy and pleasing the tastes or desires of the audience. Hearing narrations about Krishna from a person of purity and spiritual maturity allows us to understand the outward scenario of the Lord's activities and also the inner driving force – the Lord's desires and intentions.

A second component of success is the attitude and sobriety of the hearer. One who is able to properly hear Krishna's *līlās* is as rare as one who is able to speak about them:

> *śravaṇayāpi bahubhir yo na labhyaḥ*
> *śṛṇvanto 'pi bahavo yaṁ na vidyuḥ*
> *āścaryo vaktā kuśalo 'sya labdhā*
> *āścaryo 'sya jñātā kuśalānuśiṣṭaḥ*

> 'Very few people receive the opportunity to hear about the Lord. Even those who do, seldom understand anything, because it is rare to find a speaker who himself understands God. However, after hearing a true teacher, few can understand him, because a good student is as rare as a good teacher.'
> *Kaṭha Upaniṣad* 1.2.7

1 *Bśravaṇa-dvārā yat kiñcid bhūyate sati,*' Śrīla Jīva Gosvāmī, *Durgama-saṅgamanī*, in a commentary on *Bhakti-rasāmṛta-sindhu.*

To hear about God, awaken the desire to serve Him, and see Him one day, we must master the art of listening. We began our discussion on Queen Kuntī's prayers with the suggestion that true prayer is born of stillness and silence. Similarly, true hearing occurs when the mind is still and silent. When a speaker succeeds in reaching people's hearts, a genuine silence falls upon the audience. It is tangible and audible. But this happens rarely.

All discipleship boils down to training one's attention. Mahārāja Parīkṣit exemplified the perfect disciple for whom listening to scripture was literally a matter of life and death. The process is a proactive exercise where we listen carefully, try to grasp and feel what we hear, and then reflect deeply upon it. If we realize that every word of *Śrīmad-Bhāgavatam* contains something essential, we will abandon our usual absent-mindedness and attempt to listen eagerly. This is our service to the person *Bhāgavata* and to the book *Bhāgavatam – nityaṁ bhāgavata-sevayā*:

> *viśvāso guru-vākyeṣu*
> *svasmin dīnatve-bhāvanā*
> *mano-doṣa-jayaś caiva*
> *kathāyāṁ niścalā matiḥ*

> 'To obtain the fruit of hearing *Bhāgavatam*, one should hear from the spiritual master with faith and humility, feeling very fallen [*dīnatve-bhavana*]. Such a person should overcome the flaws of his mind [distraction, etc.] and fully concentrate his mind on what the spiritual master says.'
>
> *Padma Purāṇa*, *Bhāgavata Māhātmya* 5.75

In 1.8.36, Queen Kuntī includes the secondary by-product of hearing Krishna's pastimes: *bhava-pravāhoparamaṁ* – cessation of the current of rebirth. '*Pravāha*' means 'flow,' the flow of material life, the flow of karma. Since time immemorial, we have been swept up in the mighty stream of *anādi-karma*, beginningless karma. Breaking free is extremely difficult. Every action we take stems from a cause, which has its own cause, ad infinitum. We simply cannot act and live in a way different from the dictation of this chain of causes although we imagine we are free to make our choices. We may think we are always right and logical in our thoughts, actions, and judgements but we just do not realize how constrained we are.

In fact, it is our rightness that ultimately takes us to hell. This hell is not necessarily a geographical location. It is a state of being where we burn alive in the blazing fire of consequences born of our 'right' and 'logical' actions, as the stormy stream of material existence carries us into the ocean of suffering and pain.

What happens to this stream of material existence for those who learn to hear *Śrīmad-Bhāgavatam*? *Uparamam* – it dries up, and the endless turning wheel of karma stops revolving. Why? Relishing narrations of Krishna's activities and training ourselves to remember Him, transforms our worldview. We no longer 'see' through the prism of our karmic righteousness but through the prism of divine love. Havir, one of the *nava-yogendras*, describes this type of vision to Mahārāja Nimi:

> *sarva-bhūteṣu yaḥ paśyed*
> *bhagavad-bhāvam ātmanaḥ*

> 'Śrī Havir said: "The most advanced devotee sees within everything the soul of all souls, the Supreme Personality of Godhead, Śrī Kṛṣṇa. Consequently he sees everything in relation to the Supreme Lord and understands that everything that exists is eternally situated within the Lord."'
>
> *Śrīmad-Bhāgavatam* 11.2.45

One last discussion point on 1.8.36 concerns the third line which reads:

> *śṛṇvanti gāyanti gṛṇanty abhīkṣṇaśaḥ*
> *smaranti nandanti tavehitaṁ janāḥ*
> *ta* ***eva*** *paśyanty acireṇa tāvakaṁ*
> *bhava-pravāhoparamaṁ padāmbujam*

> 'They [people who chant and remember Your pastimes] will **certainly** see very soon…' (line 3)

Viśvanātha Cakravartī Ṭhākura offers an interesting commentary on this. The particle '*eva*' means 'certainly,' 'definitely,' 'necessarily,' 'exactly.' According to Sanskrit grammar, the word can also add emphasis to the word it precedes or to any word in the sentence. Therefore, if we apply *eva* to six other words in this verse, we learn of six amazing results that come from hearing about Krishna.

In combination with *janāḥ* (people), *eva* stresses that **specific** people, those who listen to God's pastimes, and no one else, can see the Lord's lotus feet and escape the wheel of karma.

In combination with *paśyanti* (seeing), *eva* asserts that such people will **certainly** see the Lord, without fail.

In combination with *acireṇa* (soon), *eva* emphasizes they will see Him **certainly very soon**. It will not take long.

In combination with *tāvakaṁ* (Your), *eva* specifies that listeners will see Krishna **in particular**, and not any other partial incarnation of the Lord.

In combination with *bhava-pravāhoparamaṁ* (stop the current of rebirth), *eva* emphasizes that service to the Lord will **undoubtedly** stop the flow of karma. Those who hear scripture will certainly be freed from the misery of material existence.

In combination with *padāmbuja* (lotus feet), *eva* stresses that listeners will **unquestionably** serve the Lord, as a person. The spirit of service will undoubtedly awaken within them as they realize that God is a person and not some indifferent, impersonal energy.

Thus, the presence of *eva* in the verse reveals the power of *bhakti* (which begins by listening to *Śrīmad-Bhāgavatam*) in six ways. Meditating on these multiple meanings removes all doubts and reinforces in absolute terms that Krishna chooses to come personally on Earth only (*eva*) to show us the path of light.

CHAPTER 10

Healing Purpose

Curing the Disease of Indifference

We have already said that Queen Kuntī's prayers can be classified as *samprārthanātmikā*, prayers to restore wholeness. Her words help us develop the spiritual emotions of surrender, which gradually reinstate our true identity. This eradicates the false ego, which is the source of our material attachments that bind us tightly to this world.

In the process of spiritual development, as we contemplate the Lord's *nāma*, *rūpa*, *guṇa* and *līlā*, we realize more and more profoundly the personal nature of the Lord and perceive His role in our lives. Krishna describes the process to Uddhava:

> *yathā yathātmā parimṛjyate 'sau*
> *mat-puṇya-gāthā-śravaṇābhidhānaiḥ*
> *tathā tathā paśyati vastu sūkṣmaṁ*
> *cakṣur yathaivāñjana-samprayuktam*

> 'When a diseased eye is treated with medicinal ointment it gradually recovers its power to see. Similarly, as a conscious living entity cleanses himself of material contamination by hearing and chanting the pious narrations of My glories, he regains his ability to see Me, the Absolute Truth, in My subtle spiritual form.'
>
> *Śrīmad-Bhāgavatam* 11.14.26

At the same time, our spiritual vision clears and we begin to perceive more deeply the divided state of our consciousness and the inner obstacles of material attachments and desires that separate us from God.

Our desire to enjoy ourselves independent of Him has thrust us into the material world. This desire for autonomy, or 'selfhood' is called *ahaṅkāra* – the false ego. It is a comprehensive system of self-perception as a (sovereign) material mind and material body that drives our thoughts, desires, and feelings. The false ego forms from early childhood, based on the strongest human instinct – the instinct of self-preservation. This is why it is so deeply rooted in our consciousness. Defining ourselves with labels of 'I am…' and through acquisitions of 'this is mine,' we struggle on by trying to protect ourselves from threats and creating some kind of ideal external environment.

Driven by fear, we constantly think about future threats, past losses and achievements, current pain in the gross and subtle body, and how we might improve the external circumstances of our existence. Thus, the pure consciousness of the soul is conditioned by three factors – time, the material mind and body, and external circumstances. The foolish attempt of the immortal soul to become independent in the material world results in its complete enslavement by matter.

By embarking on the spiritual path, we try to redefine ourselves by forming a new, spiritual 'I' based on a relationship with God. However, sooner or later our attempts clash with our material self-identification, for 'No one can serve two masters… You cannot serve both God and money.'[1] At a certain stage, we strive for God but become painfully aware of our attachment to matter. This stage is *anartha-nivṛtti*. Having reached it, we face a most difficult choice – to persist along the spiritual path, gradually sever all material bonds, rely on God, and give up the habit of controlling situations, or return to the habitual and relatively safe sphere of material existence.

Most prefer to go back to the known or choose to compromise, thus halting their spiritual development. This is quite understandable. The onward spiritual path narrows and

1 The Gospel of Matthew, 6:24.

challenges us, while our strong ties with matter pull at us. It is painful to break away from them. To justify our weakness to ourselves and the world, we often begin finding faults with the spiritual path and the spiritual teachers who have been guiding us, or we turn into pharisees to hide our failures behind a screen of asceticism and strict adherence to rituals. Most congregational members of religions fall into this category. Sincere seekers of truth are in the minority.

When confronted by their weakness, those rare individuals who dare to follow the spiritual path to its end, come to realize that they are unable to deal with their attachments on their own. They realize they need help and pray to God to break their bonds to matter, that is, become free from the fear of time, and spiritualize the 'I' and 'mine.' To attain this, they place themselves in even greater dependence on God, relying on His mercy. This act is *śaraṇāgati*.

The impulse to surrender to the Lord is triggered by the understanding that no one else can rescue us from the cycle of birth and death and no one else can protect us from our internal enemies. Śrīla Jīva Gosvāmī describes this in the *Bhakti-sandarbha*:

> *ṣaḍ-vargādy-avikṛta-saṁsāra-bhaya-bādhyamāna*
> *eva hi śaraṇaṁ praviśaty ananya-gatiḥ*
> *bhakti-mātra-kāmo 'pi tat-kṛta-bhagavad-vaimukhya-*
> *bādhyamānaḥ*

> 'Tormented by the fear of material existence caused by the six internal enemies (lust, anger, greed, illusion, pride and envy), one realizes that only the Lord can save him (ananya-gatiḥ). Although such a person wants to attain love of God to some extent, he realizes that he is impeded by the disease of indifference. Such a person surrenders to the Lord.'
>
> Śrīla Jīva Gosvāmī, *Bhakti-sandarbha, Anuccheda*, 236

At the initial stages of our spiritual development, our desire to serve God is speculative. Śrīla Jīva Gosvāmī writes that even at the level of *ruci*, the desire to serve Krishna is not spontaneous, but dictated by the intellect: *rucir abhilāṣa kintu buddhi-pūrvakam.*[1] We are tied down to this world by powerful and gross material emotions – lust, anger, greed, envy, etc. This bondage is impossible to sever by intellectual effort alone. To break it, we need the Lord's help. On our part, we petition the Lord by submerging in the emotions of *śaraṇāgati* and surrender ourselves to His mercy. The process consists of six components:

ānukūlyasya saṅkalpaḥ / prātikūlyasya varjanam
rakṣiṣyatīti viśvāso / goptṛtve varaṇaṁ tathā
ātma-nikṣepa-kārpaṇye / ṣaḍ-vidhā śaraṇāgatiḥ

'The six divisions of surrender are the acceptance of those things favorable to devotional service, the rejection of unfavorable things, the conviction that Kṛṣṇa will give protection, the acceptance of the Lord as one's guardian or master, full self-surrender, and humility.'

Hari-bhakti-vilāsa 11.676.
Quoted from *Caitanya-caritāmṛta*, *Madhya-līlā* 22.100)

It is important to understand that *śaraṇāgati* is not a state produced by cold reasoning. Each component is charged with certain emotions. Bhaktivinoda Ṭhākura describes the nature of these in *Jaiva Dharma*, chapter six.

The first two elements are *ānukūlyasya saṅkalpaḥ* and *prātikūlyasya varjanam*, translate into: 'I will only do that which is favorable for unalloyed *bhakti*, and I will reject all that is unfavorable.' This is *saṅkalpa*, or *pratijñā*, a solemn vow.

1 *Durgama-saṅgamanī*, commentary on *Bhakti-rasāmṛta-sindhu*, 1.4.15.

The third element is *rakṣiṣyatīti viśvāso*, which is faith in Bhagavān as one's protector: 'Bhagavān is my only protector. I can derive no benefit whatsoever from *jñāna*, yoga, or other similar practices.' This is an expression of trust.

The fourth element is *goptṛtve varaṇaṁ*, which means deliberate acceptance of Bhagavān as one's maintainer: 'I cannot obtain anything or maintain myself by my own endeavor. I will serve Bhagavān to the best of my ability, and He will take care of me.' This is dependence.

The fifth element is *ātma-nikṣepa*, which entails self-surrender: 'Who am I? I am His. My duty is to fulfill His desire.' This is surrendering oneself (*ātma-nivedana*).

The sixth element is *kārpaṇye*, which is meekness: 'I am wretched, insignificant, and materially destitute.' This is humility.

According to Śrīla Jīva Gosvāmī, the fourth dynamic (*goptṛtve varaṇaṁ*) is the essence of *śaraṇāgati* because it most fully expresses and encompasses the spirit of surrendering oneself to the Lord's will. In the prayers discussed so far, Queen Kuntī's exquisite feelings constitute the essence of surrender: determination, trust in Krishna, utter humbleness, and devotion. As if to sum up all that has been said, in the next four verses, 1.8.37-40, she expresses heartfelt sentiments of *goptṛtve varaṇaṁ* to Krishna: that she and her sons have no other protector and maintainer except Him; that she is utterly dependent on Him; and that only He can rid her of any remnants of independent thinking and indifference towards Him.

Declaration of Independence

apy adya nas tvaṁ sva-kṛtehita prabho
jihāsasi svit suhṛdo 'nujīvinaḥ
yeṣāṁ na cānyad bhavataḥ padāmbujāt
parāyaṇaṁ rājasu yojitāṁhasām

'O my Lord, You have executed all duties Yourself. Are you leaving us today, though we are completely dependent on Your mercy and have no one else to protect us, now when all kings are at enmity with us?'

Śrīmad-Bhāgavatam 1.8.37

Śrīla Prabhupāda begins his commentary on this verse by contrasting the Pāṇḍavas to those driven by their false egos and who try in vain to become self-reliant and independent of God:

'The Pāṇḍavas are most fortunate because with all good luck they were entirely dependent on the mercy of the Lord. In the material world, to be dependent on the mercy of someone else is the utmost sign of misfortune, but in the case of our transcendental relation with the Lord, it is the most fortunate case when we can live completely dependent on Him. The material disease is due to thinking of becoming independent of everything. But the cruel material nature does not allow us to become independent. The false attempt to become independent of the stringent laws of nature is known as material advancement of experimental knowledge. The whole material world is moving on this false attempt of becoming independent of the laws of nature. Beginning from Rāvaṇa, who wanted to prepare a direct staircase to the planets of heaven, down to the present age, they are trying to overcome the laws of nature. They are trying now

to approach distant planetary systems by electronic mechanical power.'

Śrīmad-Bhāgavatam 1.8.37, purport

The presumptuous and doomed attempts of mankind to attain independence from God and the laws of material nature have brought about innumerable problems. Humans have proudly praised these demonic endeavors as the 'progress of experimental science,' and destroyed themselves and the world. Experimental science, for all its impressive achievements, has increased human suffering exponentially. It is not for nothing that Śrīla Prabhupāda mentions Rāvaṇa, the great demon and first great scientist, who sought to bestow happiness to mankind by constructing a staircase leading to the Heavens. He failed. The staircase remained unfinished. But since then, scientists have never stopped trying to forcibly restore humans to their 'lost paradise.'

According to the Bible all our problems began when our imprudent forefathers tasted the fruit from the tree of the knowledge of good and evil. As the tree of 'knowledge' continues bearing abundant fruit, and we continue to eat its fruit, the more 'God-like' we become, as promised. Alas, all attempts to exist free of God have invariably ended in human self-destruction. By attempting to destroy the root of our existence, we inevitably destroy ourselves. The more we assume ourselves to be God and distance ourselves from Him, the more we become miserable and embittered, and the darker and more meaningless our lives are.

Modern science is mankind's collective effort to protect itself from the power of a 'jealous' and 'wayward' God who condemns people to endless misery, and to take His place. Darwin's theory of evolution legitimized these pursuits; once humans appropriated the topmost position on the evolutionary ladder, there was no need to be grateful to any creator or revere His creation. Freed from restraint, we could consider ourselves entitled to do whatever we please with material nature.

Scientists' quest to correct the 'design flaws' of Earth and create and maintain an ideal external environment have become a permanent war with material nature. Ivan Michurin, a famous Russian plant biologist of the early twentieth century, expressed the essence of this absurd idea most frankly, 'We cannot wait for favors from Nature. To take them from it – that is our task.' Some laugh at this notion, but nevertheless do not stop their attempts to rape and plunder material nature. The Earth is rapidly turning into a promised paradise, which suspiciously resembles hell.

All advances in material science designed to relieve us of our struggle for existence have paradoxically led to an increase in stress levels. Modern science was supposed to make our lives easier, but instead our lives are busier, faster, and overwhelmed. Moreover, we are trapped in the never-ending race for the latest conveniences that scientists keep inventing because advertising imposes the idea that it is impossible to live without these things. Thus, we are compelled to spend our lives acquiring symbols of material success.

Furthermore, science has largely spared us the need for physical labor which used to help relieve tension in the mind. As a result, modern people experience severe levels of stress, which undermines their mental and physical health. This is the 'blessing' brought by technocratic civilization.

The worst plague generated by modern civilization for us neurotic humans is not just our physical and mental deterioration, but that we are much more dependent on matter than the humans of the past. Due to science, human life is much more complicated, and our way of thinking has become more materialistic. We are focused on our own selves, our bodies, and our problems. Stress hormones focus our consciousness on the external and make us aggressive and incapable of going within to experience the sublime emotions of gratitude, compassion, and love. In other words, in this stressful state, the knot of the false ego binds the soul even more tightly to matter. Human striving for independence from God has resulted in deeper dependence on matter.

We have paid a high price for the 'easy life' promised by scientists. Man was not created to idle around, but to work under the Lord's guidance, says Śrīla Prabhupāda, who articulates the spiritual model:

> *'But the highest goal of human civilization is to work hard under the guidance of the Lord and become completely dependent on Him. The highest achievement of perfect civilization is to work with valor but at the same time depend completely on the Lord. The Pāṇḍavas were the ideal executors of this standard of civilization. Undoubtedly they were completely dependent on the good will of Lord Śrī Kṛṣṇa, but they were not idle parasites of the Lord. They were all highly qualified both by personal character and by physical activities. Still they always looked for the mercy of the Lord because they knew that every living being is dependent by constitutional position.'*
>
> *Śrīmad-Bhāgavatam* 1.8.37, purport

The Labor of Love

Śrīla Prabhupāda explains Queen Kuntī's use of *anujīvinaḥ* in 1.8.37 to mean 'those who live in dependence.' The Pāṇḍavas voluntarily made themselves dependent on the Lord. This was not something humiliating but sweet, which is why Queen Kuntī says, 'We are Your friends (*suhṛdaṁ*), completely dependent on You. Are You really going to leave us today?'

Of course, the Lord never abandons His friends who have rendered themselves dependent on Him. As soon as we proclaim our need for God and accept His protection, He will always play a part in our lives, visibly or invisibly. For those who declare themselves self-governing and independent, He may not manifest Himself in their lives. Why would He impose Himself? He waits for us to take the first step. Thereafter, He acts. When Vibhīṣaṇa abandoned his demon brother, Rāvaṇa, and entreated Rāma for shelter, the Lord made a solemn vow:

sakṛd eva prapanno yas
tavāsmīti ca yācate
abhayaṁ sarvadā tasmai
dadāmy etad vrataṁ mama

> 'I promise that anyone who asks for My protection, and at least once sincerely entrusts himself to Me with the words, "My dear Lord, from this day on I belong to You," will be immediately relieved of all fears by Me. From that moment on, he will always be safe. This is my vow.'
>
> *Rāmāyaṇa, Yuddha-khaṇḍa* 18.33.
> Also quoted in *Caitanya-caritāmṛta, Madhya-līlā* 22.34

Śrīla Prabhupāda emphasizes that surrendering to Krishna's will does not imply a lazy, careless existence. Often, we oscillate between extremes. Either we work hard for our personal welfare with a resounding sense that 'It's all down to me,' or we become fatalists and resign ourselves to the flow of fate with the words, 'I have surrendered to God. I don't need to do anything.' Both are manifestations of the human ego swinging like a pendulum between *bhoga* or *tyāga* – in thirst for material pleasures or rejecting them. We are unable to stop in the middle.

Our lives become perfect and bring true satisfaction when we find balance: externally we work tirelessly, and internally depend on the Lord. The Pāṇḍavas were the most powerful warriors of their time. They fought enemies and performed great feats, but internally they always relied on the Lord and not on their own strength. They had no material ego, no voice inside that said, 'I am a great hero.' This blissful and balanced state of consciousness is devotion.

When we raise our consciousness to this state, the Lord begins acting through us. We become a conductor of His energy. 'Become an instrument in My hands, O Savyasācī!'[1] says Krishna to Arjuna. In doing so, *bhakta* and Bhagavān experience deep happiness.

Sweet Burden

Sane people understand that they are dependent on all things around them. Only the self-sufficient can be independent in this world. Anyone who cannot produce everything necessary for existence is dependent. Humans need assistance from others for everything. Dependency and incompleteness are synonymous. If someone claims to be independent of everyone, then for the sake of consistency, they must stop eating, drinking, and breathing.

The notion of independence is faulty. It does not exist in nature because everything in the material world is interrelated. Humans, animals, trees, plants, microorganisms live in sync. Acknowledging our dependence on God is an acknowledgment of reality. Everything we have comes from God and we need to acknowledge this fact. An aphorism from the *Nīti Śāstra* says it all:

yena sukla kṛta hamsam
sukas ca hariti-kritah mayūras citritā
yena sa te vrittim vidhāsyati

1 *'nimitta-mātraṁ bhava savya-sācin,' Bhagavad-gītā* 11.33.

> 'The one who created the swan white, the parrot green, and the peacock colorful, will take care of you, too.'
>
> *Hitopadeśa* 1.172

By definition, a particle cannot be independent of the whole. Separated and isolated from the whole, it is incomplete and deprived of its meaning of existence. If we disassemble a new car into parts, then each component is useless. Parts can function normally only as a portion of the whole. In the same way, man is a part of the whole. When such a particle foolishly and proudly declares its independence, its connection to the whole severs, and it deprives itself of its existential meaning. This is why Śrīla Prabhupāda writes that we come to know the true meaning of our lives when we make ourselves dependent on the Lord.

Such dependence is the perfection of life, for God is the complete whole. He does not need anything from us. He is selfless because self-interest is a symptom of incompleteness, which creates constant cravings for more. By encouraging us to become instruments in His hands, He wants to endow us with the experience of love.

However, we suspect Him of merciless exploitation, as expressed by the third servant in the parable, 'I knew that you are a hard man, harvesting where you have not sown and gathering where you have not scattered seed.' Indeed, in human interactions, being dependent on someone who is himself dependent and in need, inevitably leads to exploitation. But what does God have to do with that? He is brimming with inner bliss. He asks living beings to work for Him so they may 'share their master's happiness.' He wants us to join in His bliss.

Therefore, Śrīla Prabhupāda taught that dependence on God is the happy state of a free person. After entrusting ourselves, we can say,

'I do not want to depend on anyone else. My Lord and Master is God and I serve Him. I will serve others too, not because I need something from them, but because I am God's servant. Since God is connected to everyone, I can serve everyone. In doing so, I enter relationships with others as a free person.'

In truth, absolute dependence on God is the only true freedom available to us. Otherwise, we are entrapped, vulnerable, alone, and in danger. Srila Prabhupāda describes this state:

> *'Those who try to become falsely independent of the Lord are called* anātha, *or without any guardian, whereas those who are completely dependent on the will of the Lord are called* sanātha, *or those having someone to protect them. Therefore we must try to be* sanātha *so that we can always be protected from the unfavorable condition of material existence.'*
> *Śrīmad-Bhāgavatam* 1.8.37, purport

Śrīla Prabhupāda refers us to a verse by Yāmunācārya in the *Stotra-ratna*:

> *bhavantam evānucaran nirantaraḥ*
> *praśānta-niḥśeṣa-mano-rathāntaraḥ*
> *kadāham aikāntika-nitya-kiṅkaraḥ*
> *praharṣayiṣyāmi sa-nātha-jīvitam*

> 'O my Lord! I have been constantly serving You and only You! All my material desires are gone. Please, let me know when I will rejoice at Your agreeing to become My master (*sa-nātha-jīvitam*) and engaging Me as Your eternal servant, who has no other goal of life.'
>
> *Stotra-ratna*, 43.
> Quoted in *Caitanya-caritāmṛta, Madhya-līlā* 8.73

According to Yāmunācārya, to have a good master is a sign of good luck. In India, stray dogs roam the streets. They usually make a pitiful sight because they are skinny, fearful, with sad, guilty eyes. Once, while walking with his disciples along Juhu beach in Bombay, Śrīla Prabhupāda saw a large stray dog approach a shaggy little pug trotting alongside its haughty owner. The pug burst into ringing barks and charged at the stray dog. Although the stray was ten times larger, it was frightened, and with tail between its legs, retreated to a safe distance. 'Do you see the difference? Śrīla Prabhupāda said. 'The little dog has an owner. That is why it is so confident. The big dog has no owner, so it is unhappy.'

Denying our dependence on God, we are forced to depend on many partial manifestations of God's energy – the elements, the forces of nature, and people such as officials, doctors, relatives, employers, and sponsors. Since none of these require absolute surrender, we retain the illusion of independence. The last word remains with us, we can choose whom to depend on. Afraid of losing this 'privilege,' we avoid dealing with God.

Accepting the Lord as our patron means that we don't need to turn to anyone else for protection (*goptṛtve varaṇaṁ*). From now on, God is our only master. Yāmunācārya emphasizes this twice in the verse: *bhavanti **eva** anucaran* and *aikāntika kiṅkaraḥ*. The understanding that the Lord alone can solve all our problems is *ananya-gatitva*. Precisely this, as Śrīla Jīva Gosvāmī notes (see above), is the motivating impulse to surrender to the Lord's will, as illustrated by a story from the *Viṣṇu-dharma-purāṇa*.[1]

1 Quoted from *Bhakti-sandarbha*, *Anuccheda* 106.

* * *

Once Mahārāja Ambarīṣa, the great ruler and saint of Mathurā, took a vow to fast. He kept a grueling abstinence while worshiping the Lord. When Lord Viṣṇu saw that Mahārāja Ambarīṣa had completed the fast, He decided to test the purity of the king's faith. The Lord took the form of Indra and transformed Garuḍa into Airāvata, the elephant. In the guise of the mighty demigod, ruler of the heavenly planets, Lord Viṣṇu rode the colossal white elephant to Mahārāja Ambarīṣa's palace and said, 'Ask from me whatever you want.'

Demigods seldom appear before mortals, but when they do, they must bestow a blessing. This is the only reason people worship them.[1] Mahārāja Ambarīṣa bowed to the unbidden guest with great respect, offered a *pūjā*, and then politely said, 'Unfortunately, I cannot accept anything from You. My Lord is Viṣṇu. I only depend on His grace.'

'Indra' began to insist, 'You must ask me for blessings! I can give you everything that Lord Viṣṇu can give. What difference does it make who fulfills your wish?'

Mahārāja Ambarīṣa made no reply and simply smiled. Seeing this, his guest shouted, 'I can't leave without giving you something. Such a thing has never happened since the dawn of time. You will disgrace me to the world if you do not ask for anything,' the guest shouted.

Mahārāja Ambarīṣa again politely declined by saying 'I'm sorry, but I cannot break my vow of loyalty to my Master!'

1 Those whose intelligence has been stolen by material desires surrender unto demigods and follow the particular rules and regulations of worship according to their own natures.' *Bhagavad-gītā* 7.20.

Furious, 'Indra' seized His deadly weapon, the *vajra*, ready to hurl it towards the king. Mahārāja Ambarīṣa didn't flinch.

'You can burn me to ashes on the spot, but I will not accept any blessings from you. I depend on my Lord alone and desire no help from anyone else,' he said.

Satisfied with Mahārāja Ambarīṣa's steadfastness, Lord Viṣṇu assumed His original form, as did Garuḍa, and said with a beaming smile, 'Now ask.'

Ananya-Gatitva

Exceptional dependence on the Lord (*ananya-gatitva*), based on absolute trust in Him, helps us gain inner completeness, integrates our divided and chaotic mind, and enables us to feel part of the Whole. It gives a feeling of complete security, inner freedom, and strength. We will always feel peaceful, for we know, 'I have a master. I don't have to worry about anything myself. He will take care of me. I just need to serve him.'

In contrast, those who try to control every situation on their own, are in a state of constant anxiety. They struggle for survival, always worrying about acquiring everything they need in life. As a result, their disrupted mind accumulates irritation, fatigue, and stress.

Many people accuse God of jealousy when they misunderstand the first commandment of Christianity and Judaism: 'I am the Lord thy God… Thou shalt have no other gods before Me.'[1] In fact, when scriptures enjoin that we make ourselves exclusively dependent on God, it is for our own good. Only in such a state of deep inner dependence can we begin to feel the

1 Exodus 20:3-5.

Lord's presence, and become causelessly happy, 'entering into the joy of the master.'

Śrīla Jīva Gosvāmī says that without surrendering in this exclusive way, the soul is unable to feel belonging to God (*tadīyatva*).[1] Complete and unconditional surrender to the will of the Lord enables us to achieve complete perfection. This is why Śrīla Prabhupāda writes, 'The perfection of life is, therefore, to become dependent on the will of the Lord, instead of becoming falsely independent in the material world.'

The last words of 1.8.37 that we will focus on are *praharṣayiṣyāmi sanātha jīvitam* – 'We ... have no one else to protect us, now when all kings are at enmity with us.' Queen Kuntī says this at a time when the Pāṇḍavas have gained victory in battle and Mahārāja Yudhiṣṭhira has become emperor. All is finally well for them. Duryodhana and his cronies, who considered themselves arch enemies of the Pāṇḍavas, are destroyed. Yet, she portrays the world as hostile towards her and her sons. Why?

Queen Kuntī reminds us that this world is a hostile environment. We often forget this. The atmosphere is charged with enmity and competition. Everyone envies one another. Consciously or unconsciously, we strive for power, fame, fortune, titles, respect, validation, security. In a word, we seek supremacy, or as Śrīla Prabhupāda used to say it, 'we want to become the Lord of all we survey.' Humans participate in constant one-upmanship just as predators eat each other in the animal kingdom.

Unfortunately, the perils do not end when we start walking the spiritual path. We face even greater hostility as the world

1 *'asyās ca pūrva tvam taṁ vinā tadīyātvāsiddhiḥ/tatra yadyapi śaraṇapattyaiva sarvaṁ sidhyati.'* Śrīla Jīva Gosvāmī, *Bhakti-sandarbha*, *Anuccheda* 237.

takes up arms against us. Oftentimes, our dearest and nearest become resentful and opposed. As a result, we have extra reason to seek Krishna's shelter, and Krishna has an extra excuse to come and save us. In this way, the two fears – fear of internal enemies, (such as lust, greed) and the fear of external dangers – prompt us to surrender to God and break our bondage to matter.

The Glance that Awakens Life

Śaraṇāgati entails our efforts to redefine ourselves through our relationship with the Lord. Presently our personality is formed by memories of the past, fears of the future, the shape of our body, our current circumstances, and others' opinions of us. In other words, we define our material personality by looking at this world and capturing the gaze of the 'other' upon us. We form and reform our sense of self based on what others say they see and what we imagine others see of us.

Śaraṇāgati is our attempt to turn away from the material world and seek the gaze of the Lord that once brought us to life. Queen Kuntī prays for this in the next verse:

> ***ke vayaṁ nāma-rūpābhyāṁ***
> ***yadubhiḥ saha pāṇḍavāḥ***
> ***bhavato 'darśanaṁ yarhi***
> ***hṛṣīkāṇām iveśituḥ***

> 'As the name and fame of a particular body is finished with the disappearance of the living spirit, similarly if You do not look upon us, all our fame and activities, along with the Pāṇḍavas and Yadus, will end at once.'
> *Śrīmad-Bhāgavatam* 1.8.38

In the previous verse, Queen Kuntī confided that she and her sons are completely dependent on Krishna, and that if He does not protect them, then surrounded by enemies, they will be defenseless. In response, Krishna might object,

'You are not defenseless or surrounded by enemies. You have such powerful heroic sons. Arjuna and Bhīma are mighty and unmatched. Your eldest son is the embodiment of righteousness. The Yādavas are your powerful allies. What are you afraid of?'

Anticipating this brush off, Queen Kuntī says in this verse, 'Without You, all our strength will diminish. The eyes, ears, and nose can see, hear, and smell as long as the soul animates the body. If You turn Your back on us, we are no more alive than a corpse.'

She uses the words *bhavataḥ adarśanam*, which means 'not seeing You.' Thus, a literal translation would be, 'When we stop seeing You, all our strength will come to an end ...' but Śrīla Prabhupāda reverses it to *'If You do not look upon us, all our strength will come to an end...'* There is a deep philosophy behind his translation.

According to the teachings of the *Upaniṣads*, this entire world was brought to life by the Lord's glance: *sa aikṣata lokān u sṛja*[1] – 'The Lord cast a glance and created the worlds.' We, tiny living entities, are also called to life by the glance of the Lord: *tad aikṣata bahu syāṁ prajāyeya.*[2] Śukadeva Gosvāmī confirms this:

karoti viśva-sthiti-saṁyamodayaṁ
yasyepsitaṁ nepsitam īkṣitur guṇaiḥ

1 *Aytareya Upaniṣad* 1.1.1.

2 *Chāndogya Upaniṣad* 6.2.3.

māyā yathāyo bhramate tad-āśrayaṁ
grāvṇo namas te guṇa-karma-sākṣiṇe

'O Lord, You do not desire the creation, maintenance or annihilation of this material world, but You perform these activities for the conditioned souls by Your creative energy. Exactly as a piece of iron moves under the influence of a lodestone, inert matter moves when You glance over the total material energy.'

Śrīmad-Bhāgavatam 5.18.38

Here, we can hardly resist the temptation of drawing an analogy with the phenomena called the 'observer effect' in quantum physics, which claims that quantum particles alter in behaviour if subjected to the act of observation. What this means is that under the gaze of an observer, a quantum object stops being a wave and transforms from a potential state into a localized one. This is called a 'wave function collapse.' Some researchers believe the collapse is not just a mathematical model but a reflection of an actual physical process where the observer's glance transforms an invisible wave into a particle and fixes it in space.[1]

The *Vedas* describe the emergence of matter from a potential, unmanifest state in a similar way. By casting His glance over the unmanifest material energy (*pradhāna*), the Lord manifests the entire material creation of myriad universes (*guṇa-karma-sākṣiṇe*). That same gaze is also the driving force of all 'being.'

mayādhyakṣeṇa prakṛtiḥ
sūyate sa-carācaram
hetunānena kaunteya
jagad viparivartate

1 Roger Penrose, *The Large, the Small and the Human Mind.*

> 'This material nature, which is one of My energies, is working under My direction, O son of Kuntī, producing all moving and nonmoving beings. Under its rule this manifestation is created and annihilated again and again.'
>
> *Bhagavad-gītā* 9.10

The act of observation involves three elements: the observer (*draṣṭā*), the object of observation (*dṛśya*) and the process of observation (*darśana*). When the soul's consciousness is extraverted and directed towards material nature, it considers itself an observer, forgetting that its own self as well as the entire material world exist only due to the energy of the Lord's gaze. In truth, God is the *draṣṭā* and we are the *dṛśya*, the object of His *darśana*. The ancient tradition of coming for a *darśana* before the temple Deity should remind us of this fact. Sometimes we mistakenly think the point of visiting a temple is to see God. Out of habit, the human wants to turn God into the object of his observation, that is, exploitation. In truth, we go to the temple so God can see us and, thereby, affirm and confirm our existence.

A spark deprived of its connection to the fire it originated from, quickly goes out. In the same way, having turned away from God, we are deeply insecure of our existence. Consequently, we constantly need validation. Glory, honor, and attention, so much sought in this world are external sources of confirmation. We crave to know, 'I am seen, heard, acknowledged, and loved. I am valued. I count. I exist.'

Thus, we depend on others' opinions, and the more materialistic we are, the more we need these confirmations. Disregard, disrespect, or neglect by others hurts us because we perceive this as a denial of our existence. Social media, a recent genius invention, is so popular because it satisfies our deepest need for recognition.

Sounds, images, touches, tastes, and smells coming in from the outside world through our senses also confirm our existence. Therefore, we enjoy (and crave) them and have become overly reliant on them. Those with an extroverted consciousness, always looking outward, need praise and sensory impressions. Otherwise, they experience deprivation[1] with all its ensuing consequences of inner frustration, insignificance, and scarcity. In an endless, feverish interaction with the external environment, we waste our precious energy, and dissipate our consciousness. The latest inventions of science, all manner of gadgets and technologies, happily and treacherously facilitate us in doing this.

Exhausted by the senseless waste of energy spent in interacting with the world and maintaining our status in it, some of us try to pull away from material energy and look inward. However, oftentimes we turn our gaze into the heart and find only emptiness. Taking up various spiritual traditions, some of us efface the material ego to become nobody and nothing, and dissolve in the boundless emptiness and silence of the unrestrained consciousness. This kind of spiritual experience is like deep sleep, as dreamt of by Mikhail Lermontov:

> No, for I hope no longer,
> And do not regret the past at all;
> I seek freedom and repose, while longing
> To obtain them in a sleep withal!
> But it's not a deathlike sleep I crave for
> I would rather fall asleep, yet live,
> For my dormant chest might keep its vigor,
> For my dormant chest might mutely heave...[2]

1 Deprivation (Latin: *deprivatio* – loss, deprivation): a state of anxiety and fear caused by a sense of loss and lack of access to something highly desirable or urgently needed.

2 Mikhail Lermontov, 'I'm alone on the path just taken...'. Translated by Evgeny Sokolovskiy. Lermontov was a pre-eminent poet and writer of Russian Romanticism.

In this kind of experience, practitioners certainly get some consolation, but eventually they get bored of monotonous 'spiritual' sleep and return to stormy material reality. Even if they believe God is behind the emptiness and silence, they are unable to see Him. Their mistake is their attempt to invoke God by their own efforts, instead of directing their attention inward and waiting patiently in prayer to catch His life-awakening gaze.

The hope of receiving God's merciful glance upon oneself is the essence of the mood of service, *kṛpā-dṛṣṭi-vṛṣṭyāti-dīnaṁ... ajnam edhi akṣi-dṛśyaḥ*[1] – 'Pour on me, the fallen and unworthy, Your merciful look and let me, an ignorant person, see You.'

Śrīla Bhaktisiddhānta Sarasvatī often explained this principle. Once he was standing before the temple Deities at some distance. He was not wearing his glasses, so an accompanying disciple asked if he could see the Deities. Sarasvatī Ṭhākura smiled and said, 'We should never regard the Lord as the object of our observation. Rather, we should ponder upon what qualities we need to acquire so that He wishes to look at us. Do not think of how to get to see Him, but of whether He wants to see us and reveal Himself to us.'[2]

Śrīla Prabhupāda's translation ('if You do not look upon us') facilitates the inclusion of this rich discussion and at the same time enables complete understanding of Queen Kuntī's sentiments. The soul is a spark of consciousness that makes use of the senses of the material body. It looks through the eyes, listens through the ears, smells through the nose. The senses are instruments. When the soul stops using these, they atrophy and die off. Likewise, if we do not allow God to use our mind and body as instruments for his benevolent will and refuse to place

1 *Śrī Dāmodarāṣṭaka* 6.

2 Bhakti Vikasa Swami, *Śrī Bhaktisiddhānta Vaibhava*, Vol. 1, part 2. 'The Contemplator and the Contemplated.'

them at His disposal, we are not truly living. Effectively, we are in the process of dying.

Queen Kuntī makes specific mention that without Krishna's glance, she and her family are without fame and ability (*nāma-rūpābhyāṁ*). This is another angle that deserves exploration. *Nāma* refers to a person's name, his reputation, and the glory that accompanies him. *Rūpa* is his beauty, strength, might, power and wealth. Queen Kuntī wants to say that, 'We owe all our strength, beauty, and glory to You alone. We will lose it all, the moment You stop looking at us with mercy. All our glory and beauty will turn into the glory and beauty of a corpse.'

As long as we are alive, we possess some glory and beauty, though as soon as the soul leaves the body, all disappears in an instant. An empty shell is left. Arjuna expresses the same emptiness when he laments the disappearance of the Lord, the Soul of our soul:

tad vai dhanus ta iṣavaḥ sa ratho hayās te
so 'haṁ rathī nṛpatayo yata ānamanti
sarvaṁ kṣaṇena tad abhūd asad īśa-riktaṁ
bhasman hutaṁ kuhaka-rāddham ivoptam ūṣyām

'I have the very same Gāṇḍīva bow, the same arrows, the same chariot drawn by the same horses, and I use them as the same Arjuna to whom all the kings offered their due respects. But in the absence of Lord Kṛṣṇa, all of them, at a moment's notice, have become null and void. It is exactly like offering clarified butter on ashes, accumulating money with a magic wand or sowing seeds on barren land.'

Śrīmad-Bhāgavatam 1.15.21

Some might object, 'There have been and still are many talented brilliant people who do not serve God nor believe in Him.

This has not diminished their talents. Doesn't their existence refute your thesis?'

Our reply: 'No. The talents and abilities of individuals not engaged in God's service become a curse. Deprived of inner support, such people use their gifts to assert themselves or earn the admiration of the crowd, mistaking it for love. Instead of catching the Lord's glance, they try to catch the crowd's glance. But the delighted audience can quickly change into a hooting one. Overnight, fame and praise in this world can mute into cruel, dirty, envious gossip. Few celebrities, philosophers, artists, politicians, or scientists have been spared. In a state of depression or disappointment, exceptionally talented individuals have taken their lives. Their talents did not help them. Therefore, Vedic literature describes the merits of materially gifted people as adornments of a dead man:

bhagavad-bhakti-hīnasya
jātiḥ śāstraṁ japas tapaḥ
aprāṇasyeva dehasya
maṇḍanaṁ loka-rañjanam

> 'If one is not engaged in devotional service, then his noble birth, knowledge of the scriptures, all the ascetic deeds that he has performed, and the Vedic mantras that he has recited are like the adornments on a dead man who is dressed up for the amusement of the crowd.'
>
> *Hari-bhakti-sudhodaya* 3.12.
> Quoted from *Caitanya-caritāmṛta, Madhya-līlā* 19.75)

Refusing to place ourselves in the Lord's shelter, we expose ourselves to a perilous fate. Our fame, beauty, money, or power turn into curses and kill us. In a lecture, Śrīla Prabhupāda tells of one such tragedy:

> *'Even Mahatma Gandhi... I have read his life. The day when he was to be killed, he did not know in the morning that he was going to be killed in the evening. But as a big man, he was receiving so many letters, so many congratulations, so many condemnations. You do not know. At the end of Gandhi's later part of life, he was so disgusted with his life that he always wanted..., he spoke to his secretaries, associates, that "If death would come to me, I would be satisfied." Such a big man, such a great man.*
>
> *One of his practical difficulty was that he could not sleep soundly, partly due to his big occupation and partly due to the disturbance of the people. Wherever he will go, thousands and thousands of people will gather and will loudly speak, "Mahatma Gandhi* kī jaya.*" Even at dead of night, at twelve o'clock of night, he is passing through a train, and if the train is stopped at the middle station, people will get information and gather: "Mahatma Gandhi* kī jaya.*" So I have seen personally. When he was going through some crowd, he was closing, capping his ears like this. His brain was being unnecessarily taxed with this sound, "Mahatma Gandhi* kī jaya.*" People thought that they were glorifying Mahatma Gandhi, but Mahatma Gandhi was being killed by that voice.'*
>
> Lecture on *Bhagavad-gītā*, 25 March, 1966

* * *

Appropriating God's energy always kills the possessor. History repeats itself; the abducted Sītā Devī always becomes the cause of Rāvaṇa's death. Queen Kuntī has already warned that noble birth, wealth, strength, good education, and beauty inflate pride, and pride leads to death. A soap bubble, no matter how buoyant and colorful, is going to burst.

However, if we constantly remember with gratitude the Supreme One from whom we have received all our gifts, then the gifts will become part of our eternal spiritual personality. Gratitude will become the foundation of sublime spiritual emotions of love for God. The Pāṇḍavas possessed everything one could dream of – wealth, strength, beauty, power, and more, but they always remembered to whom they owed it all. This meant that their wealth was never a setback in their relationship with the Lord. A small episode from Rāmānujācārya's life illustrates this principle well.

The *ācārya* had a cousin called Govinda. Govinda was instructed by his guru to serve Rāmānujācārya for the rest of his days. Govinda accepted the command with such sincerity that soon he manifested the ideal qualities of a servant. For example, he could anticipate Rāmānujācārya's wishes and fulfill them without waiting for the request. Other disciples were delighted with Govinda's attitude and one day gathered to praise his service.

Govinda listened patiently and abruptly said, 'You are right. My qualities undoubtedly deserve glory.'

Such boastful words from the lips of a Vaiṣṇava greatly embarrassed the disciples who went to their guru to share their concerns. Rāmānujācārya immediately summoned Govinda and said sternly, 'You certainly possess the virtues of a true devotee – all but one. You obviously lack modesty. Be careful. Pride is like poison. Even a drop can bring death.'

'O Master, I've lived thousands of lifetimes in this material world before receiving this human body,' replied Govinda, humbly. 'After obtaining it, I still strayed from the path of perfection and wandered in the darkness. It was only by your grace that I escaped my delusions. Therefore, if someone sees merit in me, I know all my virtues have come from you. Who but me can know how fallen and lowly I am? No amount of praise will ever dissuade me from this. When someone glorifies me, I am aware that he is actually glorifying you. How can I disagree with him and not rejoice in his words?'

* * *

Material life consists of trying to please people and attract their favorable glances. We are born helpless and completely dependent on our parents' love and mercy. At school, we learn to seek the favor of teachers. Our teenage insecurities force us to seek the approval of peers and friends. In adulthood, we take care of our reputation among colleagues and acquaintances. Success in life seems determined by how many people know about our existence and are interested in us, so we try to draw attention to our achievements and merits in any way possible. And it goes on.

In this never-ending effort to please others, we lose ourselves. Not understanding who we really are, we form a concept, image of ourselves made up of the projections we broadcast outward, as well as from the fragmentary opinions of others. These opinions enslave and limit us, just as each glance thrown at us, supportive or negative, nails us to our bodies and minds.

Spiritual life begins the moment we realize that the Lord's glance has awakened us and that only under His gaze can we understand our purpose and meaning in life. Gradually, we stop looking for the meaning of our existence in the approval of worldly people. Instead, we seek the favor of those dedicated to serving the Lord. Under their gaze, for the first time, we begin to feel like a soul, and not a mortal body. Associating with them, we suddenly realize that they do not judge us. For the first time in our lives, we desire not to flatter but to serve.

The love of saintly people drives fear out of our hearts. In serving them, we realize that we can stop being slaves to lust and anger. Through negligence or bad habits, sometimes we hurt them while associating with them and immediately feel the spiritual fire in our hearts, kindled by them, start to extinguish. Both their benevolence and their discontent equally teach us that God is a person, not an impersonal energy, and that He, too, may turn away from us if we offend Him or those He loves.

As we associate with saintly persons, our desire to gain God's loving gaze grows stronger. Depending on the Lord and saintly persons becomes our greatest value. At some point, with tears in our eyes, we will begin to pray:

'Who am I and what am I without You, my Lord? This world reshapes me in its own image and likeness. But I know I don't belong to this world. I belong to You. So, please, don't leave me, my Lord. Forgive me for still clinging to my seeming independence. Take it away, but don't turn Your back on me! Your gaze is the greatest jewel in my life.'

God's Opulence

True dependence and gratitude are synonymous. Those who dream of independence accept help when they need it but reject it as soon as they meet their needs. They try to forget their benefactors. The false ego does not allow us to feel obliged to anyone. So, we try to live in such a way that our sense of gratitude does not overly darken our happiness. Our attitude towards God is similar: in troubles, we tearfully pray to Him for help, but when the difficulty is over, we forget about Him and consider our success to be our own merit.

But one who is not ashamed of depending on the Lord is grateful to Him both in sorrow and in happiness.

neyaṁ śobhiṣyate tatra
yathedānīṁ gadādhara
tvat-padair aṅkitā bhāti
sva-lakṣaṇa-vilakṣitaiḥ

'O Gadādhara [Krishna], our kingdom is now being marked by the impressions of Your feet, and therefore it appears beautiful. But when You leave, it will no longer be so.'

Śrīmad-Bhāgavatam 1.8.39

In this verse, Queen Kuntī's mood of overflowing love and gratitude towards Krishna continues. Previously, she praised His glance as life-sustaining, here she focuses on the power of the Lord's lotus feet. First, she praises the Lord as Gadādhara, He who wields the mace. Looking at Him through the prism of *aiśvarya-jñāna*, in awareness of his greatness and omnipotence, she evokes the four-armed Lord, holding a club in one hand; the same club that Krishna used to protect Mahārāja Parīkṣit in Uttarā's womb. In remembering Him this way, she thanks Him again for protecting the Pāṇḍavas.

Then, Queen Kuntī reverentially talks about Krishna's footprints, 'O Gadādhara, never has our kingdom been as beautiful since You adorned it with Your footprints. Its beauty will cease to shine as soon as You leave us.'

Krishna is the epitome of beauty. Everything about Him is beautiful. Everything that comes into direct contact with Him becomes beautiful. Vedic literature celebrates His lotus-like feet. Their specialness features in several parts of the *Śrīmad-Bhāgavatam*. The *gopīs* adore them as precious treasure:

vṛndāvanaṁ sakhi bhuvo vitanoti kīṛtiṁ
yad devakī-suta-padāmbuja-labdha-lakṣmi

'O friend, Vṛndāvana is spreading the glory of the earth, having obtained the treasure of the lotus feet of Kṛṣṇa, the son of Devakī.'

Śrīmad-Bhāgavatam 10.21.10)

Bhūmi Devī, the personified form of Earth, was so pleased that the imprints of Krishna's feet adorned her lands:

tasyāham abja-kuliśāṅkuśa-ketu-ketaiḥ
śrīmat-padair bhagavataḥ samalaṅkṛtāṅgī
trīn atyaroca upalabhya tato vibhūtiṁ
lokān sa māṁ vyasṛjad utsmayatīṁ tad-ante

'I was endowed with specific powers to supersede the fortune of all the three planetary systems by being decorated with the impressions of the flag, thunderbolt, elephant-driving rod and lotus flower, which are signs of the lotus feet of the Lord. But at the end, when I felt I was so fortunate, the Lord left me.'

Śrīmad-Bhāgavatam 1.16.33

Akrūra, the great courtier of Kaṁsa's court, caught a glimpse of the Lord's footprints, fell to the ground, and began rolling around blissfully in the dust of Vṛndāvana.

padāni tasyākhila-loka-pāla-
kirīṭa-juṣṭāmala-pāda-reṇoḥ
dadarśa goṣṭhe kṣiti-kautukāni
vilakṣitāny abja-yavāṅkuśādyaiḥ
tad-darśanāhlāda-vivṛddha-sambhramaḥ
premṇordhva-romāśru-kalākulekṣaṇaḥ
rathād avaskandya sa teṣv aceṣṭata
prabhor amūny aṅghri-rajāṁsy aho iti

'In the cowherd pasture Akrūra saw the footprints of those feet whose pure dust the rulers of all the planets in the universe hold on their crowns. Those footprints of the Lord, distinguished by such marks as the lotus, barleycorn and elephant goad, made the ground wonderfully beautiful. Increasingly agitated by ecstasy at seeing the Lord's footprints, his bodily hairs standing on end because of his pure love, and his eyes filled with tears, Akrūra jumped down from his chariot and began rolling about among those footprints, exclaiming, "Ah, this is the dust from my master's feet!"'

Śrīmad-Bhāgavatam 10.38.25-26

Vaiṣṇavas apply *tilaka* on their bodies which symbolizes Krishna's footprints.[1] In their eyes, this is the best decoration, which mirrors the desire that Krishna take over their lives as master.

In the next verse, Queen Kuntī speaks again of the power of the Lord's glance. She has already celebrated how His glance gives life, value, significance, security, and bliss to all people that He looks at. Now, she appreciates how places, nature and environments become balanced and at their best after Krishna sweeps His eyes over them.

ime jana-padāḥ svṛddhāḥ
supakvauṣadhi-vīrudhaḥ
vanādri-nady-udanvanto
hy edhante tava vīkṣitaiḥ

'All these cities and villages are flourishing in all respects because the herbs and grains are in

1 '*Śāstras* explain that these vertical signs [*tilaka*] symbolize either the Lord's footprints, or that the body of a Vaiṣṇava becomes a temple to Hari.' Bhaktivinoda Ṭhākura, *Pañca-saṁskāra*.

> abundance, the trees are full of fruits, the rivers are flowing, the hills are full of minerals and the oceans full of wealth. And this is all due to Your glancing over them.'
>
> *Śrīmad-Bhāgavatam* 1.8.40

Krishna's gaze infuses life, sustenance, vitality, and prosperity. Contrary to popular belief, material prosperity does not necessarily impede spiritual development. This verse suggests otherwise. It is probably not mere chance that the words for 'God' and 'wealth' in Russian come from the same root. Krishna's presence brings wholesome balance in nature and nourishment to all. We see this most strikingly in the Pāṇḍavas' kingdom after the battle was over. They were pure devotees, yet they lived in astounding abundance. Later in the First Canto, Sūta Gosvāmī describes the beautiful landscape:

> 'During the reign of Mahārāja Yudhiṣṭhira, the clouds showered all the water that people needed, and the earth produced all the necessities of man in profusion. Due to its fatty milk bag and cheerful attitude, the cow used to moisten the grazing ground with milk. The rivers, oceans, hills, mountains, forests, creepers, and active drugs, in every season, paid their tax quota to the King in profusion. Because of the King's having no enemy, the living beings were not at any time disturbed by mental agonies, diseases, or excessive heat or cold.'
>
> *Śrīmad-Bhāgavatam* 1.10.4-6

> 'O *brāhmaṇas*, the opulence of the King was so enchanting that the denizens of heaven aspired for it. But because he was absorbed in the service of the Lord, nothing could satisfy him except the Lord's service.'
>
> *Śrīmad-Bhāgavatam* 1.12.6

Sūta Gosvāmī stresses the point: a devotee can endure poverty or prosperity with nonchalance when absorbed in Krishna's service. Internally, Mahārāja Yudhiṣṭhira felt satiated. Thus, the Lord bestowed upon him untold wealth, which the King used in service to others. This brought all the auspiciousness upon his personal dealings, rulership, and subjects. Śrīla Prabhupāda's analysis brings further light:

> *'The whole material world is full of hungry living beings. The hunger is not for good food, shelter or sense gratification. The hunger is for the spiritual atmosphere. Due to ignorance only they think that the world is dissatisfied because there is not sufficient food, shelter, defense and objects of sense gratification. This is called illusion. When the living being is hungry for spiritual satisfaction, he is misrepresented by material hunger. But the foolish leaders cannot see that even the people who are most sumptuously materially satisfied are still hungry. And what is their hunger and poverty? This hunger is actually for spiritual food, spiritual shelter, spiritual defense and spiritual sense gratification. These can be obtained in the association of the Supreme Spirit, Lord Śrī Kṛṣṇa.'*
>
> *Śrīmad-Bhāgavatam* 1.12.6 purport

We are looking for fullness and satisfaction. Our deepest need is for God but unfortunately, we project the need outward into the world of luxurious foods and objects. We just don't believe that connection to God can satisfy us and bring prosperity.

Some might say Mahārāja Yudhiṣṭhira's opulence is a mythical tale of glorious antiquity. But a legacy of riches in palaces, temples and in the soils of India remained for later centuries. Unfortunately, hungry foreign invaders plundered much of it because they believed happiness and power came from appropriating stones and metals.

Pre-invasion, India (the land of dharma) was the richest country in the world. Its fabulous wealth was legendary. A Persian historian, Abdul Razzaq Samarqandi visited Vijayanagar in South India, during the reign of Mahārāja Krishnadev and was struck to see precious stones such as diamonds, rubies, pearls and emeralds sold in heaps on streets and in open bazaars.[1] After the conquest of Vijayanagar, Malik Naib, the governor of the Delhi Sultan, carried away 96,000 *manas* of gold, which is about 80 tons![2]

Similarly, after the Persian Shah, Mahmud Ghaznavi plundered Mathurā for the seventeenth time (!) he needed a caravan of 100 camels to carry away the gold, silver and precious stones. Then he razed to the ground Krishna's magnificent temple located at the place of the Lord's birth. The temple was so huge and beautiful that Mahmoud wrote, 'If someone would wish to build a structure equal to it, he would need one hundred million gold dinars, a whole army of skilled craftsmen and two hundred years of time.'[3] Since he did not possess such funds, Mahmoud decided to destroy the temple.

The famous 'Peacock Throne' of the Mughal rulers, crafted upon Shah Jahan's order, was taken from India to Iran by Nadir Shah. According to an eyewitness, 'it weighed a little less than two tons of pure gold. Only the rubies, emeralds and diamonds set in gold, weighing more than five tons, had to be carried away on twenty-one camels, with small diamonds weighing up to half a ton; they didn't even bother to count the pearls.'[4]

1 Kamaluddin Abdul-Razzaq Samarqandi, Mission to Calicut and Vijayanagar. In A Century of Princes: Sources on Timurid History and Art, selected and translated by W. M. Thackston.

2 Manikant Shah, The Fabulous Wealth of Pre-British India, essay appears on www.indianscience.org

3 The accounts by Mahmud of Ghazni were translated and published in History of India as told by its own Historians, by J. Dowson and H.M. Elliot, originally in London 1867-1877.

4 O. E. Nepomnin, Living History of the East.

We could go on giving examples without end. But what is the point? People would still not believe that connection with God brings about prosperity. Five thousand years ago, Śrīla Vyāsadeva foresaw the upcoming Age of *Kali* and placed a bitter verse at the end of *Mahābhārata*:

> *ūrdhva bāhur vīraumy eṣa na ca kāścic srinoti me*
> *dharmād arthac ca kāmāś ca sa kim artham na sevyate*

> 'Throwing up my arms to the sky, I shout, "Dharma brings wealth and prosperity (*artha*). Dharma grants pleasure and fulfills desires (*kāma*). Is there any reason not to follow the path of dharma?" But who will hear me?'
>
> *Mahābhārata, Svargārohana-parva* 5.49

Truly, it is but a cry in the wilderness. Ordinary righteousness, not to mention devotion to the Supreme Lord, which is the supreme dharma of all living beings, brings material prosperity. In a wonderful purport, Śrīla Prabhupāda tries to appeal to human intelligence. Following Vyāsadeva, he encourages us to rethink. But who will hear him? Who will believe him?

> *'Human prosperity flourishes by natural gifts and not by gigantic industrial enterprises. The gigantic industrial enterprises are products of a godless civilization, and they cause the destruction of the noble aims of human life. The more we go on increasing such troublesome industries to squeeze out the vital energy of the human being, the more there will be unrest and dissatisfaction of the people in general, although a few only can live lavishly by exploitation. The natural gifts such as grains and vegetables, fruits, rivers, the hills of jewels and minerals, and the seas full of pearls are supplied by the order of the Supreme, and as He desires, material*

nature produces them in abundance or restricts them at times. The natural law is that the human being may take advantage of these godly gifts by nature and satisfactorily flourish on them without being captivated by the exploitative motive of lording it over material nature. The more we attempt to exploit material nature according to our whims of enjoyment, the more we shall become entrapped by the reaction of such exploitative attempts. If we have sufficient grains, fruits, vegetables and herbs, then what is the necessity of running a slaughterhouse and killing poor animals? A man need not kill an animal if he has sufficient grains and vegetables to eat. The flow of river waters fertilizes the fields, and there is more than what we need. Minerals are produced in the hills, and the jewels in the ocean. If human civilization has sufficient grains, minerals, jewels, water, milk, etc., then why should it hanker after terrible industrial enterprises at the cost of the labor of some unfortunate men?'

Śrīmad-Bhāgavatam 1.8.40, purport

The Dungeon of Demons

Those who do not trust God have created an artificial civilization in which they try to secure themselves and prevent any interference from above. However, such a civilization will self-destruct despite its impressive achievements. A stem cutting placed in a nutrient solution lives for a while, but without roots it withers. Modern godless civilization is just such a stem cut off from its root.

Industrial civilization emerged in Europe and America at the end of the eighteenth and nineteenth centuries, at the crest of the great industrial revolution. Now, we live in its replacement – a post-industrial society. Encyclopedic dictionaries unanimously declare that we live a 'higher quality of life,' determined by factors such as health status, life expectancy, environmental conditions, nutrition, household comfort, social environment, satisfaction of cultural and spiritual needs, and psychological comfort. However, whichever factors we take, with the exception of household comfort, the situation is becoming catastrophic.

The environment is deteriorating. Presently, only a quarter of the Earth's landmass is free of human activity. Natural resources are depleting while toxic waste is cast-off into the atmosphere or ground. The astrophysicist, Stephen Hawking stated that we will not be able to avoid a catastrophe on Earth, 'I am convinced that humans need to leave Earth. We are running out of space. Our physical resources are being depleted at an alarming rate.'[1]

The quality of our food is degrading. Supermarket shelves, stuffed with groceries, suggest we have reached abundance. However, this plenty is based on chemical fertilizers, pesticides, insecticides, growth hormones and genetic manipulation. The so-called 'green revolution' has brought increased yields but at what cost? Depleted lands, ecosystems irreversibly destroyed, and the environment polluted. According to conservative estimates, food causes 30-50 percent of human diseases.

Though infectious diseases have receded, HIV and Ebola have replaced the plague and smallpox. Depression has become the 'plague of the 21st century' that leads to ill health, disability, and suicide. Chronic stress and anxiety are the precursors taking over society. At the same time, social structures erode as live communication between people is being almost superseded by virtual communication on social networks.

1 Stephen Hawking, Starmus Conference speech, Cambridge, 20 June 2017.

Life expectancy, contrary to current perceptions, is also reducing. The idea that in ancient times people died barely reaching the age of thirty is at least controversial. Such statistics appeared on the basis of the high infant mortality rate. However, it does not occur to anyone in our times to count the number of children that are killed in the womb. Even five thousand years ago, people lived longer and were much healthier. For example, Bhīṣma was one hundred and eighty-six years old at the time of the battle, and Yudhiṣṭhira was about ninety years old. Biblical patriarchs lived for several hundred years.

Most alarming in modern civilization is the dehumanization of man. Modern industrial enterprises have caused, in Śrīla Prabhupāda's words, 'the destruction of the noble aims of human life.' Human goals and values are eroding right before our eyes, prompting some futurologists to assert that post-industrialism is a prologue to the 'posthuman' phase where the 'posthuman' or 'superman' will be devoid of emotions.

This is the grim but logical outcome for a human society that has turned its back on God. The transformation of humans into robots who are devoid of the sublime emotions of gratitude, compassion, self-sacrifice, and love is hardly surprising. Without reading futurist theories, Śrīla Prabhupāda summarizes:

> '*... People depended on nature's gifts of fruits and flowers without industrial enterprises promoting filthy huts and slums for residential quarters. Advancement of civilization is estimated not on the growth of mills and factories to deteriorate the finer instincts of the human being, but on developing the potent spiritual instincts of human beings and giving them a chance to go back to Godhead. Development of factories and mills is called ugra-karmā, or pungent activities, and such activities deteriorate the finer sentiments*

of the human being and society to form a dungeon of demons.'

Śrīmad-Bhāgavatam 1.11.12, purport

The Vedic Alternative

Modern post-industrial society is rapidly transforming God's world into a casemate for demons. The main cause is the ideological foundation of materialism, which generates three base material emotions – attachment (*rāga*), fear (*bhaya*) and anger (*krodha*). In such a seriously ill society of crippled and unhappy people, the only reasonable alternative is the social model of Vedic society. It is based on overcoming these three stressful emotions through devotion to the Lord and the development of sublime emotions of love for Him.

vīta-rāga-bhaya-krodhā
man-mayā mām upāśritāḥ
bahavo jñāna-tapasā
pūtā mad-bhāvam āgatāḥ

'Being freed from attachment, fear and anger,
being fully absorbed in Me and taking refuge in Me,
many, many persons in the past became purified
by knowledge of Me – and thus they all attained
transcendental love for Me.'

Bhagavad-gītā 4.10

Śrīla Prabhupāda describes the main principle of such a society:

'... All these natural gifts are dependent on the mercy of the Lord. What we need, therefore, is to be obedient to the laws of the Lord and achieve the perfection of human life by devotional service.'

Śrīmad-Bhāgavatam 1.8.40, purport

Modern materialistic Western civilization inflates one's false ego. An excessively inflated false ego fosters *rāga* – attachment, thirst for enjoyments, and *dveṣa* – dislike, envy, enmity towards other people. *Rāga* and *dveṣa* are twin brothers. When we face any threats in achieving our insatiable desire to enjoy, we experience either fear (if the threat is stronger than us) or anger (if the threat is weaker). Thus, *dveṣa* manifests in the form of these two emotions – fear and anger. Attachment, fear, and anger are the three emotions of survival.

Vedic culture teaches people to resist these base emotions. Krishna says the confrontation of materialistic emotions is to practice *jñāna-tapas* – austerity in knowledge. Caring for the welfare of others, we can overcome attachment. By giving respect to and receiving protection from elders and those who are stronger than us, we overcome fear. Nurturing a friendly attitude towards all living beings helps us overcome anger.

The first principle of caring for others is to willingly feed anyone who asks, even if it means we starve. The story of Mahārāja Rantideva in the *Śrīmad-Bhāgavatam* exemplifies this. Śrīla Prabhupāda also explains that in Vedic times, before sitting down at the table, a family man would go out and call, 'Is anyone hungry? Come, we will feed everyone!' This is the sacred duty of every person: first to feed others before having the right to sit down at the table. If we cook only for ourselves, we 'eat' sin: *bhuñjate te tv aghaṁ pāpā/ye pacanty ātma-kāraṇāt.*[1]

Our connection with the material world is primarily based on attachment to food. The deep rootedness of this attachment reveals itself when we try to fast for just a day. Therefore, it is a basic commandment of Vedic culture to feed everyone and treat everyone generously. No matter what time a guest knocks on your door, feed them. God will be pleased with you. This is the main cure for attachment.

1 *Bhagavad-gītā* 3.13.

The second unshakable principle of Vedic culture is to respect seniors. We respect the principle of hierarchy when we do this, which is a fundamental law of creation. The senior is not necessarily somebody who is older than us but anyone who surpasses us in something. Respecting seniors helps us overcome fear and always feel protected. When we respect superior people, we automatically receive their blessings and guidance. Their wisdom, instructions and above all good wishes protect us in all difficulties of life.

In the Western World, a young person regards older relatives as hindrances to their enjoyment. The tragic mythical King Oedipus, who killed his father, married his mother, and became the next king, is a paradigmatic figure for all Western culture. He symbolizes the ever-existing rebellion of juniors against their elders, which deprives juniors of the blessings that come from above.

Our *dveṣa*, hatred or dislike for elders, begins when we refuse to recognize their seniority or look down on them. In the *Mahābhārata*, Krishna tells Arjuna, 'Showing disrespect to those who are worthy of respect is equal to killing them.'[1] According to Krishna, merely addressing an elder by 'you' in the singular is enough to kill him. The Pāṇḍava brothers, who unconditionally honored Yudhiṣṭhira's seniority, are an example of strict adherence to this principle. Conversely, Duryodhana personified an atheistic denial of it.

The third principle is *ahiṁsā*, non-violence or friendliness, based on the deep understanding of the equality of all living beings. By observing this principle, we overcome our tendency to exploit those who are vulnerable or weaker than us and treat them with respect. The heart-warming emotion of friendliness is the cure for anger.

1 *'yad avamānaṁ labhate mahāntaṁ tadā jīvan mṛta ity ucyate saḥ,' Mahābhārata, Karṇa-parva* 49.65.

Based on these three principles, Vedic culture helps us overcome *rāga* and *dveṣa*. Thus, we weaken the false ego and begin to eliminate our ignorant identification with the material body. Of course, these principles work only in a God-centered society, where the main driving force for all people is the desire to please the Lord. Since it is difficult to motivate a *Kali-yuga* person without promising material prosperity, Śrīla Prabhupāda explains in his purport that true material prosperity is entirely based on the Lord's favor.

* * *

Many social philosophers and thinkers agree that modern industrial and post-industrial society is seriously ill.[1] The symptoms of this disease are our increasing alienation from nature and from each other, as well as a loss of the meaning of life. The psychological consequences of such alienation are extremely deplorable: boredom, anxiety, stress, personality degradation, an increase in the number of suicides, and most importantly, our inner emptiness, which we try to backfill with feverish activities, drugs, and all sorts of entertainment.

Following the three principles of Vedic culture helps us overcome our alienation and feel connected to others. But the most important reward is the gradual restoration of our connection with God, which alone gives us wholeness and fulfillment. Therefore, in her next prayers, Queen Kuntī directly asks Krishna to reinforce that connection and take away all attachments that interfere with it.

1 See, for example: E. Fromm, The Sane Society.

Prayer for Absolute Purity

atha viśveśa viśvātman
viśva-mūrte svakeṣu me
sneha-pāśam imaṁ chindhi
dṛḍhaṁ pāṇḍuṣu vṛṣṇiṣu

'O Lord of the universe, Soul of the universe,
O Personality of the form of the universe, please,
therefore, sever my tie of affection for my kinsmen,
the Pāṇḍavas and the Vṛṣṇis.'

Śrīmad-Bhāgavatam 1.8.41

Queen Kuntī begins 1.8.41 with '*atha*' – 'therefore,' to indicate that this and the following verse are a summary, a logical conclusion, of all she has said. Thereafter, she will complete her prayers with a final verse. For now, she contemplates Krishna standing before her. She knows He is God, and she knows that firsthand. To emphasize this once again, she turns to Krishna with the words:

- ***viśveśa***, Lord of the universe – because He rules over the universe in the form of eternal time, or providence.

- ***viśvātma***, Soul of the universe – because He resides in every atom and heart of every living being as Paramātmā to maintain the universe.

- ***viśva-mūrti***, the personification of the universe – because He creates this world from His own self, thus becoming the material cause of creation, its *upādāna-kāraṇa*.

In our conditioned state, we are dependent on time, the state of our mind and body, and the circumstances of life. Using these three names, Queen Kuntī appears to say, 'O Krishna, in truth, our fate depends on You alone, our existence depends on You alone, and the circumstances of our lives depend on You alone.' She reiterates what she has already told Him in the previous four verses. After such a build-up, it is essential to understand what she asks of almighty Krishna in this verse.

Queen Kuntī could have asked for one of several things, 'You can do anything. Therefore, since all my grandchildren were killed in the war, send me new grandchildren to continue our glorious lineage.' She might have said, 'You are God. You have given us everything we have, so please go on pouring Your mercy upon us, Your faithful servants,' or 'Let us reign for a long, long time,' or 'We depend entirely on You. You protect us, so please stay with us always and never leave us.'

But no! Her request is, 'You can do anything, so please cut the knot of affection in my heart towards my sons and my father's family.'

Only by understanding the underlying logic of Queen Kuntī's plea can we say that we have understood her heart. Let us remember everything she has said so far. She began her prayers with a question, 'You come here to bestow love for Yourself (*bhakti-yoga*) upon those who are pure in heart. What are we women, whose hearts are full of so many worldly attachments, to do then?'

Answering her own question, she outlines what we (whose hearts are full of material desires) should do:

- chant God's names, which contain the seed of love.
- serve His form, full of beauty.
- cast off the sense of ownership in the material world and try to understand that God's mercy is behind all events in life.
- reflect on the stories of God's pastimes and try to see

how His unlimited love manifests in His activities in this world.
- realize that Krishna comes here in various incarnations for the sole purpose of enabling people to hear, retell and remember the pastimes – which breaks us free from the rapid current of karma and permits us to begin serving God directly.

Thus, in a few verses, Queen Kuntī has described the path of *bhakti yoga*, available to everyone. By following this path, we gradually detach our attention from the world of matter and redirect it inwards – towards God. This provides some primary spiritual experience, a glimmer of the causeless happiness that permeates spiritual existence.

Our material attachments persist not so much because of material life as from the lack of spiritual experience. In the poetic words of Osip Mandelstam, we love this 'poor land' because we have not seen any other:

I am tired of living – to death.
No longer life's beauties are welcomed.
But I love my misfortunate homeland
For I haven't known anything else.[1]

People come to God, to a church or a temple, and ask Him to fulfill their material desires only because they feel they are part of this world and material life seems the only reality. God and the spiritual dimension are too ethereal for ordinary people, even if they are believers. Godly people turn to God only to receive their 'daily' bread and resolve other equally 'pressing' problems.

Regular practice of devotional service changes our perception, step by step. Gradually, our awareness of God's love

1 Osip Mandelstam, Children's Stories – are all I shall read, 1908, Translated by Maya Jouravel.

and the visible manifestation of His mercy in our lives becomes deeper and deeper. God and spiritual existence become more and more an urgent reality.

However, our attempts to focus inwardly will inevitably meet a huge obstacle – our complete involvement in the world of matter, to which we are tied by myriads of subtle and gross bonds. In human consciousness, material self-identification does not lose ground so readily. We cling tightly to our self-image. Meantime, all the negative emotions that accompany material existence constantly pull our minds back to our bodies, which prevents us from having deep spiritual experiences.

śokāmarṣādibhir-bhāvair
ākrāntaṁ yasya mānasam
katham tatra mukundasya
sphūrttiḥ-sambhānā bhavet

> 'How can Lord Mukunda's form, even for a moment, appear in the heart of one whose mind is overwhelmed with grief, anger and other negative emotions?'
>
> *Padma Purāṇa.*
> Quoted from *Bhakti-rasāmṛta-sindhu* 1.2.115

Negative material emotions distort our consciousness and tightly bind it to the body. For those whose minds are constantly agitated, a spiritual experience remains a pale shadow, a semblance of a magical dream. Pure spiritual emotions are as incompatible with the severe material reality just as a beautiful rainforest flower is alien to the grainy dunes of a sun-scorched desert and cannot take root there.

Again and again, we might try to rise beyond mundane life but are forced back down to deal with material desires that hold us captive. We can feel doomed in our struggles with fear, grief, endless anxiety, and guilt. In his prayers, Lord Brahmā, laments the predicament:

tāvad bhayaṁ draviṇa-deha-suhṛn-nimittaṁ
śokaḥ spṛhā paribhavo vipulaś ca lobhaḥ
tāvan mamety asad-avagraha ārti-mūlaṁ
yāvan na te 'ṅghrim abhayaṁ pravṛṇīta lokaḥ

'O my Lord, the people of the world are embarrassed by all material anxieties – they are always afraid. They always try to protect wealth, body and friends, they are filled with lamentation and unlawful desires and paraphernalia, and they avariciously base their undertakings on the perishable conceptions of 'my' and 'mine.' As long as they do not take shelter of Your safe lotus feet, they are full of such anxieties.'

Śrīmad-Bhāgavatam 3.9.6

Of all material attachments, affection for family and friends is one of the strongest. We are often willing to sacrifice ourselves for the good of our loved ones. Human society praises this quality. However, affection to near and dear ones (and not to others) is a manifestation of our false ego – for what is a material person but the sum of their family ties? Is this not the weakness of heart that Queen Kuntī bemoans at the start with 'What are we, women, supposed to do?'

Even Arjuna, a valiant warrior, despaired when he realized that all his kin would die in the war. Interestingly, when he stood between the two armies, Krishna's first words to him were, 'Just behold, O Pārtha, all the Kurus assembled here.' (*Bhagavad-gītā* 1.25)

Madhusūdana Sarasvatī, the famed commentator of the scripture, wrote about this moment, '...realizing that Arjuna was overwhelmed with sorrow and illusion, [Krishna] addresses Arjuna with a sarcastic smile: "Pārtha, O Pārtha ..." He means to say, "Now your ties to Pṛthā, who, like any woman is subject to grief and illusion, have become apparent."[1] This is not a disdainful condemnation of women as such, but an impartial description of the soft feminine nature which makes women more prone to grief. Śrīla Prabhupāda describes the conflict in Queen Kuntī's heart:

> *'The Pāṇḍavas are her own sons, and the Vṛṣṇis are the members of her paternal family. Kṛṣṇa was equally related to both the families. Both the families required the Lord's help because both were dependent devotees of the Lord. Śrīmatī Kuntīdevī wished Śrī Kṛṣṇa to remain with her sons the Pāṇḍavas, but by His doing so her paternal house would be bereft of the benefit. All these partialities troubled the mind of Kuntī, and therefore she desired to cut off the affectionate tie.*
>
> *Śrīmad-Bhāgavatam* 1.8.41, purport

Eventually, any person traversing the spiritual path faces this problem: choosing between attachment for God or attachment for family and friends. Some regard this a far-fetched problem, 'How can an innocent attachment to family and children become a hindrance in our relationship with God?' they say. 'Doesn't God encourage us to "Love your neighbor as yourself?"'[2] However, they forget that this is the second most important commandment, while the first one is, 'Love the Lord your God with all your heart, and with all your soul, and with all your mind.'[3]

Thus, we can and should love our near and dear ones but only after we have surrendered all our heart, all our soul and all our mind to God. When love for family and friends is a reflection

1 Madhusudana Sarasvatī. *Gudartha-dipika*, 1.24-5.

2 The Gospel of Matthew, 22:39.

3 The Gospel of Matthew, 22:37.

of our love for God, it becomes true love that no more enslaves us nor them. But if this so-called love competes with our love for God, then it is not love at all but material attachment. Hence, Queen Kuntī's seemingly cruel words echo those of the Gospel, 'Let the dead bury the dead.'[1] Jesus spoke these words to a disciple who wanted to stay at home rather than follow Him and commit to spiritual responsibilities.

Attaining the highest goal, we simultaneously achieve all lower goals. However, if in our consciousness the lower goal is on the same plane as the higher goal, it becomes a hindrance in achieving the higher aim. Love of God includes love for everything, but independent 'love' for anyone else prevents us from completely trusting God, let alone loving Him. Vedic scriptures have presented a clear hierarchy of goals:

tyajed ekam kulasyarthe grāmasyarthe kulam tyajet
grāmam janapadāsyarthe atmarthe prithivim tyajet

'One person is to be renounced for the sake of family, family is to be renounced for the sake of village, village is to be renounced for the sake of the whole country. But for God's sake we must be ready to renounce the entire world.'
Mahābhārata, Adi-parva 107.32

Śrīla Prabhupāda expands on this:

'A pure devotee cuts off the limited ties of affection for his family and widens his activities of devotional service for all forgotten souls. The typical example is the band of Six Gosvāmīs, who followed the path of Lord Caitanya. All of them belonged to the most

1 Another of the disciples said to him, 'Lord, let me first go and bury my father.' And Jesus said to him, 'Follow me, and leave the dead to bury their own dead.' The Gospel of Matthew, 8:21-22.

enlightened and cultured rich families of the higher castes, but for the benefit of the mass of population they left their comfortable homes and became mendicants. To cut off all family affection means to broaden the field of activities. Without doing this, no one can be qualified as a brāhmaṇa, *a king, a public leader or a devotee of the Lord. The Personality of Godhead, as an ideal king, showed this by example. Śrī Rāmacandra cut off the tie of affection for His beloved wife to manifest the qualities of an ideal king. Such personalities as a brāhmaṇa, a devotee, a king or a public leader must be very broad-minded in discharging their respective duties.'*

Śrīmad-Bhāgavatam 1.8.41, purport

The *Nīti Śāstra* also shares this opinion:

ayam nijāḥ paro veti
gaṇanām laghu-cetasām
udāra-caritānām tu
vasudhaiva kutumbakam

'Only petty people always divide the world into friends and foes. To open-minded people, the whole world is one family.'

Hitopadeśa 1.71

Material attachment to some people in this world inevitably breeds enmity towards others, in accordance with the principle 'my friend's enemy is my enemy.' Or, over time it can even turn into hatred of those whom we have been 'loving.' Anger is an inseparable companion of attachments, it is *kāma*'s younger brother. It is called *kāmanuja* in Sanskrit. Spite and anger in the heart drive God out of it, for He is ruler of the universe and harbors no enmity towards anyone.

Looking deeply into her heart, Queen Kuntī realizes that material attachment for her kin and children is still present and clouding her relationship with Krishna. Just as a single, tiniest speck of dirt is stark on a snow-white sheet, so in a devotee's pure heart, any material attachment (even the most insignificant) is perceived clearly and painfully. Queen Kuntī realizes she can never uproot these attachments from her heart by herself, so she begs Krishna to do so.

Her prayer is the prayer of a purified heart for absolute purity, a prayer of a divided heart for utmost sincerity, a prayer of a humble heart for even greater humility. This is the prayer of a surrendered person for pure love. The Lord gives us everything anyway – there is no point in asking Him for anything except purity, integrity, and love. Without His mercy, we cannot attain these by ourselves. Without God's help, we can never get all the way to Him. Śrīla Prabhupāda offers concluding words on this:

> *'Śrīmatī Kuntīdevī was conscious of this fact and being weak she prayed to be free from such bondage of family affection. The Lord is addressed as the Lord of the universe, or the Lord of the universal mind, indicating His all-powerful ability to cut the hard knot of family affection. Therefore, it is sometimes experienced that the Lord, out of His special affinity towards a weak devotee, breaks the family affection by force of circumstances arranged by His all-powerful energy. By doing so He causes the devotee to become completely dependent on Him and thus clears the path for his going back to Godhead.'*
> *Śrīmad-Bhāgavatam* 1.8.41, purport

* * *

Some of us might object, 'Wait, the Pāṇḍavas and the Vṛṣṇis were pure devotees and Krishna's servants. How could attachment to them contaminate Queen Kuntī's heart?' Queen Kuntī provides an answer in the next, penultimate verse, which Śrīla Prabhupāda explains in detail.

The Unstoppable Flow of Love

tvayi me 'nanya-viṣayā
matir madhu-pate 'sakṛt
ratim udvahatād addhā
gaṅgevaugham udanvati

'O Lord of Madhu, as the Ganges forever flows to the sea without hindrance, let my attraction be constantly drawn unto You without being diverted to anyone else.'

Śrīmad-Bhāgavatam 1.8.42

Queen Kuntī may have asked Krishna to cut the knot of material attachment in her heart, but her desire isn't freedom from material attachment per se. Her actual goal is continuous, unclouded devotion to Krishna. Therefore, Viśvanātha Cakravartī begins his commentary on this verse by asking on Krishna's behalf:

'Does this mean that you want to attain Brahman? If you cut the knot of attachment to the Vṛṣṇis in your heart, you will also destroy your attachment to Me because I am one of the Vṛṣṇi clan.'

'Of course not,' replies Queen Kuntī. 'I want a mighty stream of affection and love for You (*rati*) to flood my mind (*matiḥ*). Let the flow of love for You be so swift and overpowering that it prevents my mind from distraction towards anything else (*ananya-viṣayā*). I know that Your devotees are nondifferent from You, therefore without attachment to them there can be no attachment to You. Such love for You, which excludes Your devotees will never please You. Therefore, let no other attachment remain in my mind besides affection for You and Your devotees.'

She continues, 'Yes, I asked You to break the bonds of love that bind me to the Pāṇḍavas and Yādavas, who are Your devotees. By this, I ask You to sever all *material* bonds that have arisen in my heart because of my identification with this body. I didn't ask to sever my loving attachment to You. I meant only those attachments that bind me to matter. (Italics are our emphasis.)

'May all obstacles in the form of material attachments and aversions for people of this world never break my connection with You. May they never come between us. May they prove powerless in blocking the stream of my consciousness from rushing towards You (utkarṣena vāhatat), just as nothing can stop the Ganga on its way to the ocean.

'As the Ganga always carries its waters (ogham) to the ocean, the final abode of all small and large rivers, so may my mind attain You, the abode of all devotees. May my mind always be full of attachment to You. And, as the Ganga sweeps away all obstacles on its path, so may my mind pay no heed to obstacles that arise when thinking of You.'

This prayer describes the essence (*svarūpa*) of love of Godhead. Upon attaining true love, one's consciousness turns into an unstoppable stream rushing towards the Beloved. It never dissipates. The very experience of such concentration brings one such bliss that interest in anything else, including personal happiness or grief ceases. Krishna describes the movements of this love in the *Bhagavad-gītā*, 'The thoughts of My pure devotees dwell in Me, their lives are fully devoted to Me.'[1] Such love, unlike its material surrogates, sets one absolutely free. We will explore this in greater depth.

The Bondage of Fear and the Freedom of Undivided Love

According to Śrīla Jīva Gosvāmī, the disease of the conditioned living being in the material world is aversion to God (*bhagavad-bahirmukhata*). The literal meaning of *bahirmukha* is 'one who has looked away.' Having looked away from God, the *jīva* begins to contemplate God's external, illusory energy instead. This evokes numerous material attachments in the heart, which we can expect because the soul cannot exist without having attachments. The energy of these attachments manifests as various emotions that rage in the heart. Śrīla Prabhupāda explains further:

> *'To cut off the tie of all other affections does not mean complete negation of the finer elements, like affection for someone else. This is not possible. A living being, whoever he may be, must have this feeling of affection for others because this is a symptom of life. The symptoms of life, such as desire, anger, hankerings, feelings of attraction, etc., cannot be annihilated.'*
>
> *Śrīmad-Bhāgavatam* 1.8.42, purport

In the material world, we give away a piece of our heart in each

1 *'mac-cittā mad-gata-prāṇā,' Bhagavad-gītā*, 10.9. In his *Prīti-sandarbha*, *Anuccheda* 78, Śrīla Jīva Gosvāmī quotes this verse as an illustration of *svarūpa prema*, the inner essence of pure love.

attachment – to spouse, parents, children, work, country, causes or even religion. These all become part of our false ego, turning it into a mosaic of all kinds of attachments.

According to the principles of logic (*nyāya*), anything in existence that consists of parts is destined for destruction. This is true for us as countless material goals and attachments split the stream of consciousness, rendering our minds unstable and distracted. The fragmentation and internal conflict between competing affections weaken the mind, and breed sickness in the body. The primary ancient text of Ayurveda, *Aṣṭāṅga Hṛdaya*, begins with the words *rāgādi rogaḥ* – '*rāga* is the primordial disease of the living being.'

A car cannot move smoothly on a road if its wheels are misaligned – it will bump and jolt. Same goes for those who place their material attachments, stemming from the false ego, at the center of their life – they will bump and jolt too. The egocentric world, split by countless attachments and devoid of integrity, dooms the person to destruction.

Each attachment gains power over us. The stronger the attachment, the stronger its power. Imperceptibly, we become enslaved by the attachment. The worst problem comes when our attachments clash and turn our hearts into battlefields. Each attachment wants to claim occupancy at the center of our being. In struggling over that place, our attachments create inner conflict and an inevitable sense of guilt.

Temporarily, we might succeed in reconciling opposing material attachments and appeasing everyone around us. But open conflict is as inevitable as the war at Kurukṣetra. The desire to please everyone brings about precisely the opposite effect – our so-called love generates more and more hostility within us and towards us. The inner and outer conflicts can tear us apart. Sadly, human beings become so accustomed to a state of duality and guilt that they consider it the norm, not understanding how to exist without it.

Bhagavad-gītā begins amid Arjuna's turmoil as he faces a difficult choice. He sees those dear to his heart on both sides of the battlefield. Fighting on one side means killing others. Either way, his false ego, which is the sum of his material attachments, will have to die. Thus, Arjuna is overwhelmed with guilt and fear of death, which he mistakes to be compassion.

All of us go through similar crises in our lives when the false ego disintegrates again and again. The soul, yearning for steadiness, has identified with the aging and dying body and those it is attached to, and thus lives in constant fear: *sadā samudvigna-dhiyām asad-grahāt* – 'The minds of those who cling to their material body and material attachments are always in a state of anxiety.'[1] The anxiety that torments the soul is a symptom of the false ego: 'I am in danger. Do something urgently!' Fear is the original emotion underlying material existence that causes us endless suffering. It manifests as other transient emotions such as envy, passion, affection, enthusiasm, pride, the urge to rule, the desire to defend one's righteousness, anxiety, tension, guilt, lust, anger, grief, hope, and despair. Since these emotions are generated by the fear of death, they bring suffering. Kavi Yogendra speaks about this:

bhayaṁ dvitīyābhiniveśataḥ syād
īśād apetasya viparyayo 'smṛtiḥ

'Fear arises when the living entity misidentifies himself as the material body because of absorption in the external, illusory energy of the Lord. Thus, by turning away from the Supreme Lord, the living being forgets his constitutional position as a servant of the Lord.'

Śrīmad-Bhāgavatam 11.2.37

1 Paraphrase of *Śrīmad-Bhāgavatam* 7.5.5.

Some people realize that material attachments and the emotions generated by them are the root cause of all suffering. They try to give these up, renounce the world, go to a monastery, and break all ties. However, they only numb themselves by suppressing in their minds 'the symptoms of life, such as desire, anger, hankerings, feelings of attraction' This becomes an attempt to commit spiritual suicide and is not a real solution to the problem of the fear of death and dealing with accompanying negative emotions. Therefore, Śrīla Prabhupāda and previous *ācāryas* of our *sampradāya* offer a fundamentally different solution:

> *'The symptoms of life, such as desire, anger, hankerings, feelings of attraction, etc., cannot be annihilated. Only the objective has to be changed. Desire cannot be negated, but in devotional service the desire is changed only for the service of the Lord in place of desire for sense gratification.'*

Śrīla Prabhupāda used 'objective,' another word for 'goal,' to stress that we must turn ourselves a hundred and eighty degrees to see a new goal before us – God. To make God the new object of all our efforts will completely change us. Śrīla Prabhupāda goes on to say:

> *'In the Bhagavad-gītā we can see that Arjuna desired not to fight with his brothers and relations just to satisfy his own personal desires. But when he heard the message of the Lord, Śrīmad Bhagavad-gītā, he changed his decision and served the Lord. And for his doing so, he became a famous devotee of the Lord, for it is declared in all the scriptures that Arjuna attained spiritual perfection by devotional service to the Lord in friendship. The fighting was there, the friendship was there, Arjuna was there, and Kṛṣṇa was there, but Arjuna became a different person by devotional service.'*
>
> *Śrīmad-Bhāgavatam* 1.8.42, purport

When God (and not matter) becomes the true goal of all our aspirations and yearnings, love banishes fear from the heart. Our numerous material goals and aspirations must be replaced by a single spiritual goal – Krishna. Our numerous material attachments must be ousted by a single attachment – attachment to Krishna. Only by placing God in the center can we reconcile and harmonize our numerous clashing false centers. Thus, by changing the goal, we heal. That is, we restore our heart's integrity. This brings human consciousness back to its original joyful state of unity and love. This is the deep meaning of Queen Kuntī's request – she prays for Krishna to grant her pure, unclouded love.

In everyday life, we use 'love' so often and inappropriately that it has long lost its original significance. Mistakenly, we pass off our material attachments as love but true love for another person means the desire to make them happy. The lover is always happy when the beloved is happy. Where there is love, there is no room for jealousy, which is only a sign of selfish affection. Therefore, true love never turns into hatred:

sarvathā dhvaṁsa-rahitaṁ saty
api dhvaṁsa-kāraṇe
yad bhāva-bandhanaṁ yūnoḥ
sa premā parikīrtitaḥ

> 'If lovers have every reason to break up, but despite this, they go on loving each other, the relationship that binds them together is called pure love.'
> *Ujjvala-nīlamaṇi* 14.63

Often, when saying, 'I love you,' people mean something completely different: 'I want you to make me happy.' Their so-called love is nothing more than the belief that the other is going to please them. Alas, in this world, 'love' for a person is not much different from 'love' of chocolate. The only difference is that 'love of chocolate' is never unrequited and therefore never turns into hatred.

True love is a stream of consciousness directed towards the other person. Thus, Queen Kuntī begs for her consciousness to flow towards Krishna, as the Ganges surges towards the ocean. This echoes the sentiments of true love – where the lover thinks always of the well-being of the beloved.

This is unlike material lovers who believe that love means the other person should always think about them. A woman wants the man to protect her, fulfill all her desires, and constantly think of her. A man wants the woman to take care of him, please him, and also constantly think of him. When they see someone who they imagine is capable of giving them what they lack, they feel an attachment that they mistake for love. When 'in love' they remain self-centered, and if the object of their affection does not give them what they expect, their so-called love instantly turns into its opposite. Such partners can easily justify their own infidelity, while being unable to forgive the unfaithfulness of the other.

The material affection that people of this world take for love is a product of their egocentric consciousness. In a computer's operating system, each operating system can only run programs written specifically for it. Other programs just do not work there. Similarly, our conditioned consciousness formed by the false ego is suitable for programs that generate three basic negative emotions – fear, grief, and anger. Other negative emotions like pride, envy, dejection, are also compatible with it.

In contrast, consciousness formed by the true ego as God's servant is suitable for programs that generate love. True love, just like fear, gives rise to a multitude of transient emotions – humility and pride, anxiety and delight, despair, and hope. These are the eternal companions of love. And just as material emotions caused by fear only increase suffering and pain, spiritual emotions generated by love increase joy and bliss. However, for this to happen, our attachment to God must become undivided. Kavi Yogendra advised how to do this:

tan-māyayāto budha ābhajet taṁ
bhaktyaikayeśaṁ guru-devatātm

'This bewildering, fearful condition is effected by the potency for illusion, called māyā. Therefore, an intelligent person should engage unflinchingly in the unalloyed devotional service of the Lord, under the guidance of a bona fide spiritual master, whom he should accept as his worshipable deity and as his very life and soul.'

Śrīmad-Bhāgavatam 11.2.37

Pure *bhakti* (*eka-bhakti* or *ananya-bhakti*[1]) alone can solve the problem of fear. All other mixed forms of devotional service are incapable of solving this most profound existential problem. Nothing but undivided devotion can restore integrity to our fragmented consciousness and make us happy; this is the true goal of life. Śrīla Prabhupāda writes:

'Śrīmatī Kuntī wanted to serve the Lord without diversion, and that was her prayer. This unalloyed devotion is the ultimate goal of life. Our attention is usually diverted to the service of something which is non godly or not in the program of the Lord. When the program is changed into the service of the Lord, that is to say when the senses are purified in relation with the service of the Lord, it is called pure unalloyed devotional service. Śrīmatī Kuntīdevī wanted that perfection and prayed for it from the Lord.'

Śrīmad-Bhāgavatam 1.8.42, purport

Such love is Bhagavān's exclusive property, and He is in no

1 To describe pure *bhakti*, scriptures use many different words of similar meaning: *ananya*, *avyabhicāri*, *uttama*, *śuddha*, *ekānta*, etc.

hurry to bestow it in hearts that harbor extraneous motives. Śukadeva Gosvāmī warns, 'Those engaged in getting the Lord's favor attain liberation from the Lord very easily, but He does not very easily give the opportunity to render direct service unto Him.'[1]

Thus, undivided love is preceded by an *undivided desire* for such love – and not some coldish intellectual endeavor but a genuine, ardent yearning that has become a part of our personality. Before Krishna can believe our prayer for love of God, we ourselves must believe it. That is why Kavi Yogendra mentions the spiritual master: *guru-devatātmā*. For transformation to take place, one must begin serving the spiritual master.

In a relationship with the spiritual master, a sincere person will be able to understand what the spiritual master wants. The disciple will give due consideration to the spiritual teacher rather than expect consideration for themselves. We can purge ourselves of the age-old habit to offend and learn to serve in the proper way. Moreover, by serving the spiritual master, we can purify our desire to attain love of Krishna and imbibe the guru's desire and mood to serve the Lord.

At the *sādhana* stage, the spiritual master and service to him will temporarily occupy the central part of the disciple's consciousness. If the yearning to serve the spiritual master is sincere, a prayer will spontaneously spring from the spiritual master's heart, 'O Lord! Grant my disciple love for You. Let no other desires remain in his heart!' As soon as the disciple is ready, the guru will gladly give up his place in the disciple's heart so Krishna can take over.

However, if our attachment to devotees and the spiritual master is materially motivated, then it will not turn into love

1 *'muktiṁ dadāti karhicit sma na bhakti-yogam,'* *Śrīmad-Bhāgavatam* 5.6.18.

nor help us remember God. Instead, it will lead to offenses and resentment. Outwardly, material and spiritual attachments look similar, which is why it is important to learn to discriminate. For example, a disciple may love the guru because he is kind and treats him well. This relationship may look spiritual from the outside, but the real motivation behind this 'love' is purely material and betrays itself the moment the disciple feels that the guru does not pay him enough attention. Spiritual attachment to the guru is starkly different. Dedicated to the guru's mood, instruction and purpose, the disciple seeks solely to serve him under any circumstances.

Gold and brass are outwardly almost indistinguishable, but when placed in acid, the gold shines all the more brightly, while the brass is corroded by the acid and tarnishes. The analogy fits well with a disciple's inner relationship with their spiritual master or indeed with others. Obstacles and trials make true love even stronger and destroy counterfeit material 'love.'

Material attachments make us suffer, while real love brings about endless happiness. Attachment pushes us to focus on ourselves, while love opens our heart towards everyone. Attachment hardens the heart, while love makes it softer and more compassionate. Attachment blinds and deepens ignorance, while spiritual love helps us gain true vision. Attachment enslaves, and spiritual love sets us free. Śrīla Prabhupāda gives further insight into recognizing the difference between spiritual and material relationships:

> *'Her affection for the Pāṇḍavas and the Vṛṣṇis is not out of the range of devotional service because the service of the Lord and the service of the devotees are identical. Sometimes service to the devotee is more valuable than service to the Lord. But here the affection of Kuntīdevī for the Pāṇḍavas and the Vṛṣṇis was due to family relation. This tie of affection*

in terms of material relation is the relation of māyā because the relations of the body or the mind are due to the influence of the external energy. Relations of the soul, established in relation with the Supreme Soul, are factual relations. When Kuntīdevī wanted to cut off the family relation, she meant to cut off the relation of the skin. The skin relation is the cause of material bondage, but the relation of the soul is the cause of freedom. This relation of the soul to the soul can be established by the medium of the relation with the Supersoul. Seeing in the darkness is not seeing. But seeing by the light of the sun means to see the sun and everything else which was unseen in the darkness. That is the way of devotional service.'
Śrīmad-Bhāgavatam 1.8.42, purport

Trying to love others in this world is like trying to see something in pitch darkness. The soul naturally yearns to love and feel kinship with other souls, like eyes are eager to enjoy colors and shapes. But just as attempts to see the world in the dark cause pain to the eyes, and even a complete loss of sight, so our efforts to love others exclusively and independent of God often harden the heart instead of softening it.

Of course, when the eyes get used to the darkness, one may discern some likeness to forms. The faint light of a candle may show snatches of colors for a brief moment. In the same way, a brief experience of material love can open our hearts and offer a glimmer of enlightenment of the infinite bliss of spiritual love. Bella Akhmadulina captures the feeling in a line, 'Love for the beloved is tenderness for everyone, near and far.'[1] We are granted this experience to intensify the craving for the sun of love of God to rise in our hearts as soon as possible. In this light we will be able to see and love the entire world. Such is the path of devotional service.

1 Bella Akhmadulina, 'House'.

Queen Kuntī prays for pure love because she understands that it includes everything else: knowledge, freedom, peace, happiness, security, strength, life, and even material prosperity, if necessary. This is the essence of her prayers. We can follow her and pray to Krishna,

'Let my connection with You become uninterrupted! Let me always feel this connection in my heart and always think lovingly of You!'

Repeating this prayer over and over, one day we will also realize that we need nothing but love, and that love alone can make us happy. We will ourselves believe in this prayer, and then Krishna will also believe us and respond. Outwardly, everything will remain as it is – the battles and the friendships – while inside we will feel an inextricable connection with Krishna, and tears of gratitude will flow spontaneously from our eyes. Hare Krishna Hare Krishna Krishna Krishna Hare Hare/Hare Rāma Hare Rāma Rāma Rāma Hare Hare.

Śrī Krishna, Krishna's Friend

śrī-kṛṣṇa kṛṣṇa-sakha vṛṣṇy-ṛṣabhāvani-dhrug-
rājanya-vaṁśa-dahanānapavarga-vīrya
govinda go-dvija-surārti-harāvatāra
yogeśvarākhila-guro bhagavan namas te

'O Kṛṣṇa, O friend of Arjuna, O chief amongst the descendants of Vṛṣṇi, You are the destroyer of those political parties which are disturbing elements on this earth. Your prowess never deteriorates. You are the proprietor of the transcendental abode, and You descend to relieve the distresses of the cows, the brāhmaṇas and the devotees. You possess all mystic powers, and You are the preceptor of the entire universe. You are the almighty God, and I offer You my respectful obeisances.'

Śrīmad-Bhāgavatam 1.8.43

In asking Krishna for undivided love for Him in the previous verse, Queen Kuntī simultaneously asked for true love for the Pāṇḍavas and Yādavas. One who loves Krishna cannot but love His devotees. The devotees become an inexhaustible source of inspiration, '*uddīpana*' – something that ignites love. Our love for Krishna gets stronger when we remember how others love Him and how He reciprocates their love. By worshiping the love that others have for Krishna, we can, to some extent, share in their love. *Sādhu-saṅga* is based on this principle. Therefore, our reason to love devotees is because of *their love for Krishna*, not their attitude towards us.

Queen Kuntī closes her prayers saying this. Directly and indirectly, she lists those who love Krishna, and by offering her obeisance to Krishna, she simultaneously offers her respect and love to all of them. She begins by calling Krishna 'friend of Arjuna' with the words '*Kṛṣṇa-sakha*.' At first sight, this seems strange. '*Kṛṣṇa-sakha*' translates to 'friend of Krishna,' which doesn't make sense in this context because it seems she is saying, 'O Krishna, who is friend of Krishna.' The logical name to use would have been '*Arjuna-sakha*.' But there is sweetness and depth to her choice.

Elsewhere in the *Mahābhārata*[1] we learn that Arjuna has ten other names. When he has to prove his identity to Prince Uttara, Arjuna recites his less known names and retells their origins. In his explanation, he reveals that he has also been named 'Krishna.' *kṛṣṇa ity eva daśamaṁ nāma cakre pīta mama/krisnava datasya sataḥ priya tvad bālakasya vai* – 'And my tenth name, Krishna, was given to me by my father out of love for me, his dark-skinned son, who was pious from birth (*sataḥ*).'

1 *Mahābhārata*, *Virāṭa-parva*, ch. 44.

Arjuna's use of '*sataḥ*' is ambiguous because apart from 'pious from birth,' it could mean 'eternal,' 'honest,' 'spiritual,' or 'connected to God.' Therefore, this line could easily translate to 'My father called me Krishna, knowing that I am eternally bound to the Supreme Lord Krishna.' Therefore, by calling Krishna '*Kṛṣṇa-sakha*,' Queen Kuntī expresses her admiration for the abiding love that binds her son to the Lord.

In the third line, Queen Kuntī calls Krishna 'Govinda', which usually denotes Krishna as the one who gives pleasure to cows. Śrīla Prabhupāda gives the name an unusual translation of 'proprietor of Golokadhāma, the transcendental abode.' In the Twelfth Canto, Sūta Gosvāmī recites a similar verse with the same meaning of the name:

> *śrī-kṛṣṇa kṛṣṇa-sakha vṛṣṇy-ṛṣabhāvani-dhrug-*
> *rājanya-vaṁśa-dahanānapavarga-vīrya*
> *govinda gopa-vanitā-vraja-bhṛtya-gīta*
> *tīrtha-śravaḥ śravaṇa-maṅgala pāhi bhṛtyān*

> 'O Kṛṣṇa, O friend of Arjuna, O chief among the descendants of Vṛṣṇi, You are the destroyer of those political parties that are disturbing elements on this earth. Your prowess never deteriorates. You are the proprietor of the transcendental abode, and Your most sacred glories, which are sung by Vṛndāvana's cowherd men and women and their servants, bestow all auspiciousness just by being heard. O Lord, please protect Your devotees.'
>
> *Śrīmad-Bhāgavatam* 12.11.25

The usage of 'Govinda' and its meaning by Queen Kuntī, Sūta Gosvāmī and Śrīla Prabhupāda concur because they want to show that Krishna is inextricably connected to his devotees. God is a person. Sweet loving bonds bind Him to the eternal inhabitants of the spiritual world. When He descends to the material world, He does so only to glorify His eternal devotees' love and to help people of this world attain that same love. This is the essence that Queen Kuntī expresses in her last prayers. Śrīla Prabhupāda summarizes her feelings:

> *'A summary of the Supreme Lord Śrī Kṛṣṇa is made herein by Śrīmatī Kuntīdevī. The almighty Lord has His eternal transcendental abode where He is engaged in keeping surabhi cows. He is served by hundreds and thousands of goddesses of fortune. He descends to the material world to reclaim His devotees and to annihilate the disturbing elements in groups of political parties and kings who are supposed to be in charge of administration work. He creates, maintains and annihilates by His unlimited energies, and still He is always full with prowess and does not deteriorate in potency. The cows, the brāhmaṇas and the devotees of the Lord are all objects of His special attention because they are very important factors for the general welfare of living beings.'*
>
> *Śrīmad-Bhāgavatam* 1.8.43, purport

Again, at the end of her last prayer, Queen Kuntī addresses Krishna as guru of the entire world (*akhila-guro*) thus expressing her gratitude to the Supreme Lord who descends into this world just to teach people the meaning of pure love.

Epilogue

sūta uvāca
pṛthayetthaṁ kala-padaiḥ
pariṇūtākhilodayaḥ
mandaṁ jahāsa vaikuṇṭho
mohayann iva māyayā

'Sūta Gosvāmī said: The Lord, thus hearing the prayers of Kuntīdevī, composed in choice words for His glorification, mildly smiled. That smile was as enchanting as His mystic power.'
Śrīmad-Bhāgavatam 1.8.44

Śrīla Prabhupāda expands on this:

'Anything that is enchanting in the world is said to be a representation of the Lord. The conditioned souls, who are engaged in trying to lord it over the material world, are also enchanted by His mystic powers, but His devotees are enchanted in a different way by the glories of the Lord, and His merciful blessings are upon them. His energy is displayed in different ways, as electrical energy works in manifold capacities. Śrīmatī Kuntīdevī has prayed to the Lord just to enunciate a fragment of His glories. All His devotees worship Him in that way, by chosen words, and therefore the Lord is known as Uttamaśloka. *No amount of chosen words is sufficient to enumerate the Lord's glory, and yet He is satisfied by such prayers as the father is satisfied even by the broken linguistic attempts of the growing child. The word māyā is used both in the sense of delusion and mercy. Herein the word māyā is used in the sense of the Lord's mercy upon Kuntīdevī.'*

Śrīmad-Bhāgavatam 1.8.44, purport

Krishna said nothing in answer to Queen Kuntī's prayers. He did not change His decision to leave Hastināpura. Externally, it might even seem that He did not hear her requests. Sometimes it seems the same to neophyte devotees – that God is deaf to their prayers. Those who newly embark on the path of love for God imagine that God is obliged to answer in their usual language. They expect thunder from the heavens or clear signs, or, at least, instant fulfillment of their desires. But most often, nothing like that happens. Life goes on as usual. The prayers, initially fervent, cool down and become routine words or give way to disappointment. However, those who are truly sincere expect no miracles. They know that God hears them. They go inward and try to listen to their hearts and feel the healing mercy as it pours down out of the silence.

Acknowledgements

Our deepest gratitude to His Divine Grace A.C. Bhaktivedanta Swami Prabhupāda, founder of the International Society for Krishna Consciousness. Without him, we would know nothing about *bhakti* nor the *Śrīmad Bhāgavatam*. Our heartfelt thanks to our spiritual master His Holiness Rādhānāth Swami for inspiring us by his example.

We gratefully acknowledge the invaluable contribution of Jānakī Rāṇī Devī Dāśī and Kṛṣṇāmṛta Devī Dāśī for translation work, Śucirāṇī Devī Dāśī for Sanskrit work, Acintya Kṛṣṇa Das for the cover and design layout, Jagadīśvarī Rādha Devī Dāśī and Lakṣmīmonī Devī Dāśī for proofreading, Vṛndā Kumārī Devī Dāśī for editing and Rādha Pramod Das for managing the project. We also thank Yaśodā Gopikā Devī Dāśī and Bhadra Yamunā Devī Dāśī for their help.

Finally, we extend our sincere gratitude to Tulsi Publications for their generous support in facilitating the publication of the book. And we also wish to acknowledge Vira Books, a division of the Vaishnava International Relief Association, Inc., headed by Kaśīśvar Das, for their dedicated efforts in printing and distributing this work throughout North America.

Manufactured by Amazon.ca
Acheson, AB

16742447R00215